BLACK PANTHER
SHURI

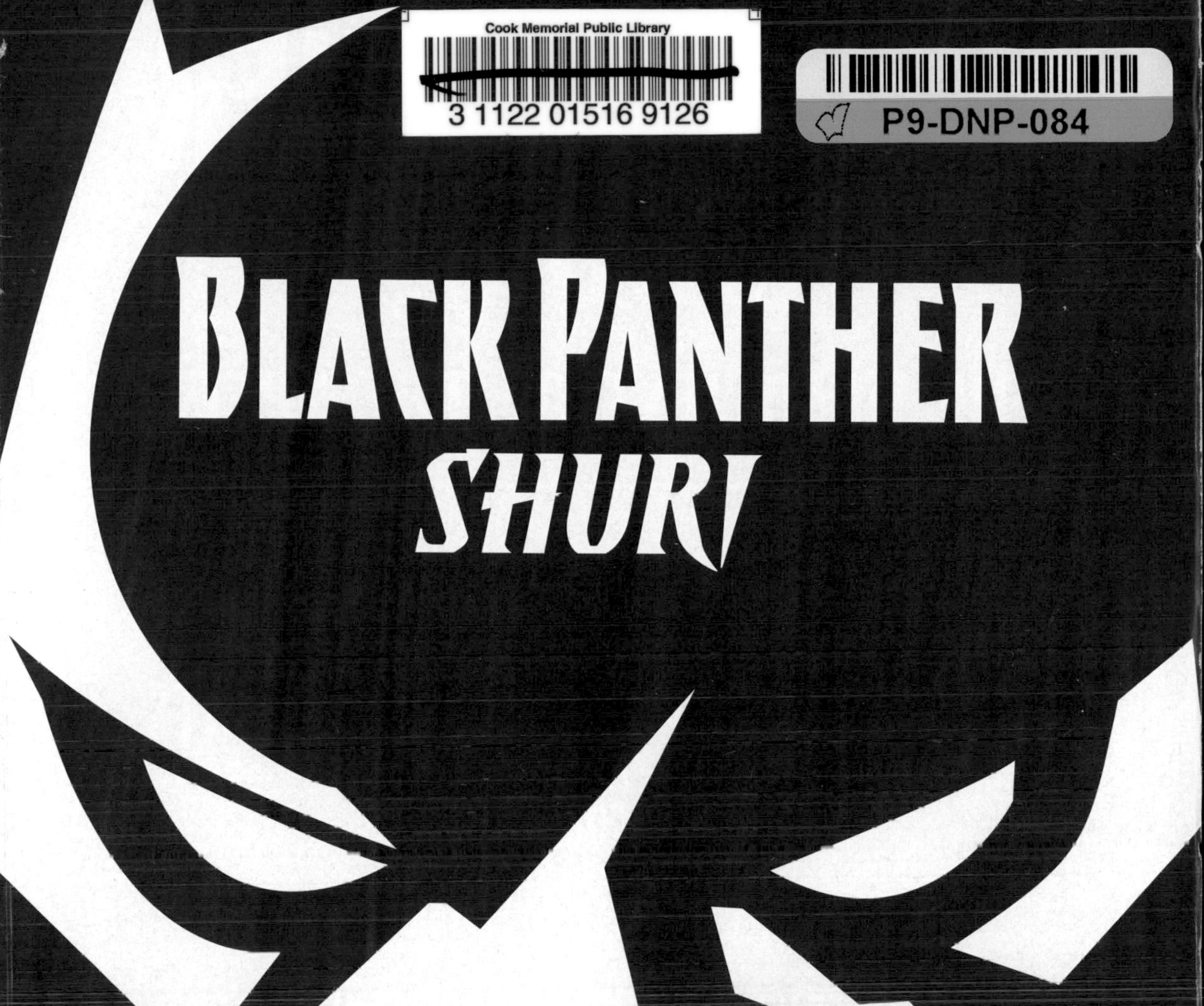

THE DEADLIEST OF THE SPECIES

BLACK PANTHER
SHURI
THE DEADLIEST OF THE SPECIES

WRITER
REGINALD HUDLIN

PENCILS
KEN LASHLEY

INKS
PAUL NEARY

COLORS
PAUL MOUNTS

LETTERS
VC'S CORY PETIT

COVER ART
J. SCOTT CAMPBELL & EDGAR DELGADO

ASSISTANT EDITORS
SEBASTIAN GIRNER & JODY LEHEUP

EDITOR
AXEL ALONSO

Special thanks to Jonathan Maberry & Enrica Jang

Black Panther created by Stan Lee & Jack Kirby

Collection Editor
JENNIFER GRÜNWALD

Assistant Editor
CAITLIN O'CONNELL

Associate Managing Editor
KATERI WOODY

Editor, Special Projects
MARK D. BEAZLEY

VP Production & Special Projects
JEFF YOUNGQUIST

SVP Print, Sales & Marketing
DAVID GABRIEL

Book Design
JEFF POWELL

Editor in Chief
C.B. CEBULSKI

Chief Creative Officer
JOE QUESADA

President
DAN BUCKLEY

Executive Producer
ALAN FINE

BLACK PANTHER: SHURI — THE DEADLIEST OF THE SPECIES. Contains material originally published in magazine form as BLACK PANTHER #1-6. Second edition. First printing 2018. ISBN 978-1-302-91419-6. Published by MARVEL WORLDWIDE, INC., a subsidiary of MARVEL ENTERTAINMENT, LLC. OFFICE OF PUBLICATION: 135 West 50th Street, New York, NY 10020. Copyright © 2018 MARVEL No similarity between any of the names, characters, persons, and/or institutions in this magazine with those of any living or dead person or institution is intended, and any such similarity which may exist is purely coincidental. **Printed in Canada.** DAN BUCKLEY, President, Marvel Entertainment; JOHN NEE, Publisher; JOE QUESADA, Chief Creative Officer; TOM BREVOORT, SVP of Publishing; DAVID BOGART, SVP of Business Affairs & Operations, Publishing & Partnership; DAVID GABRIEL, SVP of Sales & Marketing, Publishing; JEFF YOUNGQUIST, VP of Production & Special Projects; DAN CARR, Executive Director of Publishing Technology; ALEX MORALES, Director of Publishing Operations; SUSAN CRESPI, Production Manager; STAN LEE, Chairman Emeritus. For information regarding advertising in Marvel Comics or on Marvel.com, please contact Vit DeBellis, Custom Solutions & Integrated Advertising Manager, at vdebellis@marvel.com. For Marvel subscription inquiries, please call 888-511-5480. **Manufactured between 3/6/2018 and 3/20/2018 by SOLISCO PRINTERS, SCOTT, QC, CANADA.**

10 9 8 7 6 5 4 3 2 1

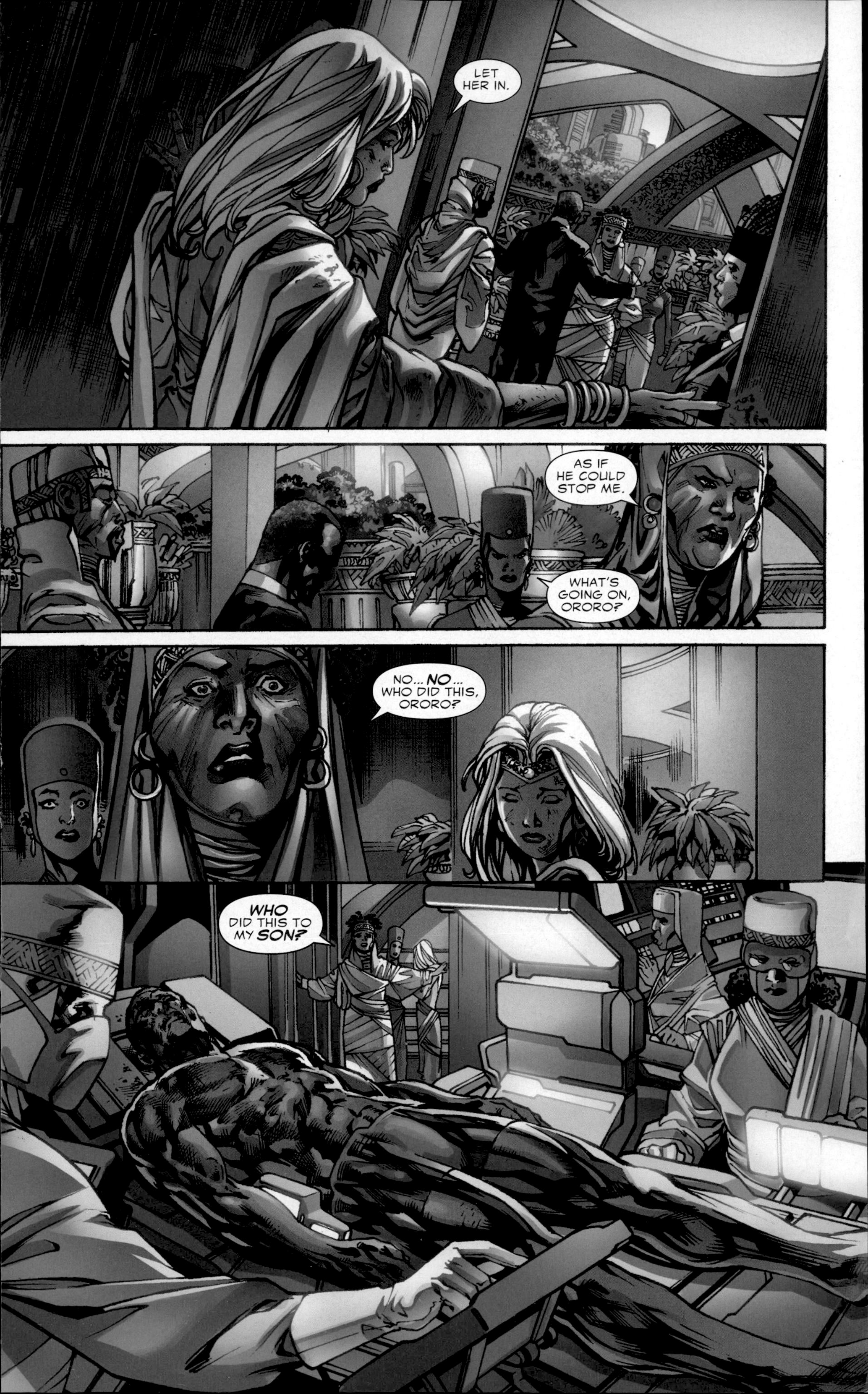
LET HER IN.
AS IF HE COULD STOP ME.
WHAT'S GOING ON, ORORO?
NO... NO... WHO DID THIS, ORORO?
WHO DID THIS TO MY SON?

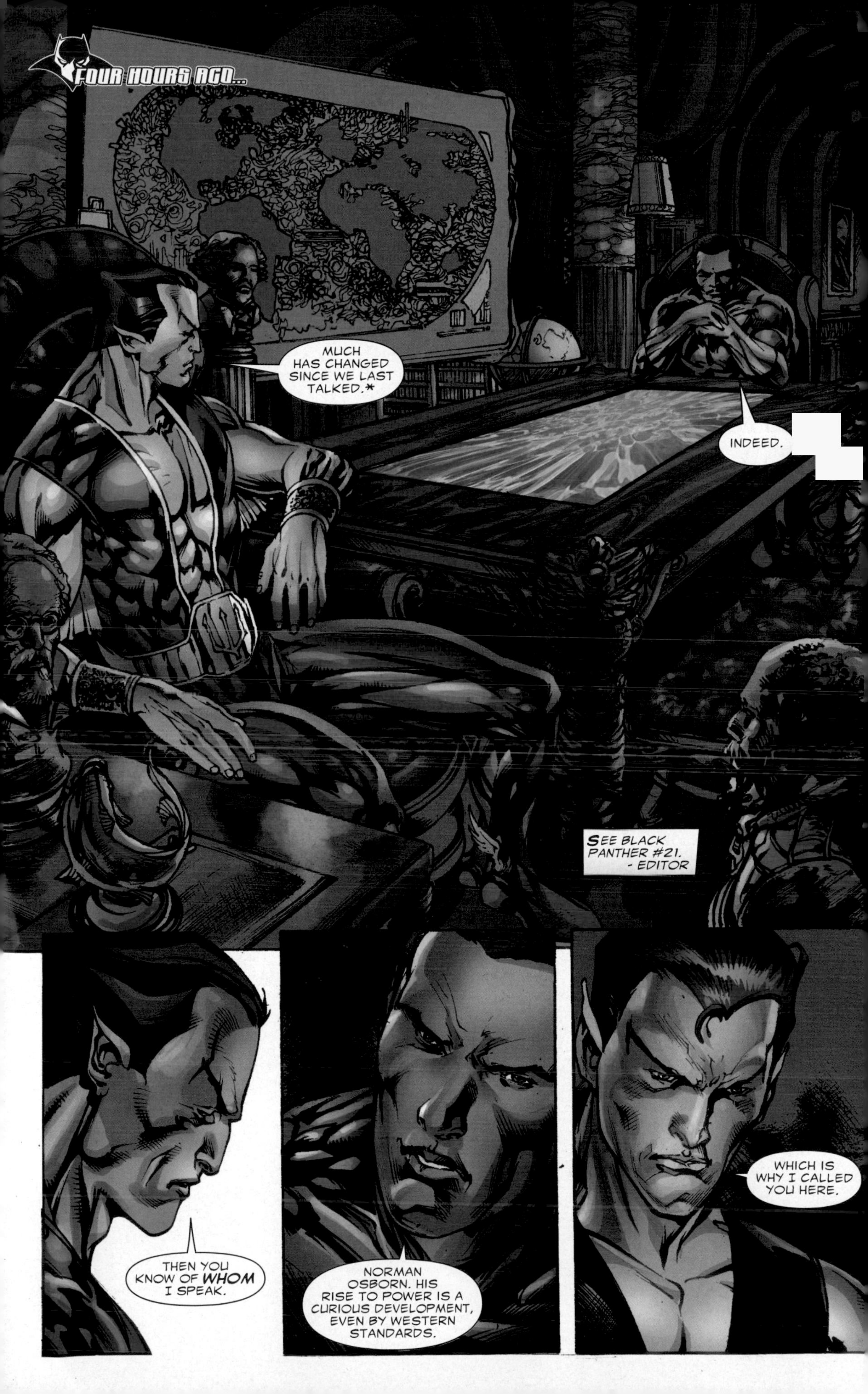

FOUR HOURS AGO...
MUCH HAS CHANGED SINCE WE LAST TALKED.*
INDEED.
SEE BLACK PANTHER #21. - EDITOR
THEN YOU KNOW OF WHOM I SPEAK.
NORMAN OSBORN. HIS RISE TO POWER IS A CURIOUS DEVELOPMENT, EVEN BY WESTERN STANDARDS.
WHICH IS WHY I CALLED YOU HERE.

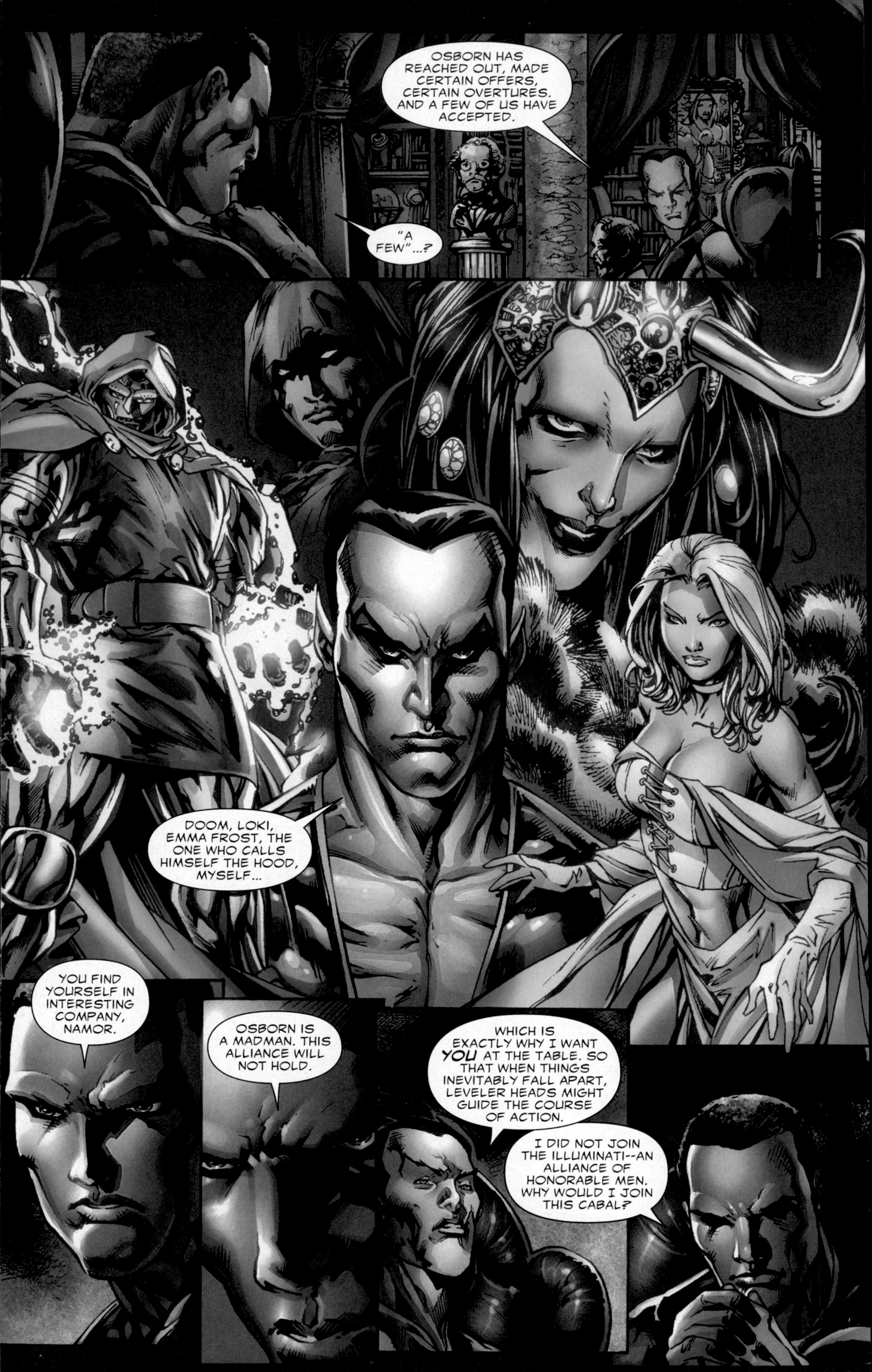
OSBORN HAS REACHED OUT, MADE CERTAIN OFFERS, CERTAIN OVERTURES. AND A FEW OF US HAVE ACCEPTED.
"A FEW"...?
DOOM, LOKI, EMMA FROST, THE ONE WHO CALLS HIMSELF THE HOOD, MYSELF...
YOU FIND YOURSELF IN INTERESTING COMPANY, NAMOR.
OSBORN IS A MADMAN. THIS ALLIANCE WILL NOT HOLD.
WHICH IS EXACTLY WHY I WANT YOU AT THE TABLE. SO THAT WHEN THINGS INEVITABLY FALL APART, LEVELER HEADS MIGHT GUIDE THE COURSE OF ACTION.
I DID NOT JOIN THE ILLUMINATI--AN ALLIANCE OF HONORABLE MEN. WHY WOULD I JOIN THIS CABAL?

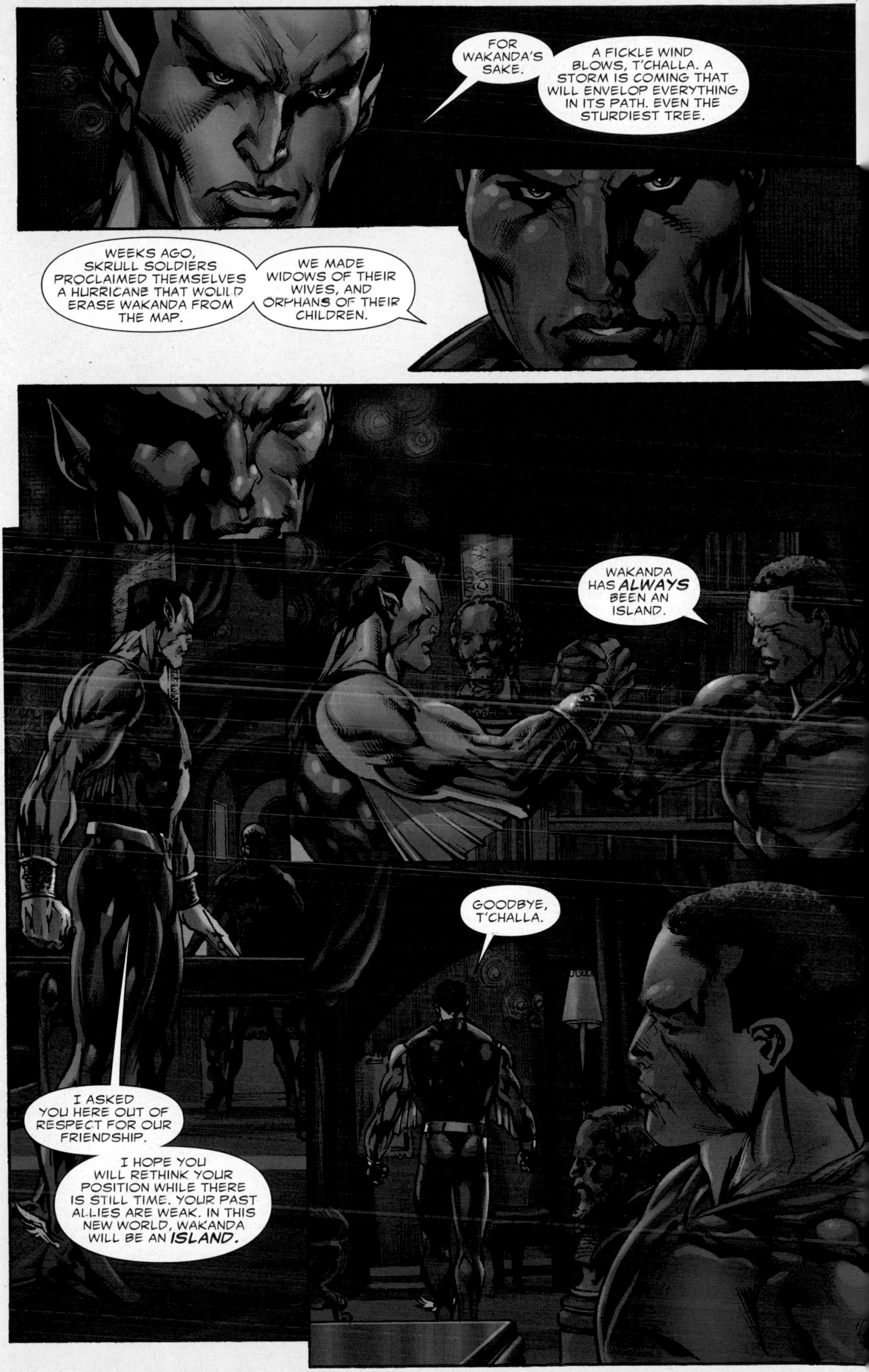
FOR WAKANDA'S SAKE.
A FICKLE WIND BLOWS, T'CHALLA. A STORM IS COMING THAT WILL ENVELOP EVERYTHING IN ITS PATH. EVEN THE STURDIEST TREE.
WEEKS AGO, SKRULL SOLDIERS PROCLAIMED THEMSELVES A HURRICANE THAT WOULD ERASE WAKANDA FROM THE MAP.
WE MADE WIDOWS OF THEIR WIVES, AND ORPHANS OF THEIR CHILDREN.
WAKANDA HAS ALWAYS BEEN AN ISLAND.
I ASKED YOU HERE OUT OF RESPECT FOR OUR FRIENDSHIP.
I HOPE YOU WILL RETHINK YOUR POSITION WHILE THERE IS STILL TIME. YOUR PAST ALLIES ARE WEAK. IN THIS NEW WORLD, WAKANDA WILL BE AN ISLAND.
GOODBYE, T'CHALLA.

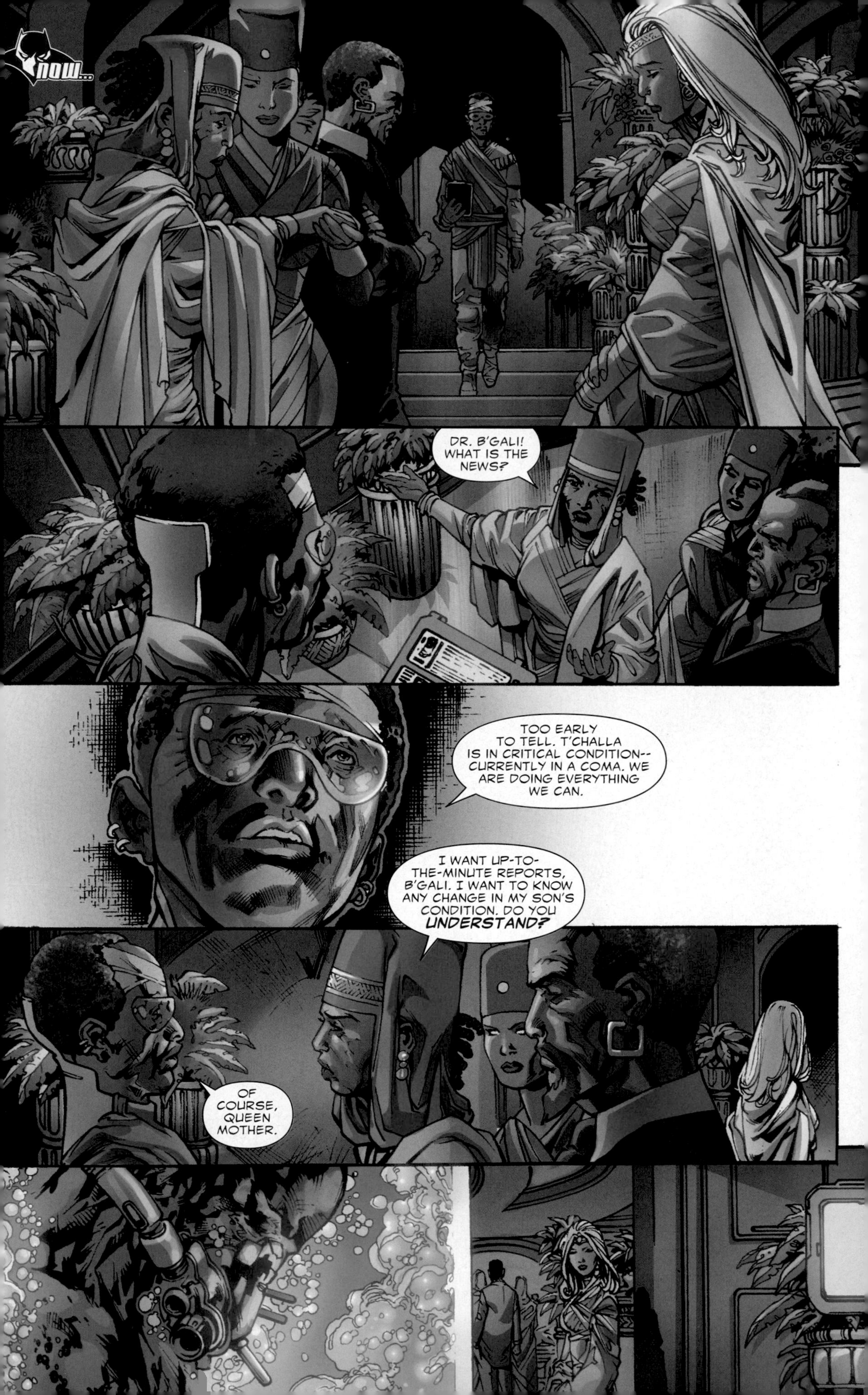
NOW...
DR. B'GALI! WHAT IS THE NEWS?
TOO EARLY TO TELL. T'CHALLA IS IN CRITICAL CONDITION-- CURRENTLY IN A COMA. WE ARE DOING EVERYTHING WE CAN.
I WANT UP-TO-THE-MINUTE REPORTS, B'GALI. I WANT TO KNOW ANY CHANGE IN MY SON'S CONDITION. DO YOU UNDERSTAND?
OF COURSE, QUEEN MOTHER.

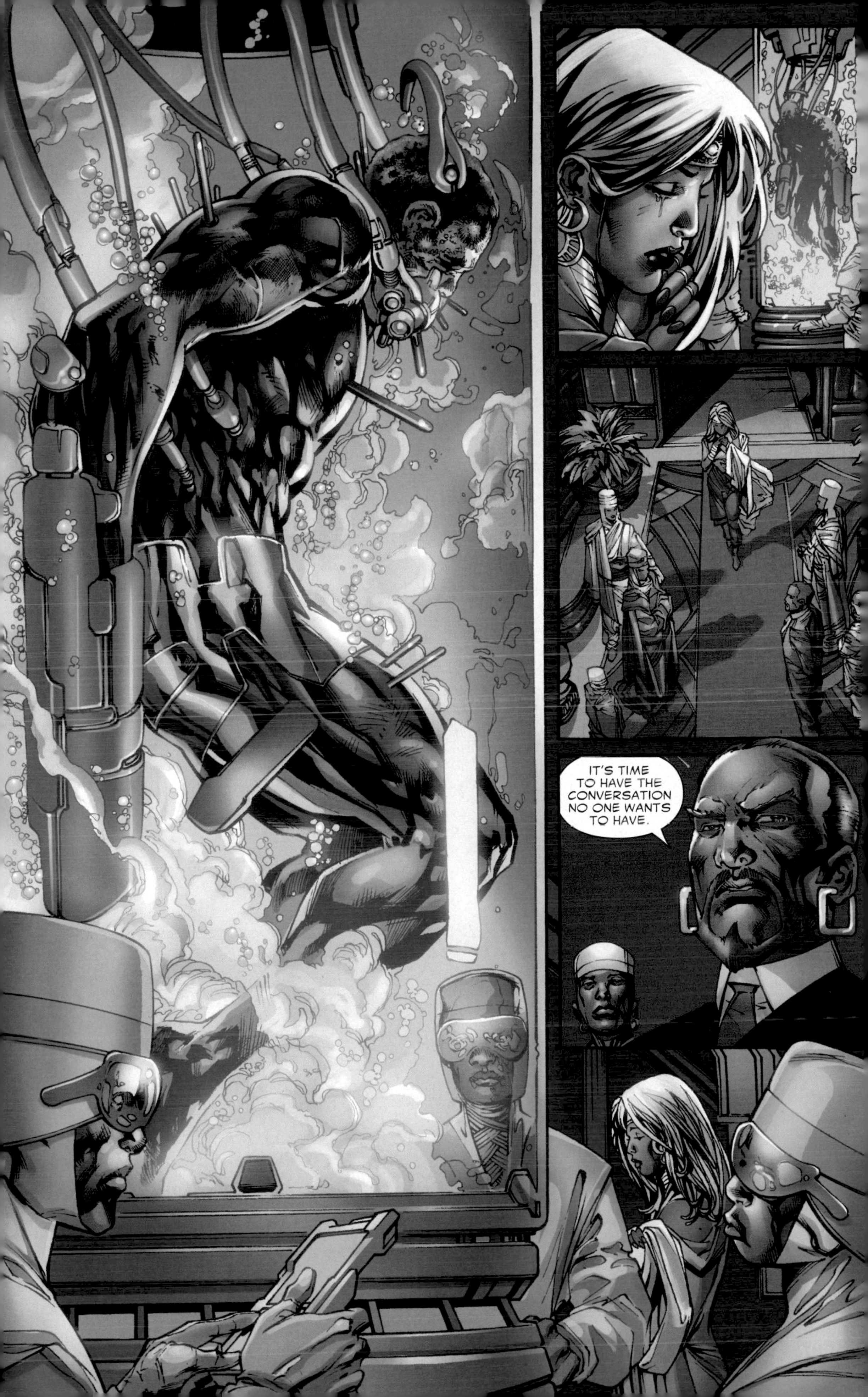
IT'S TIME TO HAVE THE CONVERSATION NO ONE WANTS TO HAVE.

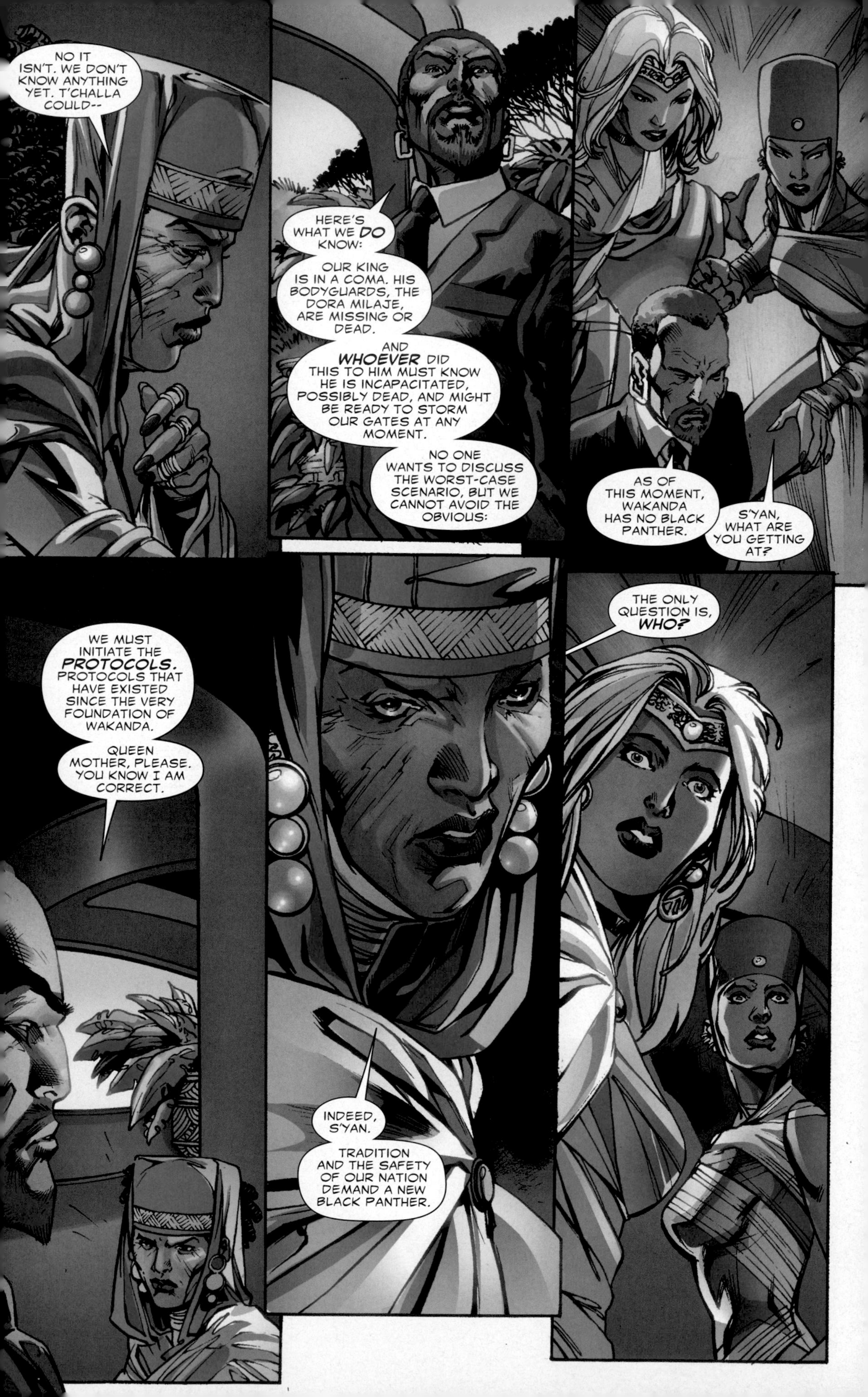
NO IT ISN'T. WE DON'T KNOW ANYTHING YET. T'CHALLA COULD--
HERE'S WHAT WE DO KNOW:
OUR KING IS IN A COMA. HIS BODYGUARDS, THE DORA MILAJE, ARE MISSING OR DEAD.
AND WHOEVER DID THIS TO HIM MUST KNOW HE IS INCAPACITATED, POSSIBLY DEAD, AND MIGHT BE READY TO STORM OUR GATES AT ANY MOMENT.
NO ONE WANTS TO DISCUSS THE WORST-CASE SCENARIO, BUT WE CANNOT AVOID THE OBVIOUS:
AS OF THIS MOMENT, WAKANDA HAS NO BLACK PANTHER.
S'YAN, WHAT ARE YOU GETTING AT?
WE MUST INITIATE THE PROTOCOLS. PROTOCOLS THAT HAVE EXISTED SINCE THE VERY FOUNDATION OF WAKANDA.
QUEEN MOTHER, PLEASE. YOU KNOW I AM CORRECT.
INDEED, S'YAN.
TRADITION AND THE SAFETY OF OUR NATION DEMAND A NEW BLACK PANTHER.
THE ONLY QUESTION IS, WHO?

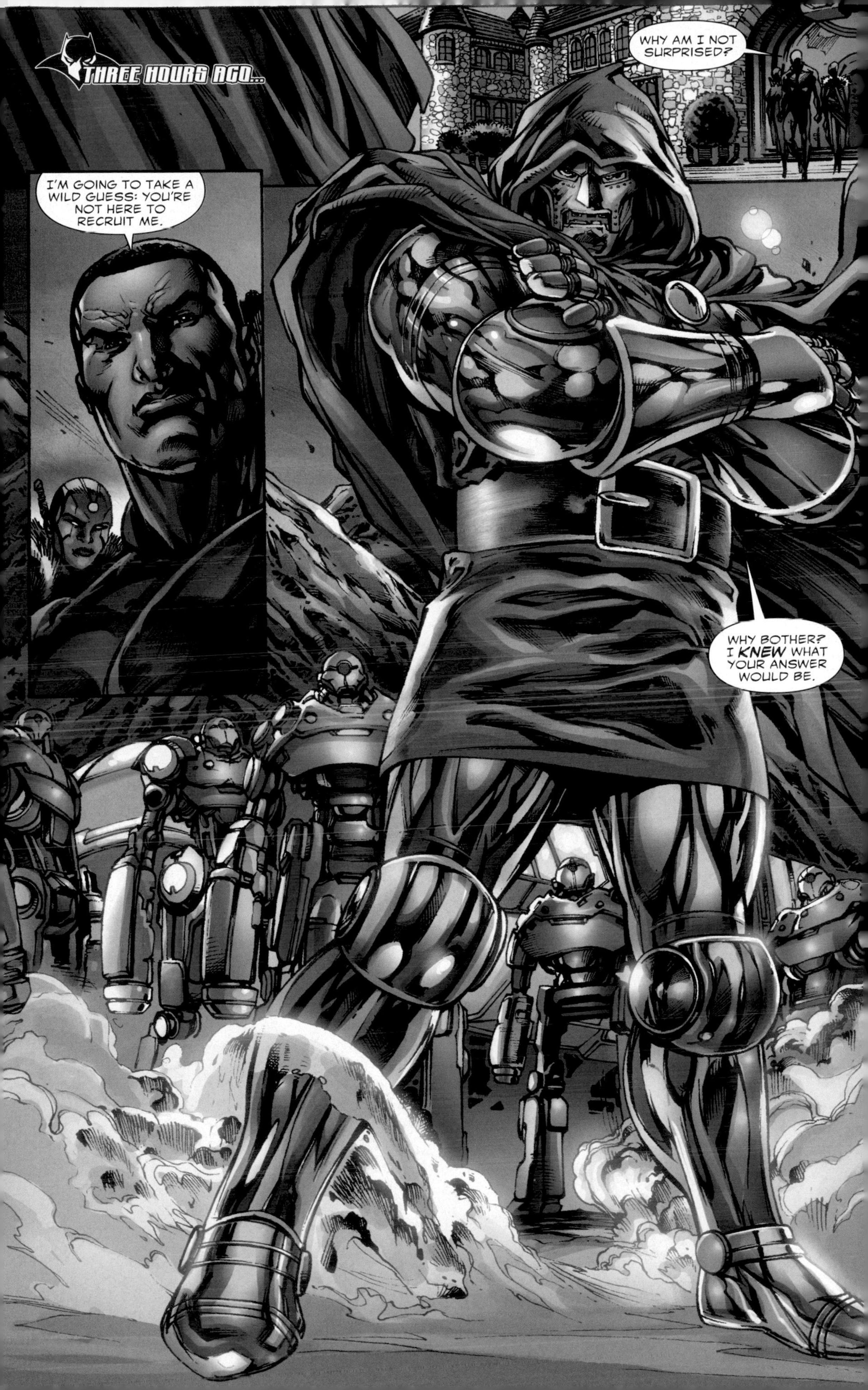
THREE HOURS AGO...
I'M GOING TO TAKE A WILD GUESS: YOU'RE NOT HERE TO RECRUIT ME.
WHY AM I NOT SURPRISED?
WHY BOTHER? I KNEW WHAT YOUR ANSWER WOULD BE.

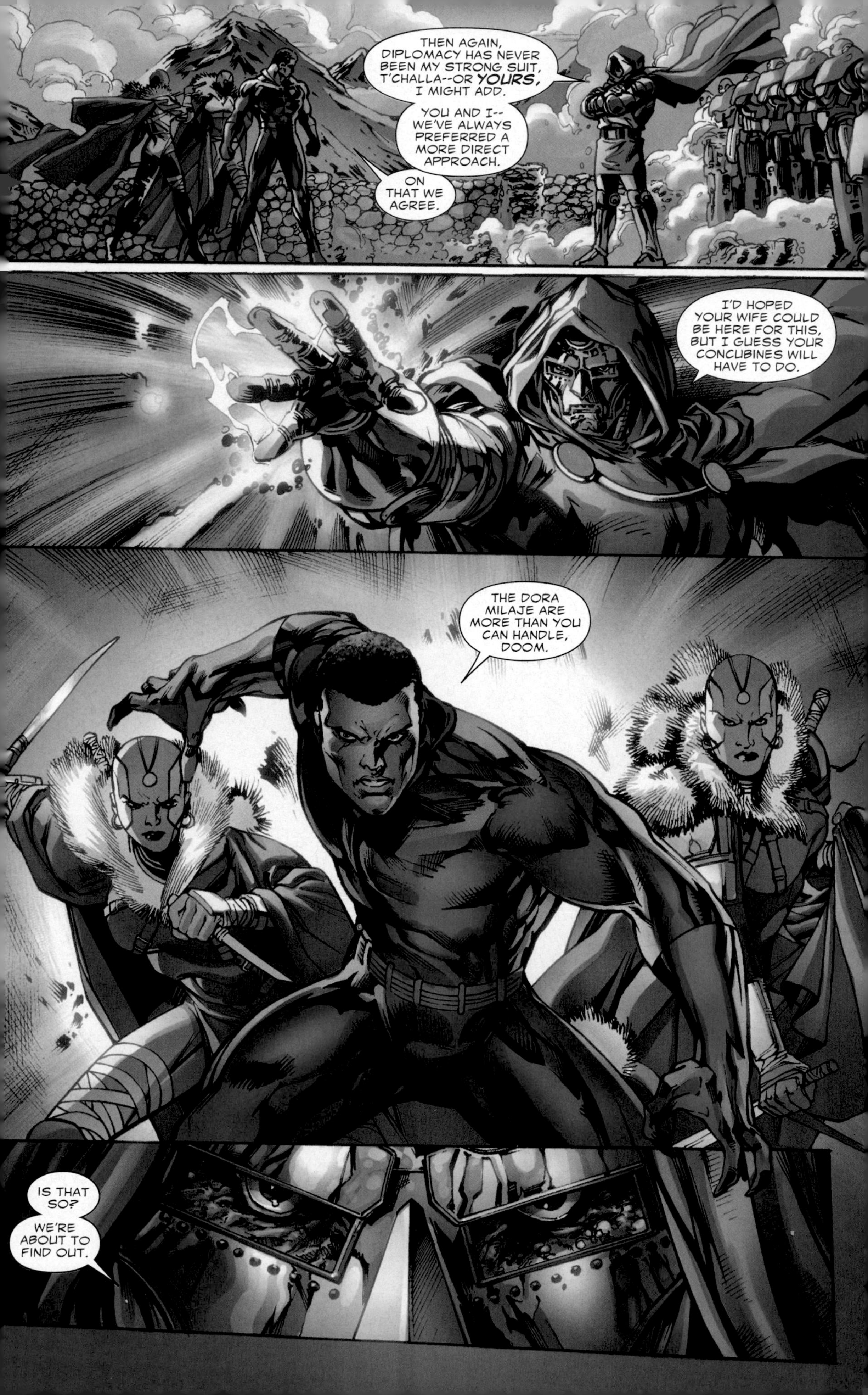
THEN AGAIN, DIPLOMACY HAS NEVER BEEN MY STRONG SUIT, T'CHALLA--OR *YOURS,* I MIGHT ADD.
YOU AND I-- WE'VE ALWAYS PREFERRED A MORE DIRECT APPROACH.
ON THAT WE AGREE.
I'D HOPED YOUR WIFE COULD BE HERE FOR THIS, BUT I GUESS YOUR CONCUBINES WILL HAVE TO DO.
THE DORA MILAJE ARE MORE THAN YOU CAN HANDLE, DOOM.
IS THAT SO?
WE'RE ABOUT TO FIND OUT.

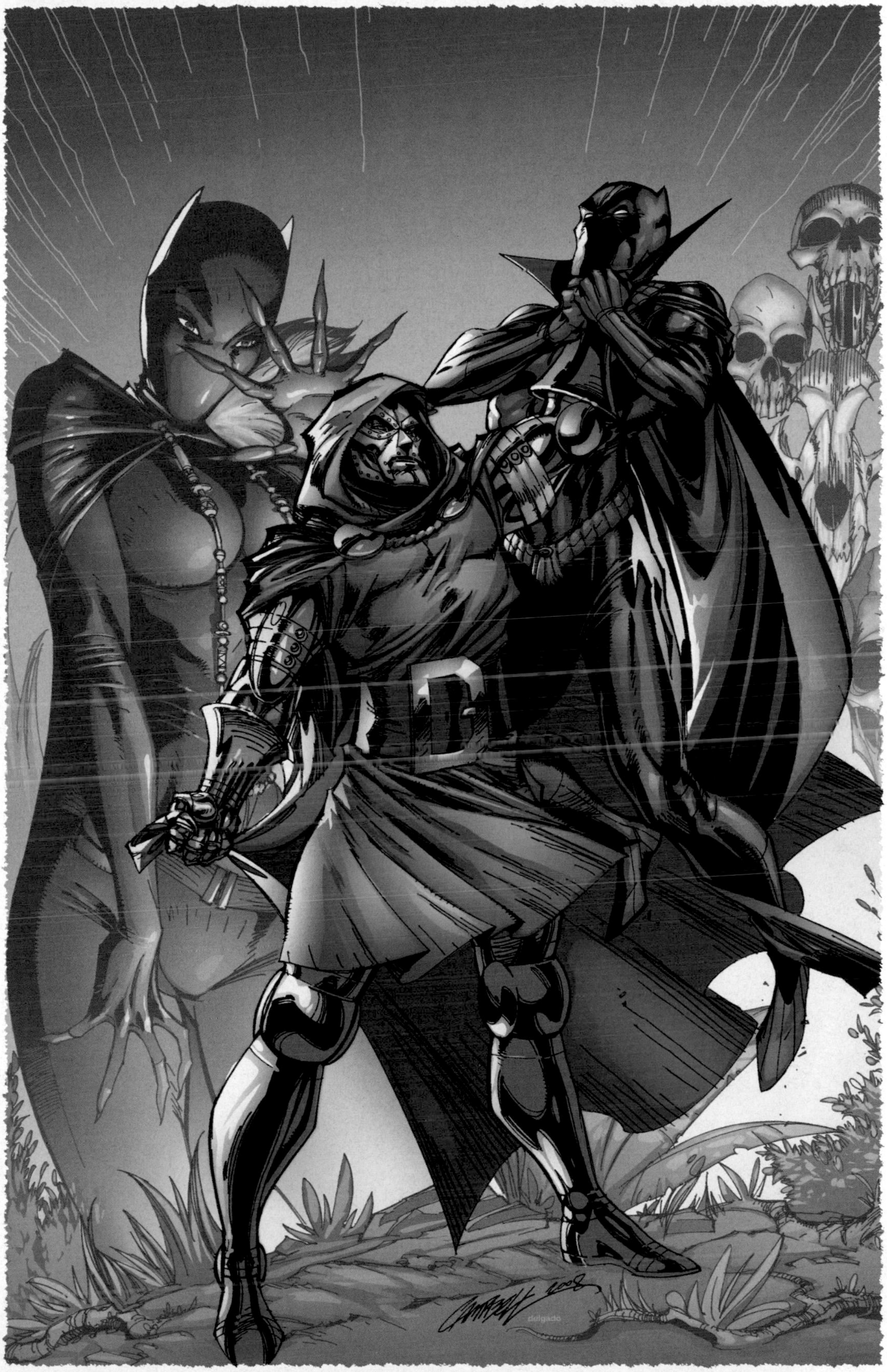

2

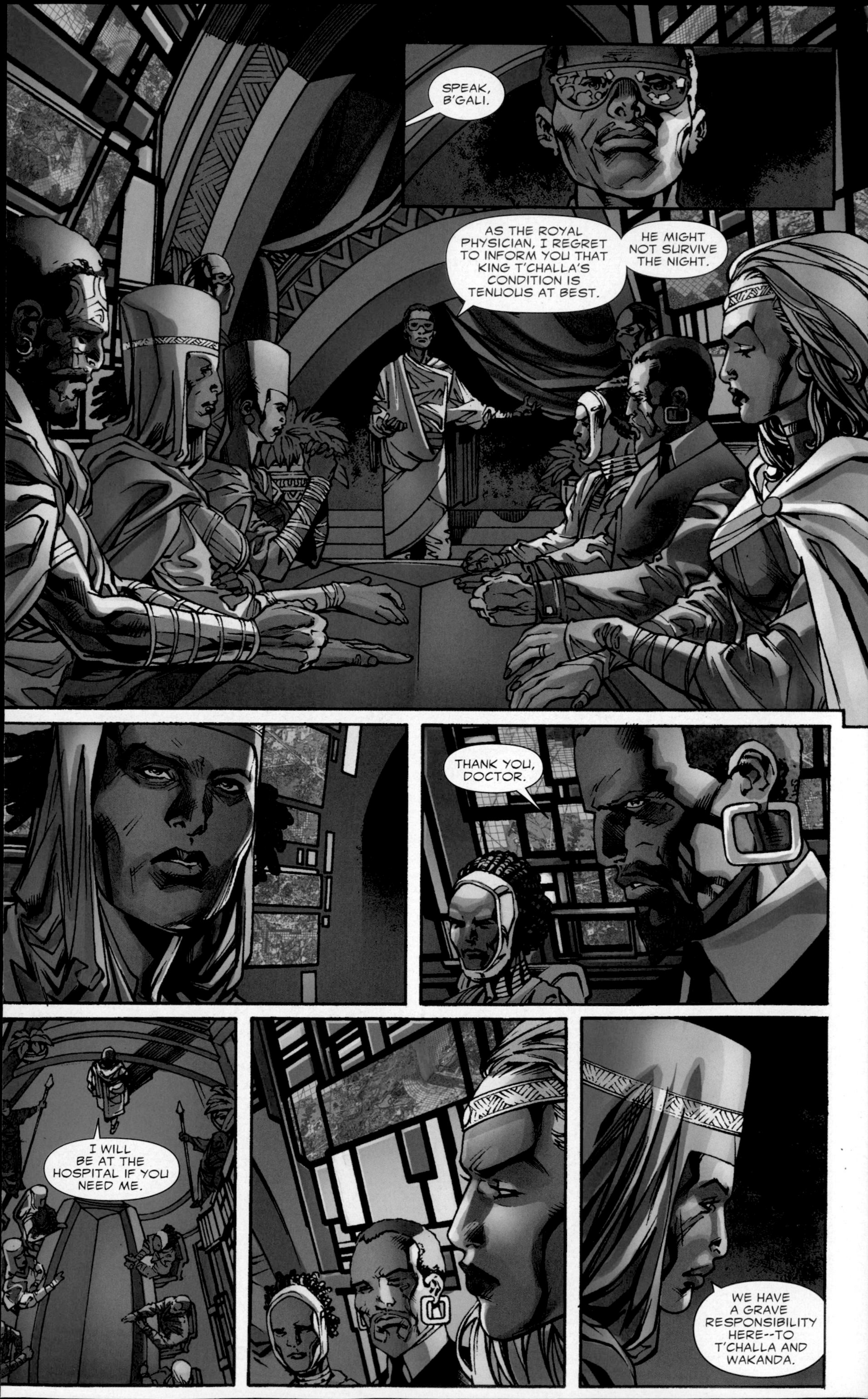
SPEAK, B'GALI.
AS THE ROYAL PHYSICIAN, I REGRET TO INFORM YOU THAT KING T'CHALLA'S CONDITION IS TENUOUS AT BEST.
HE MIGHT NOT SURVIVE THE NIGHT.
THANK YOU, DOCTOR.
I WILL BE AT THE HOSPITAL IF YOU NEED ME.
WE HAVE A GRAVE RESPONSIBILITY HERE--TO T'CHALLA AND WAKANDA.

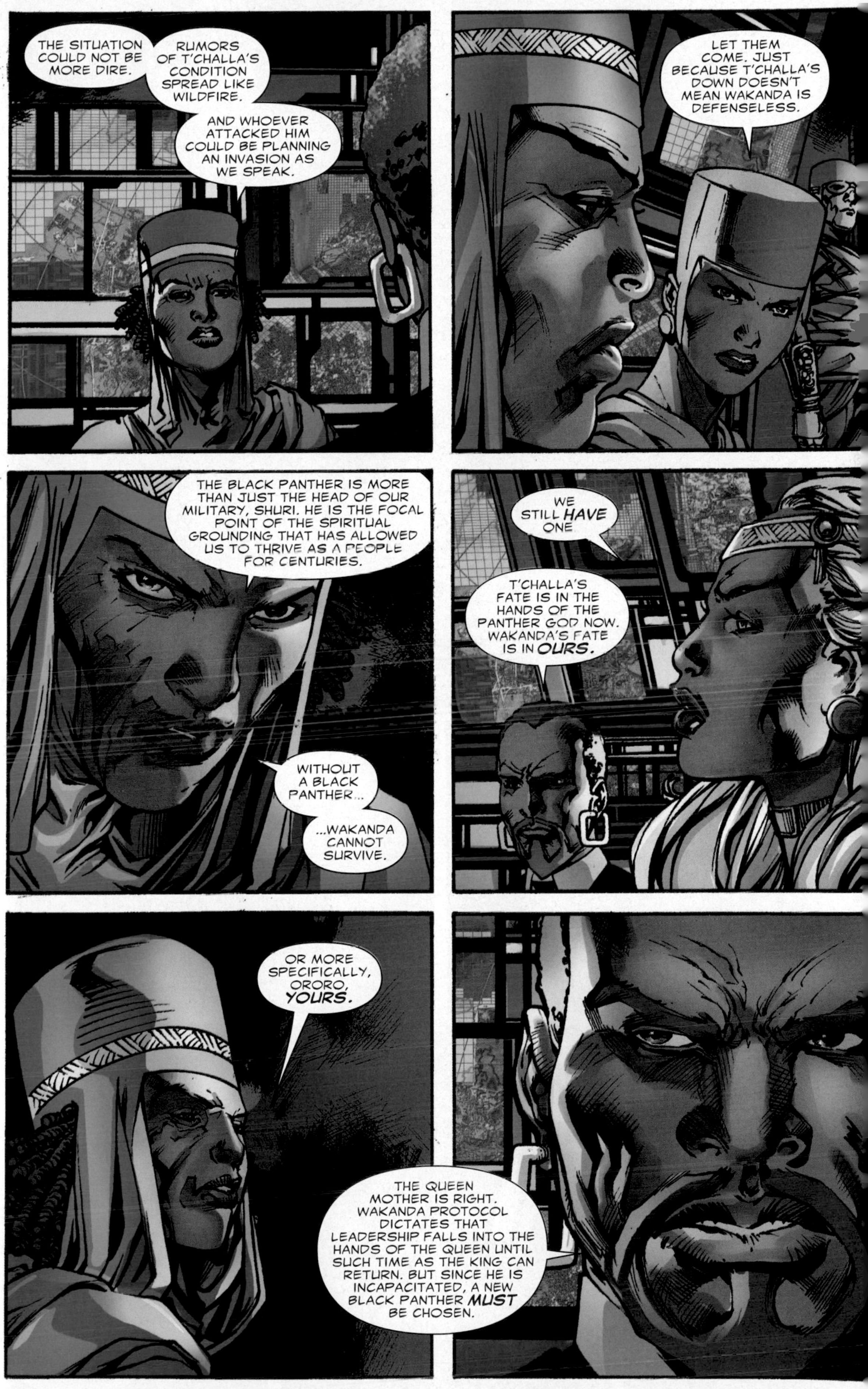
THE SITUATION COULD NOT BE MORE DIRE.
RUMORS OF T'CHALLA'S CONDITION SPREAD LIKE WILDFIRE.
AND WHOEVER ATTACKED HIM COULD BE PLANNING AN INVASION AS WE SPEAK.
LET THEM COME. JUST BECAUSE T'CHALLA'S DOWN DOESN'T MEAN WAKANDA IS DEFENSELESS.
THE BLACK PANTHER IS MORE THAN JUST THE HEAD OF OUR MILITARY, SHURI. HE IS THE FOCAL POINT OF THE SPIRITUAL GROUNDING THAT HAS ALLOWED US TO THRIVE AS A PEOPLE FOR CENTURIES.
WITHOUT A BLACK PANTHER...
...WAKANDA CANNOT SURVIVE.
WE STILL HAVE ONE.
T'CHALLA'S FATE IS IN THE HANDS OF THE PANTHER GOD NOW. WAKANDA'S FATE IS IN OURS.
OR MORE SPECIFICALLY, ORORO, YOURS.
THE QUEEN MOTHER IS RIGHT. WAKANDA PROTOCOL DICTATES THAT LEADERSHIP FALLS INTO THE HANDS OF THE QUEEN UNTIL SUCH TIME AS THE KING CAN RETURN. BUT SINCE HE IS INCAPACITATED, A NEW BLACK PANTHER MUST BE CHOSEN.

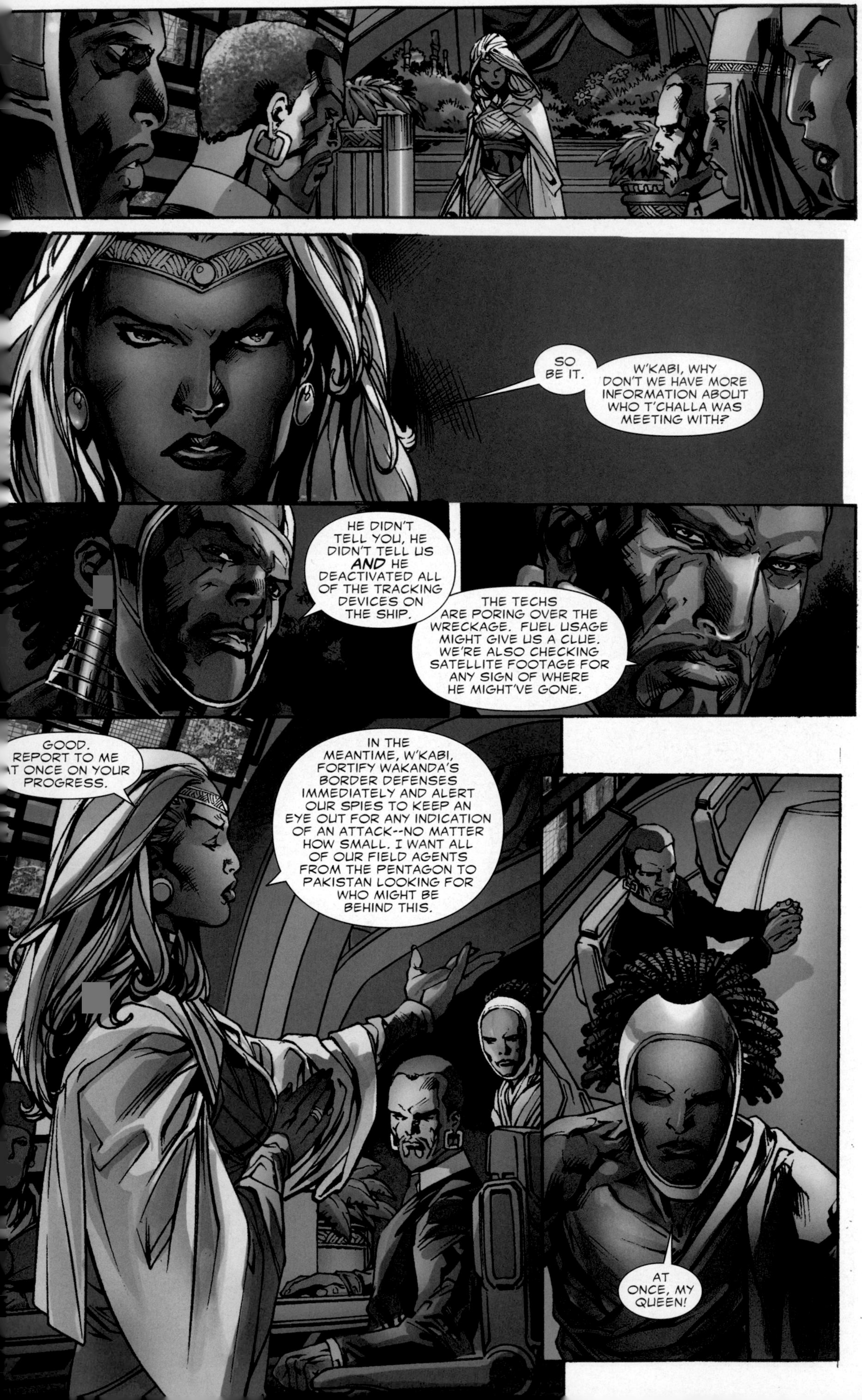
SO BE IT.
W'KABI, WHY DON'T WE HAVE MORE INFORMATION ABOUT WHO T'CHALLA WAS MEETING WITH?
HE DIDN'T TELL YOU, HE DIDN'T TELL US *AND* HE DEACTIVATED ALL OF THE TRACKING DEVICES ON THE SHIP.
THE TECHS ARE PORING OVER THE WRECKAGE. FUEL USAGE MIGHT GIVE US A CLUE. WE'RE ALSO CHECKING SATELLITE FOOTAGE FOR ANY SIGN OF WHERE HE MIGHT'VE GONE.
GOOD. REPORT TO ME T ONCE ON YOUR PROGRESS.
IN THE MEANTIME, W'KABI, FORTIFY WAKANDA'S BORDER DEFENSES IMMEDIATELY AND ALERT OUR SPIES TO KEEP AN EYE OUT FOR ANY INDICATION OF AN ATTACK--NO MATTER HOW SMALL. I WANT ALL OF OUR FIELD AGENTS FROM THE PENTAGON TO PAKISTAN LOOKING FOR WHO MIGHT BE BEHIND THIS.
AT ONCE, MY QUEEN!

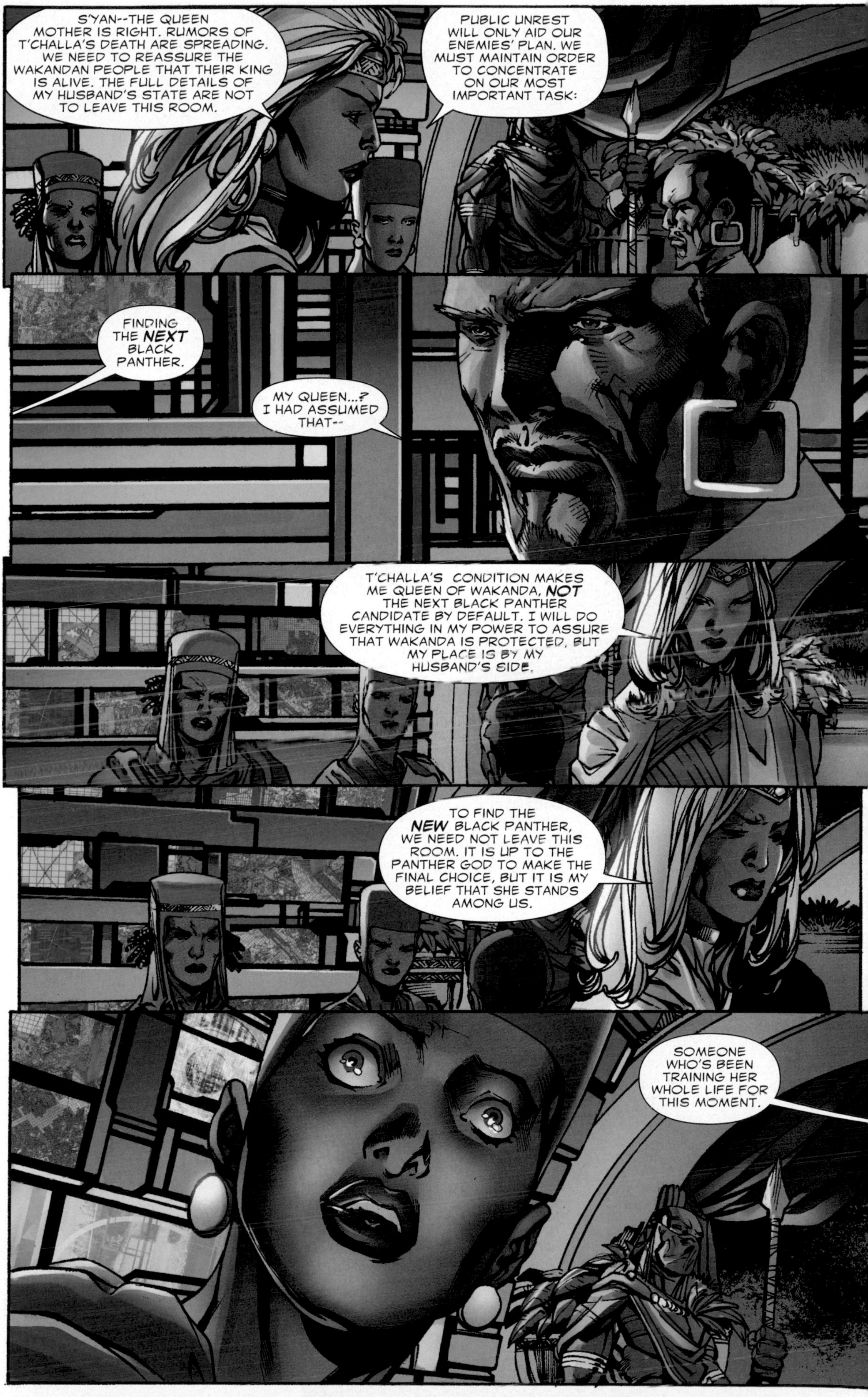
S'YAN--THE QUEEN MOTHER IS RIGHT. RUMORS OF T'CHALLA'S DEATH ARE SPREADING. WE NEED TO REASSURE THE WAKANDAN PEOPLE THAT THEIR KING IS ALIVE. THE FULL DETAILS OF MY HUSBAND'S STATE ARE NOT TO LEAVE THIS ROOM.
PUBLIC UNREST WILL ONLY AID OUR ENEMIES' PLAN. WE MUST MAINTAIN ORDER TO CONCENTRATE ON OUR MOST IMPORTANT TASK:
FINDING THE NEXT BLACK PANTHER.
MY QUEEN...? I HAD ASSUMED THAT--
T'CHALLA'S CONDITION MAKES ME QUEEN OF WAKANDA, NOT THE NEXT BLACK PANTHER CANDIDATE BY DEFAULT. I WILL DO EVERYTHING IN MY POWER TO ASSURE THAT WAKANDA IS PROTECTED, BUT MY PLACE IS BY MY HUSBAND'S SIDE.
TO FIND THE NEW BLACK PANTHER, WE NEED NOT LEAVE THIS ROOM. IT IS UP TO THE PANTHER GOD TO MAKE THE FINAL CHOICE, BUT IT IS MY BELIEF THAT SHE STANDS AMONG US.
SOMEONE WHO'S BEEN TRAINING HER WHOLE LIFE FOR THIS MOMENT.

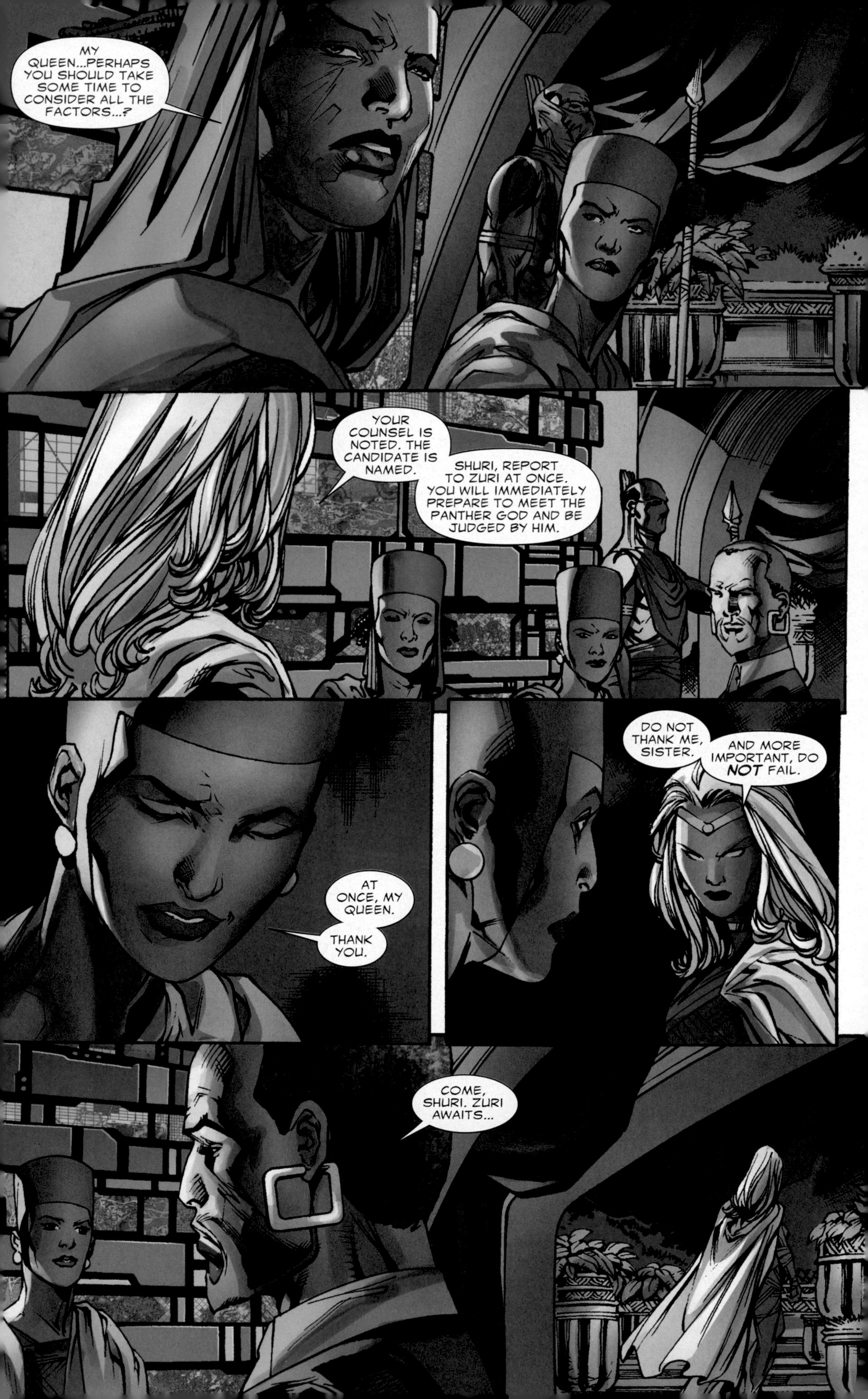
MY QUEEN...PERHAPS YOU SHOULD TAKE SOME TIME TO CONSIDER ALL THE FACTORS...?
YOUR COUNSEL IS NOTED. THE CANDIDATE IS NAMED.
SHURI, REPORT TO ZURI AT ONCE. YOU WILL IMMEDIATELY PREPARE TO MEET THE PANTHER GOD AND BE JUDGED BY HIM.
AT ONCE, MY QUEEN.
THANK YOU.
DO NOT THANK ME, SISTER.
AND MORE IMPORTANT, DO NOT FAIL.
COME, SHURI. ZURI AWAITS...

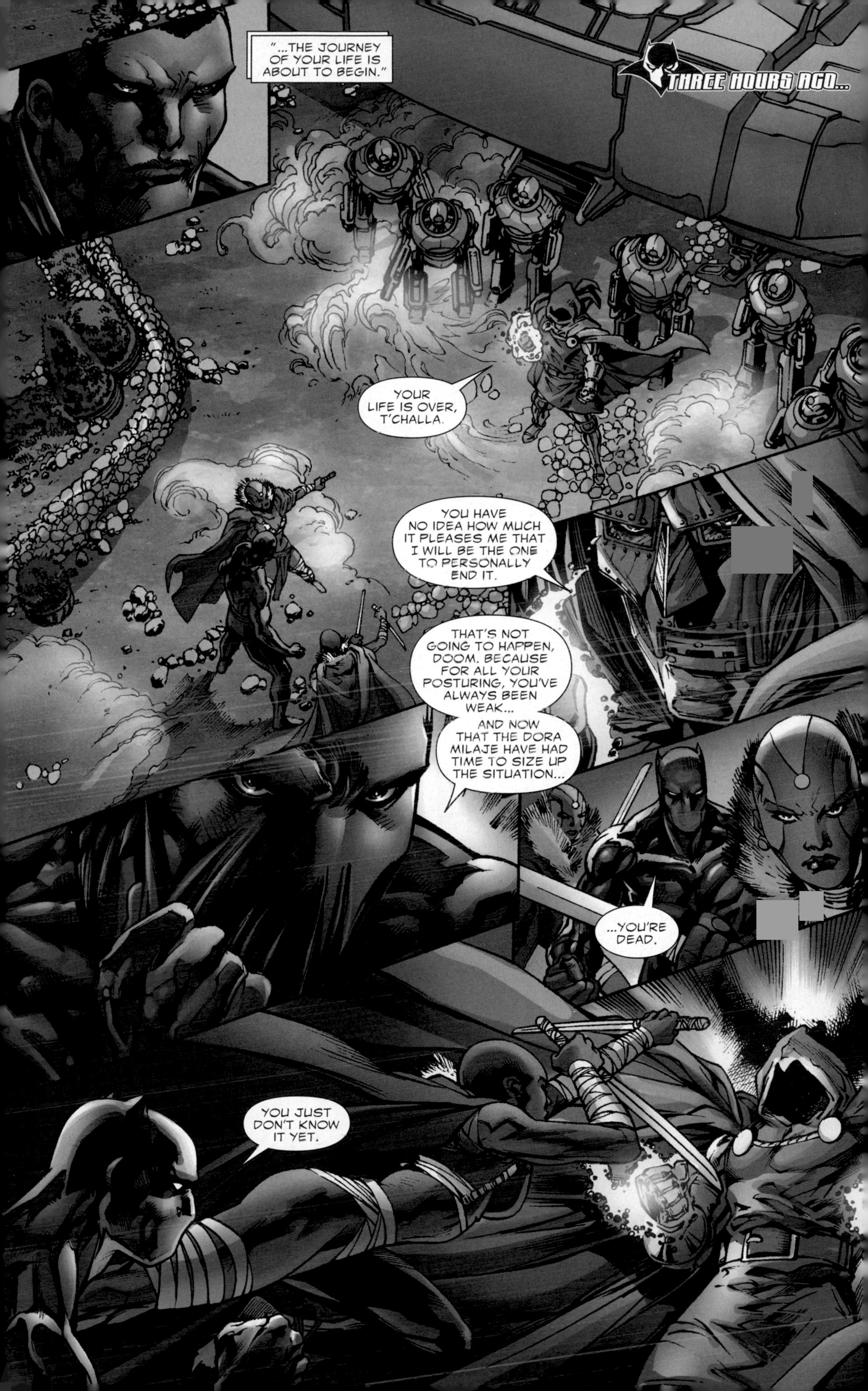
"...THE JOURNEY OF YOUR LIFE IS ABOUT TO BEGIN."
THREE HOURS AGO...
YOUR LIFE IS OVER, T'CHALLA.
YOU HAVE NO IDEA HOW MUCH IT PLEASES ME THAT I WILL BE THE ONE TO PERSONALLY END IT.
THAT'S NOT GOING TO HAPPEN, DOOM. BECAUSE FOR ALL YOUR POSTURING, YOU'VE ALWAYS BEEN WEAK...
AND NOW THAT THE DORA MILAJE HAVE HAD TIME TO SIZE UP THE SITUATION...
...YOU'RE DEAD.
YOU JUST DON'T KNOW IT YET.

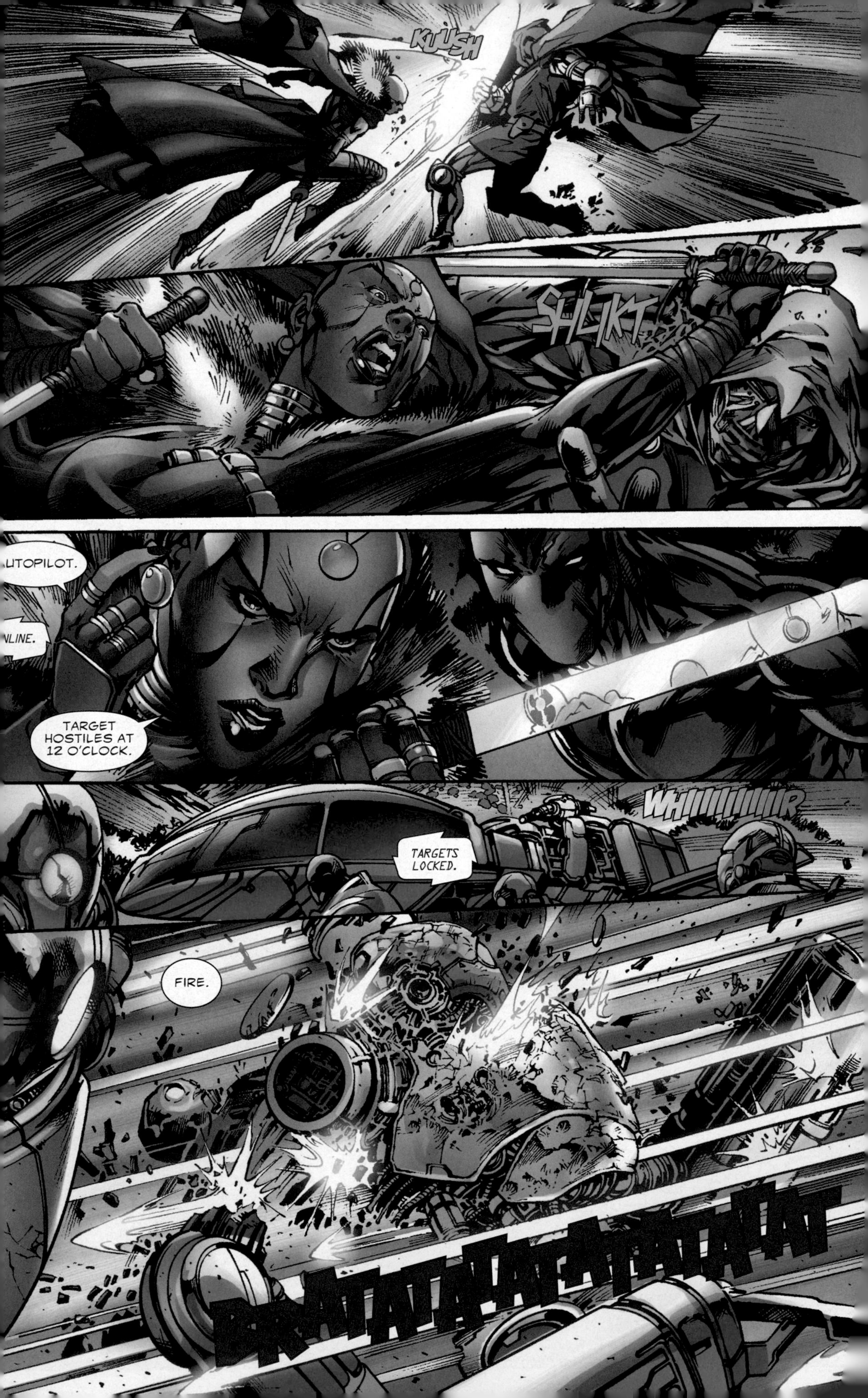
KUUSH
SHLIKT
UTOPILOT.
NLINE.
TARGET HOSTILES AT 12 O'CLOCK.
WHIIIIIIIIR
TARGETS LOCKED.
FIRE.

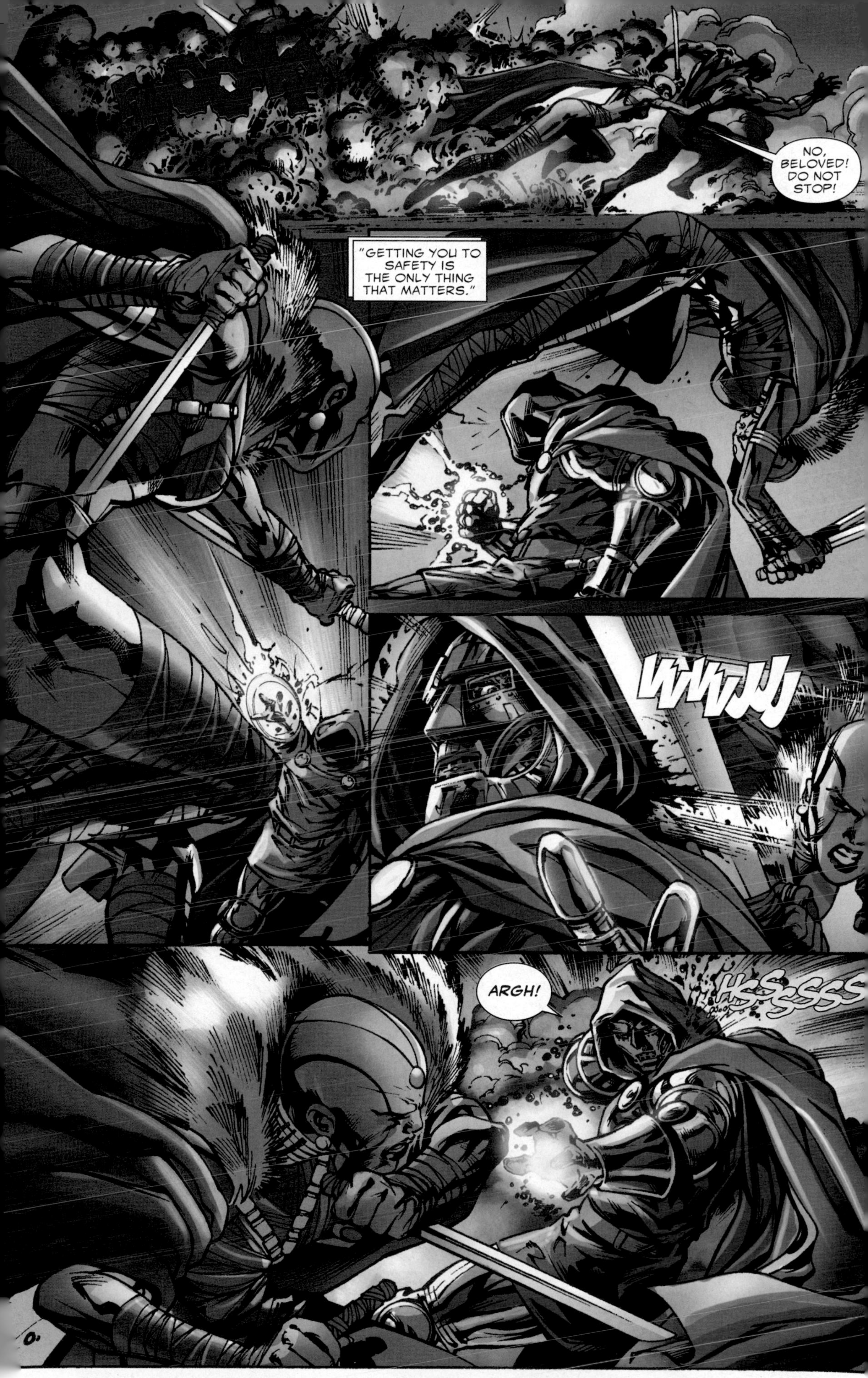
NO, BELOVED! DO NOT STOP!
"GETTING YOU TO SAFETY IS THE ONLY THING THAT MATTERS."
WWWM
ARGH!
HSSSSSS

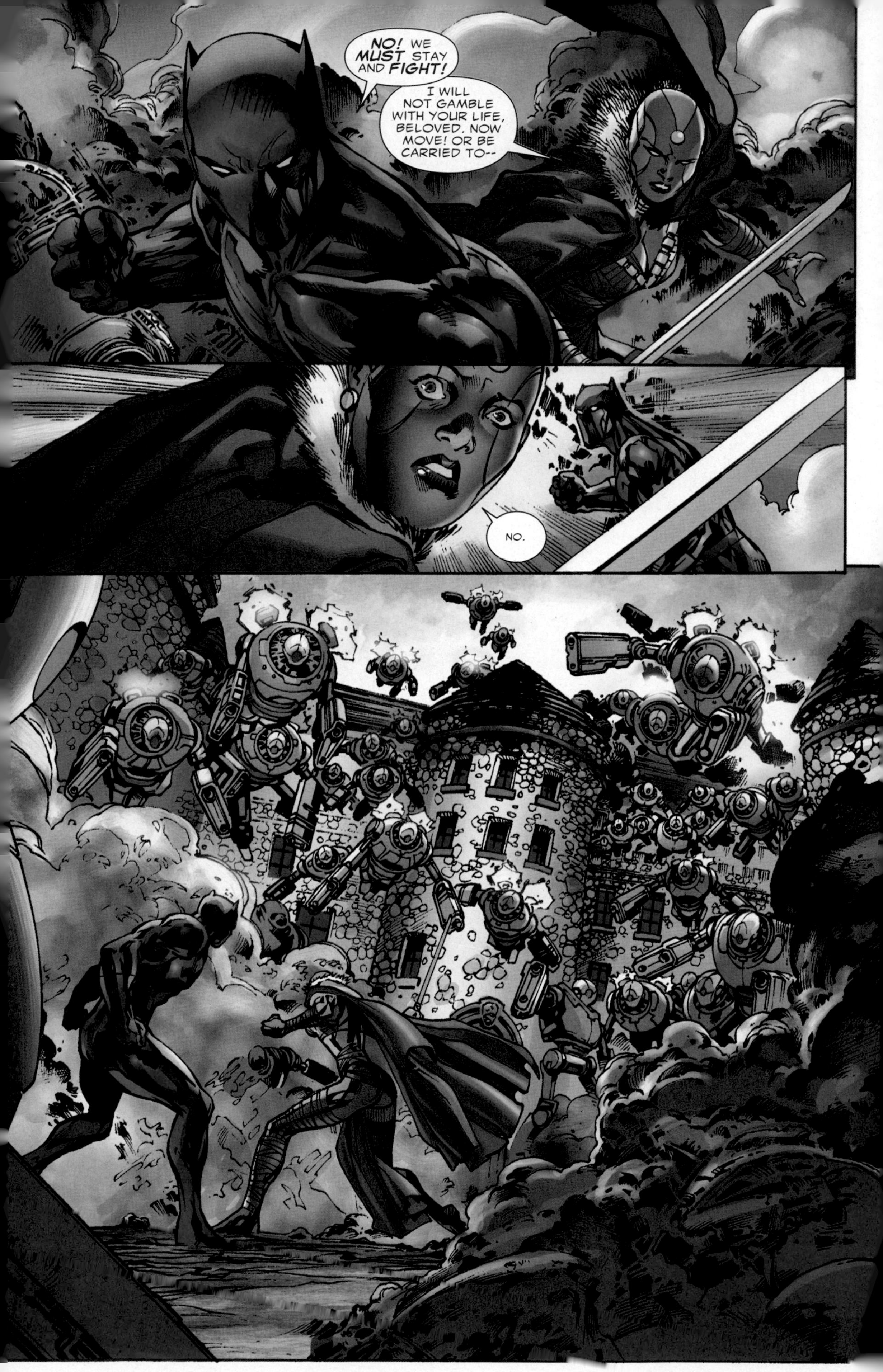
NO! WE MUST STAY AND FIGHT!
I WILL NOT GAMBLE WITH YOUR LIFE, BELOVED. NOW MOVE! OR BE CARRIED TO--
NO.

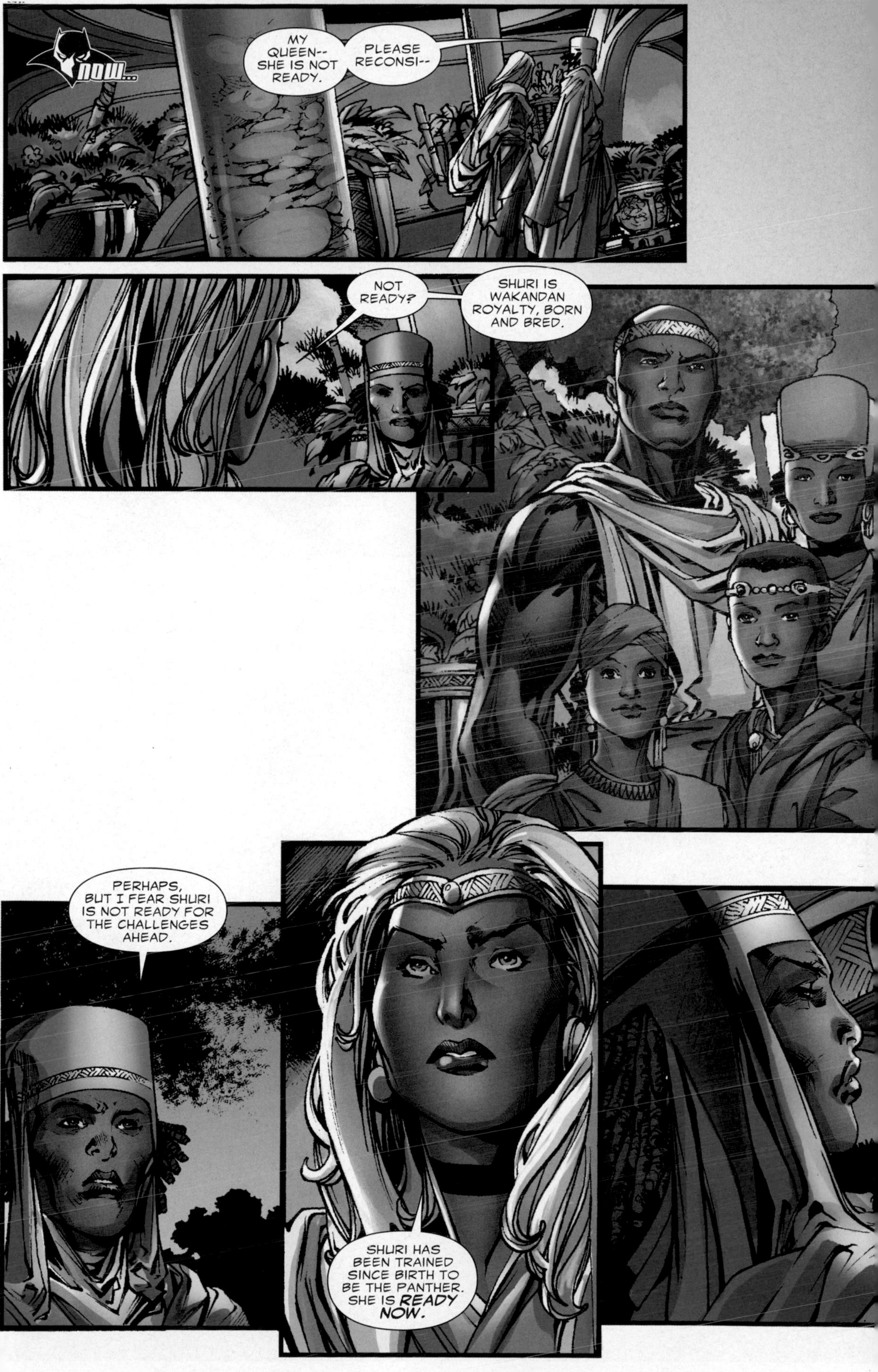
NOW...
MY QUEEN-- SHE IS NOT READY.
PLEASE RECONSI--
NOT READY?
SHURI IS WAKANDAN ROYALTY, BORN AND BRED.
PERHAPS, BUT I FEAR SHURI IS NOT READY FOR THE CHALLENGES AHEAD.
SHURI HAS BEEN TRAINED SINCE BIRTH TO BE THE PANTHER. SHE IS *READY NOW.*

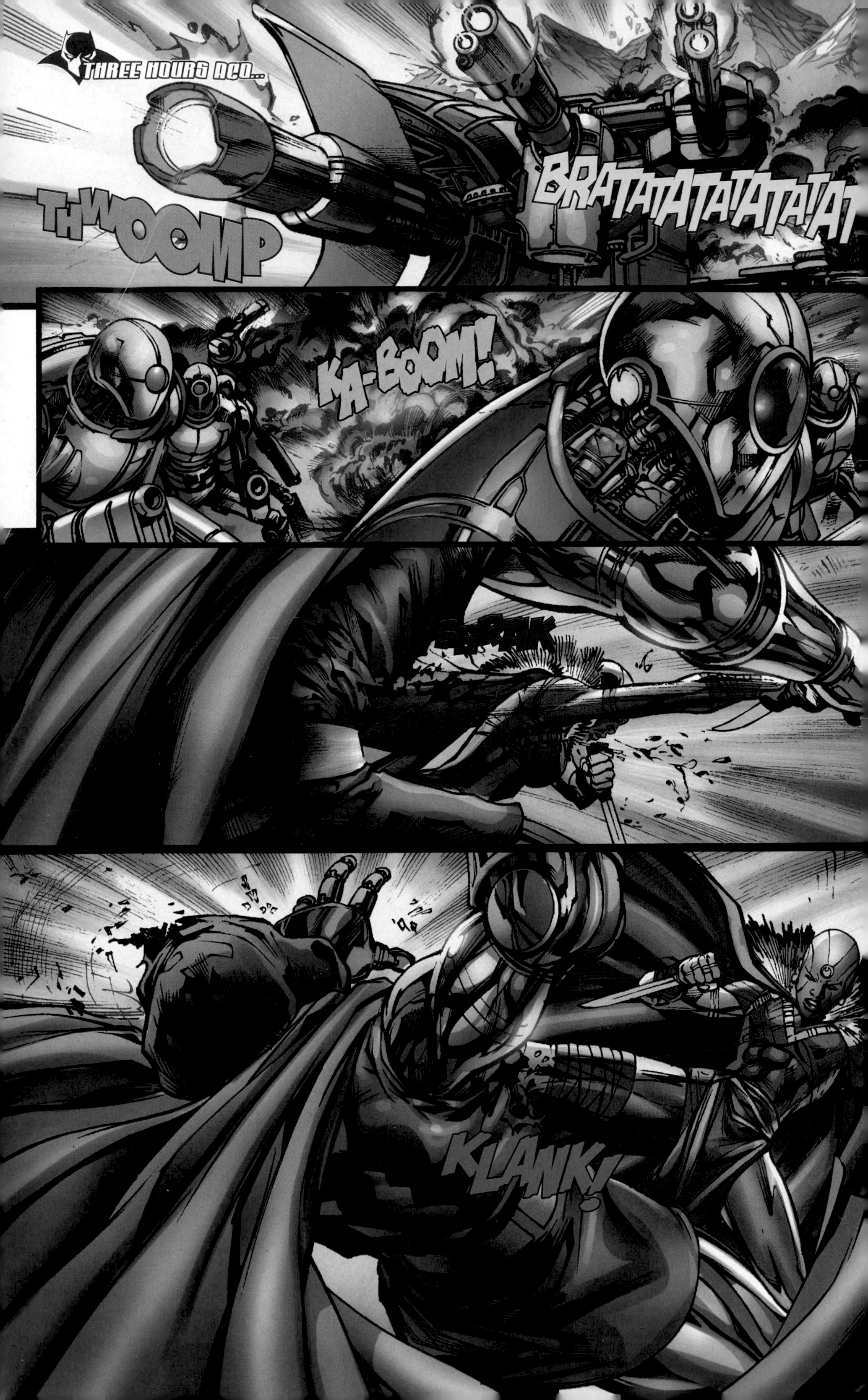
THREE HOURS AGO...
THWOOMP
BRATATATATATATAT
KA-BOOM!
KLANK!

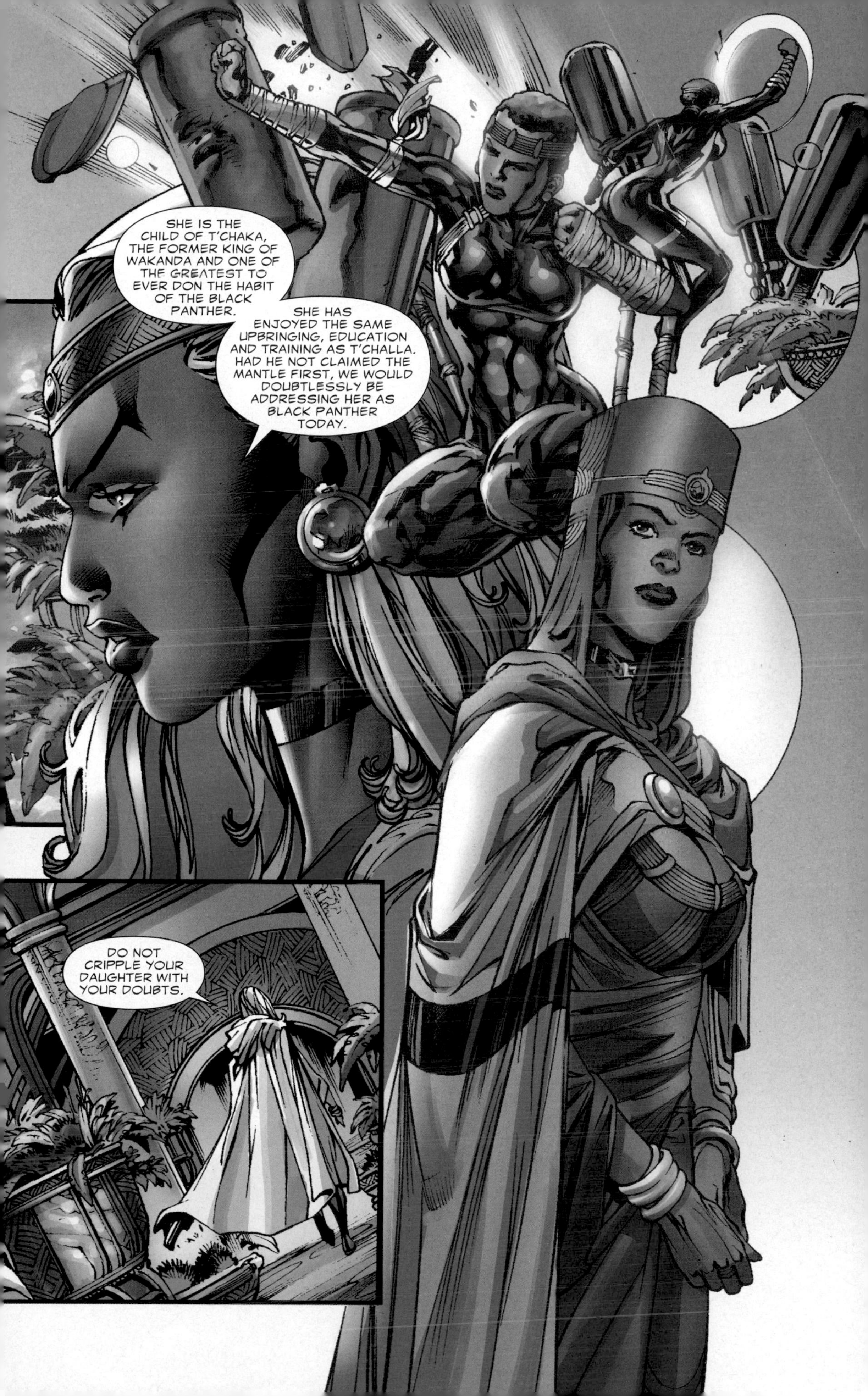
SHE IS THE CHILD OF T'CHAKA, THE FORMER KING OF WAKANDA AND ONE OF THE GREATEST TO EVER DON THE HABIT OF THE BLACK PANTHER.
SHE HAS ENJOYED THE SAME UPBRINGING, EDUCATION AND TRAINING AS T'CHALLA. HAD HE NOT CLAIMED THE MANTLE FIRST, WE WOULD DOUBTLESSLY BE ADDRESSING HER AS BLACK PANTHER TODAY.
DO NOT CRIPPLE YOUR DAUGHTER WITH YOUR DOUBTS.

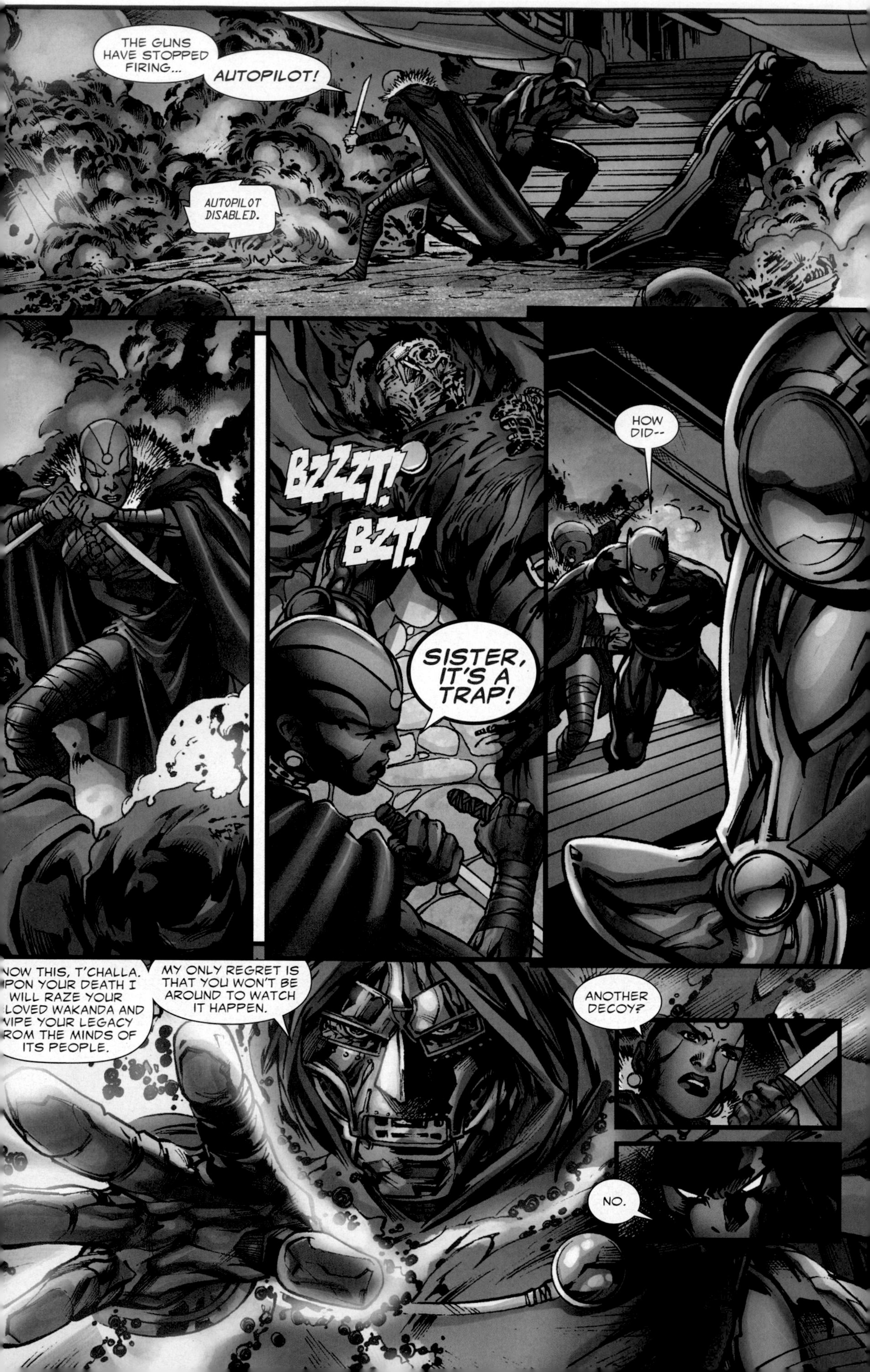
THE GUNS HAVE STOPPED FIRING...
AUTOPILOT!
AUTOPILOT DISABLED.
BZZZT! BZT!
SISTER, IT'S A TRAP!
HOW DID--
NOW THIS, T'CHALLA. UPON YOUR DEATH I WILL RAZE YOUR BELOVED WAKANDA AND WIPE YOUR LEGACY FROM THE MINDS OF ITS PEOPLE.
MY ONLY REGRET IS THAT YOU WON'T BE AROUND TO WATCH IT HAPPEN.
ANOTHER DECOY?
NO.

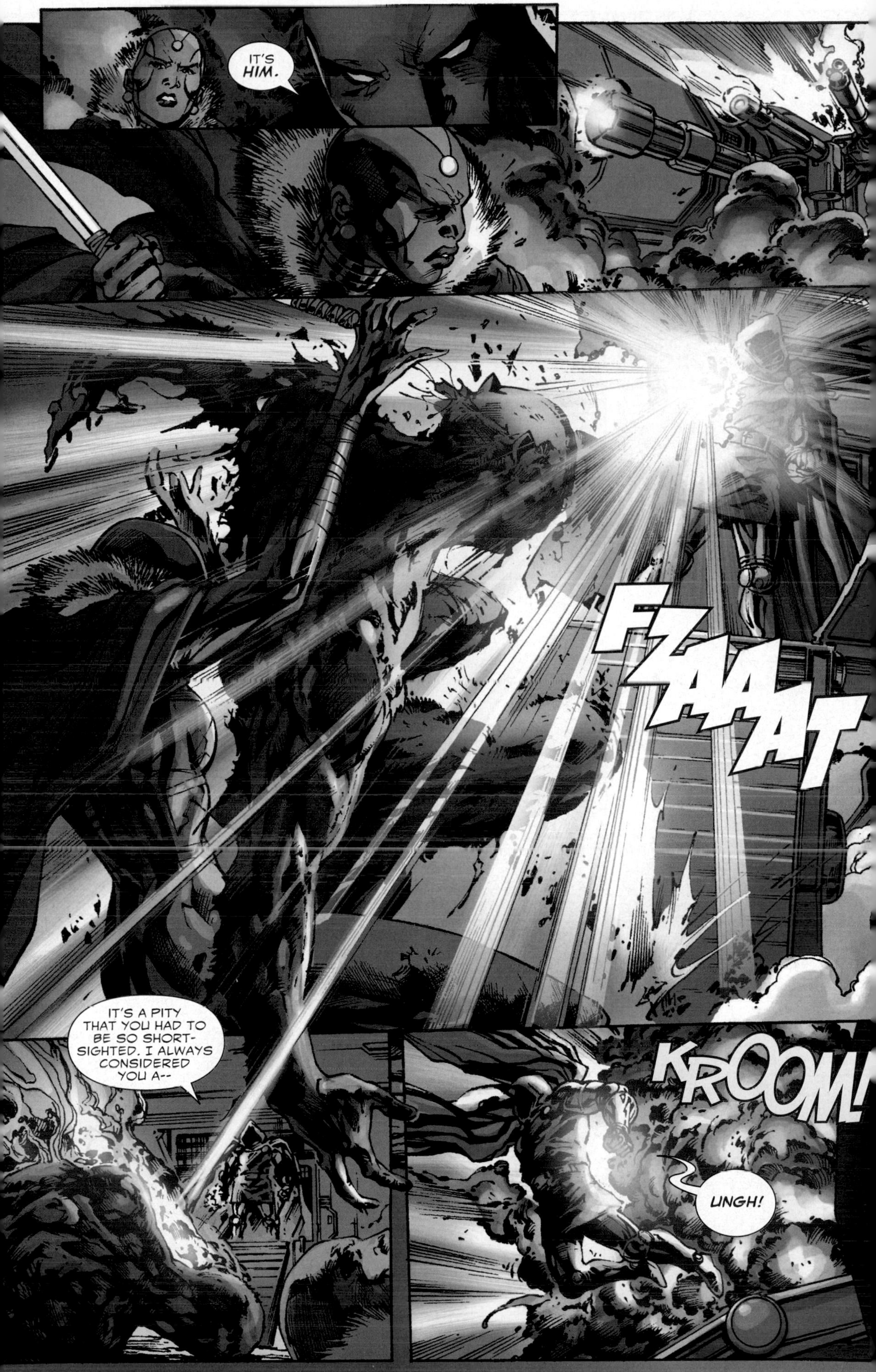
IT'S HIM.
FZAAAT
IT'S A PITY THAT YOU HAD TO BE SO SHORT-SIGHTED. I ALWAYS CONSIDERED YOU A--
KROOM!
UNGH!

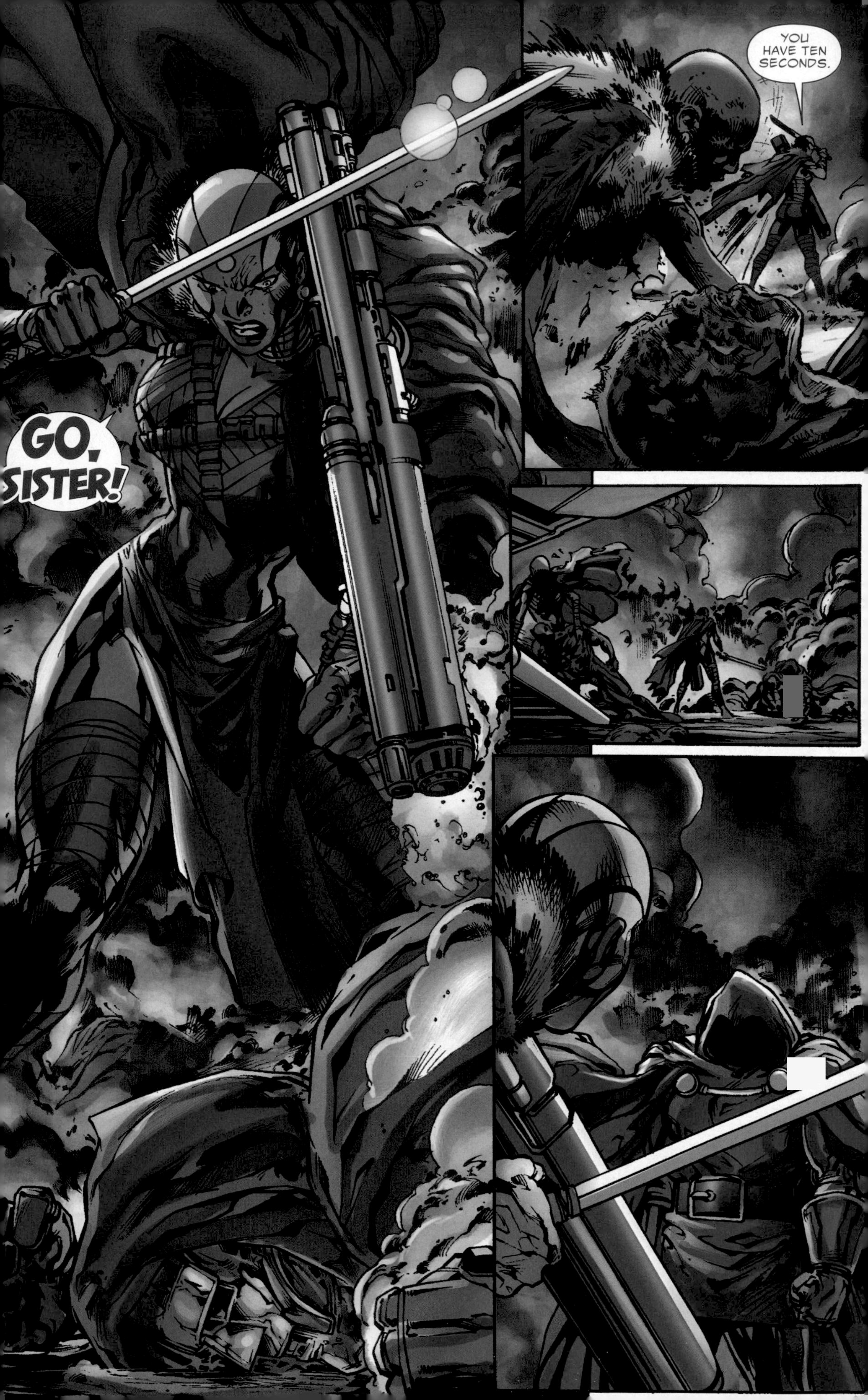
GO, SISTER!
YOU HAVE TEN SECONDS.

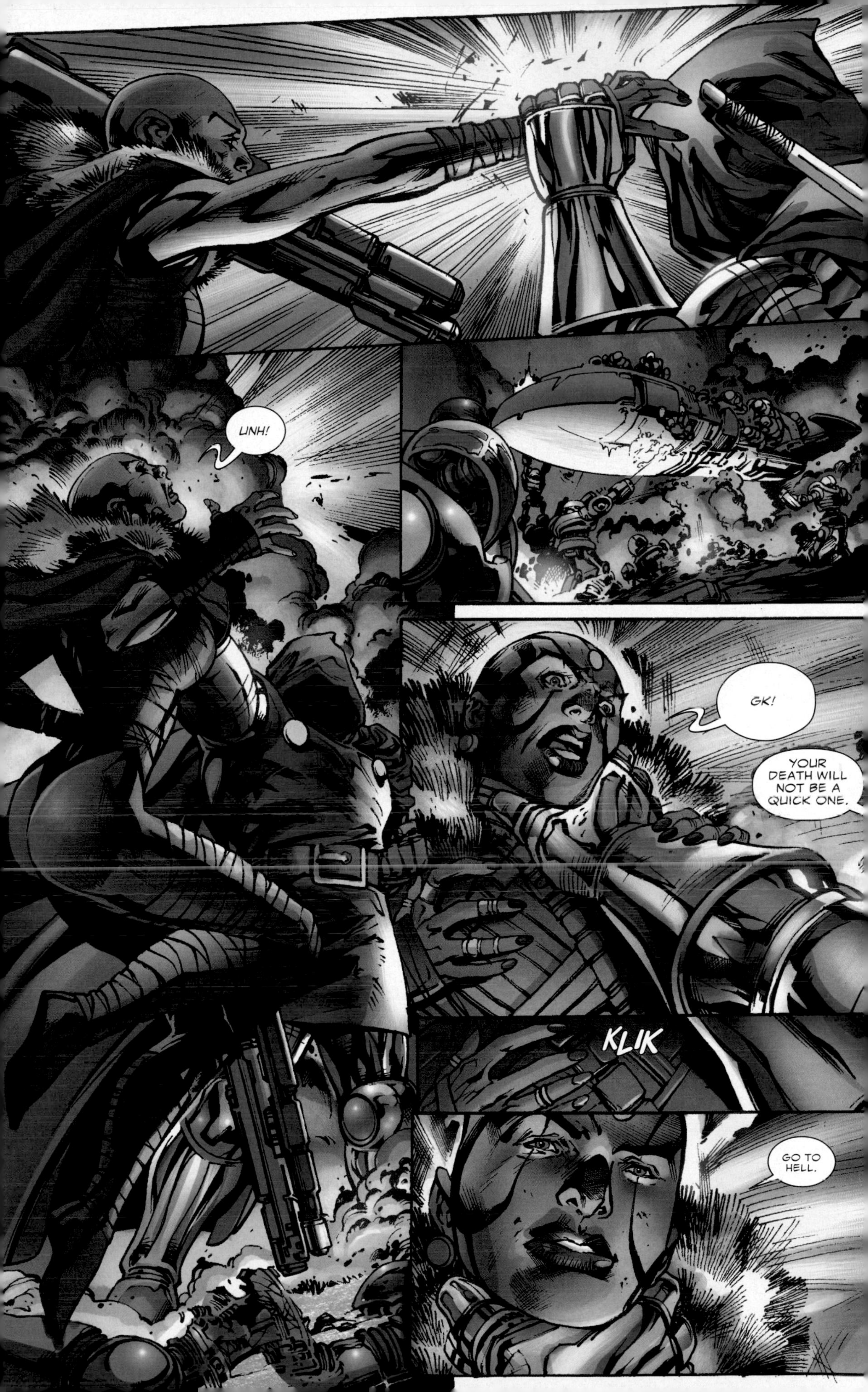
UNH!
GK!
YOUR DEATH WILL NOT BE A QUICK ONE.
KLIK
GO TO HELL.

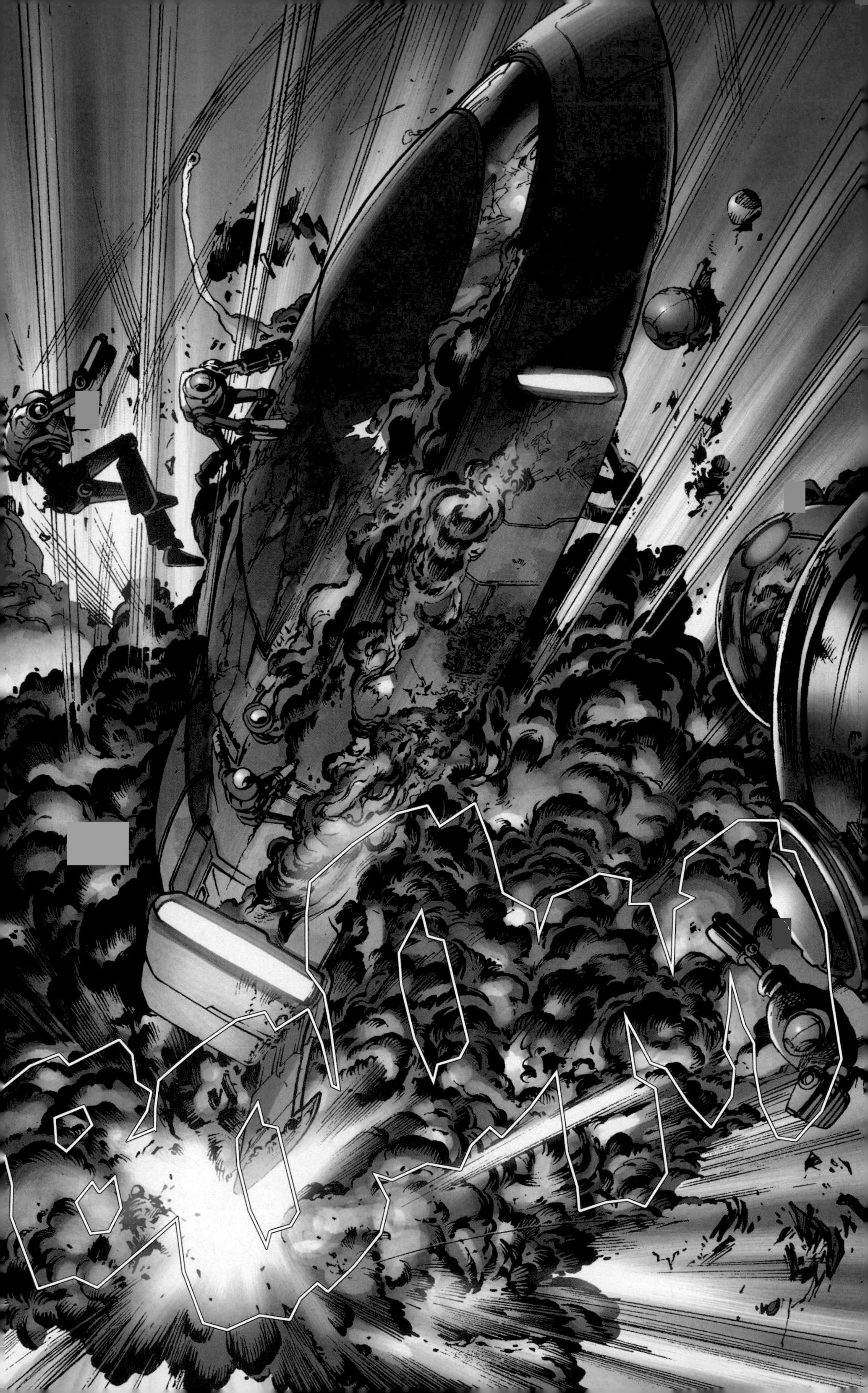

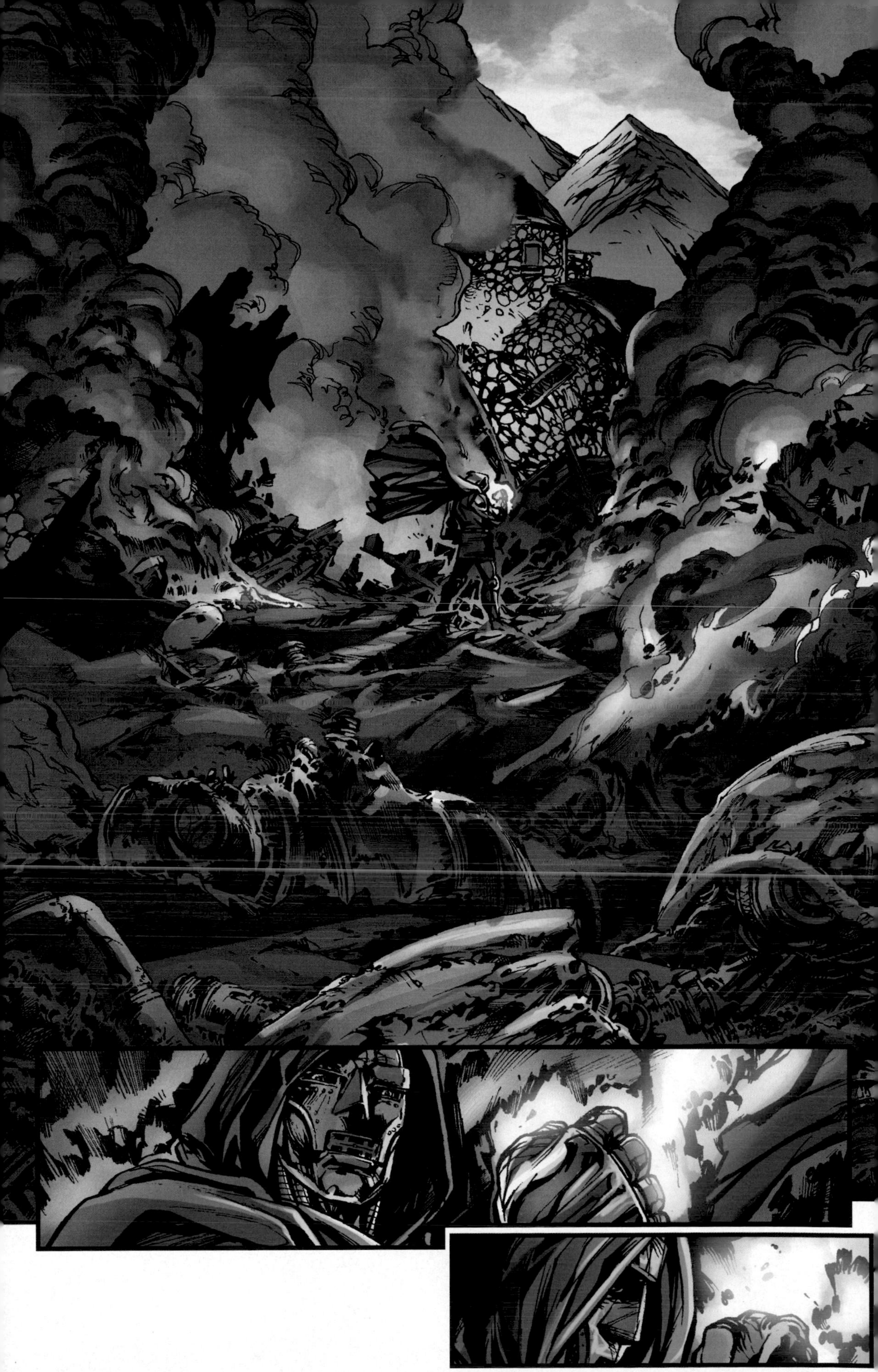

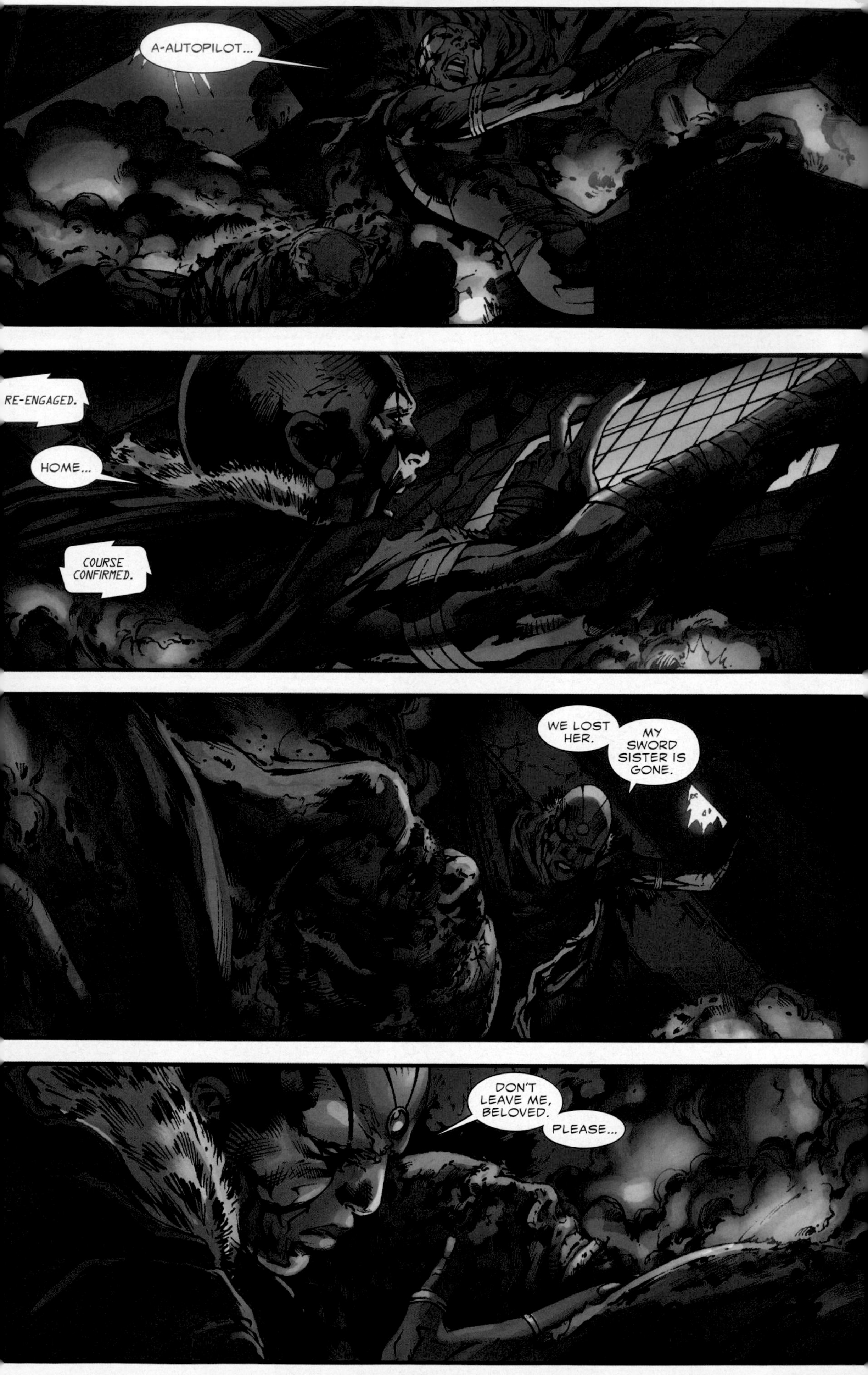
A-AUTOPILOT...
RE-ENGAGED.
HOME...
COURSE CONFIRMED.
WE LOST HER.
MY SWORD SISTER IS GONE.
DON'T LEAVE ME, BELOVED.
PLEASE...

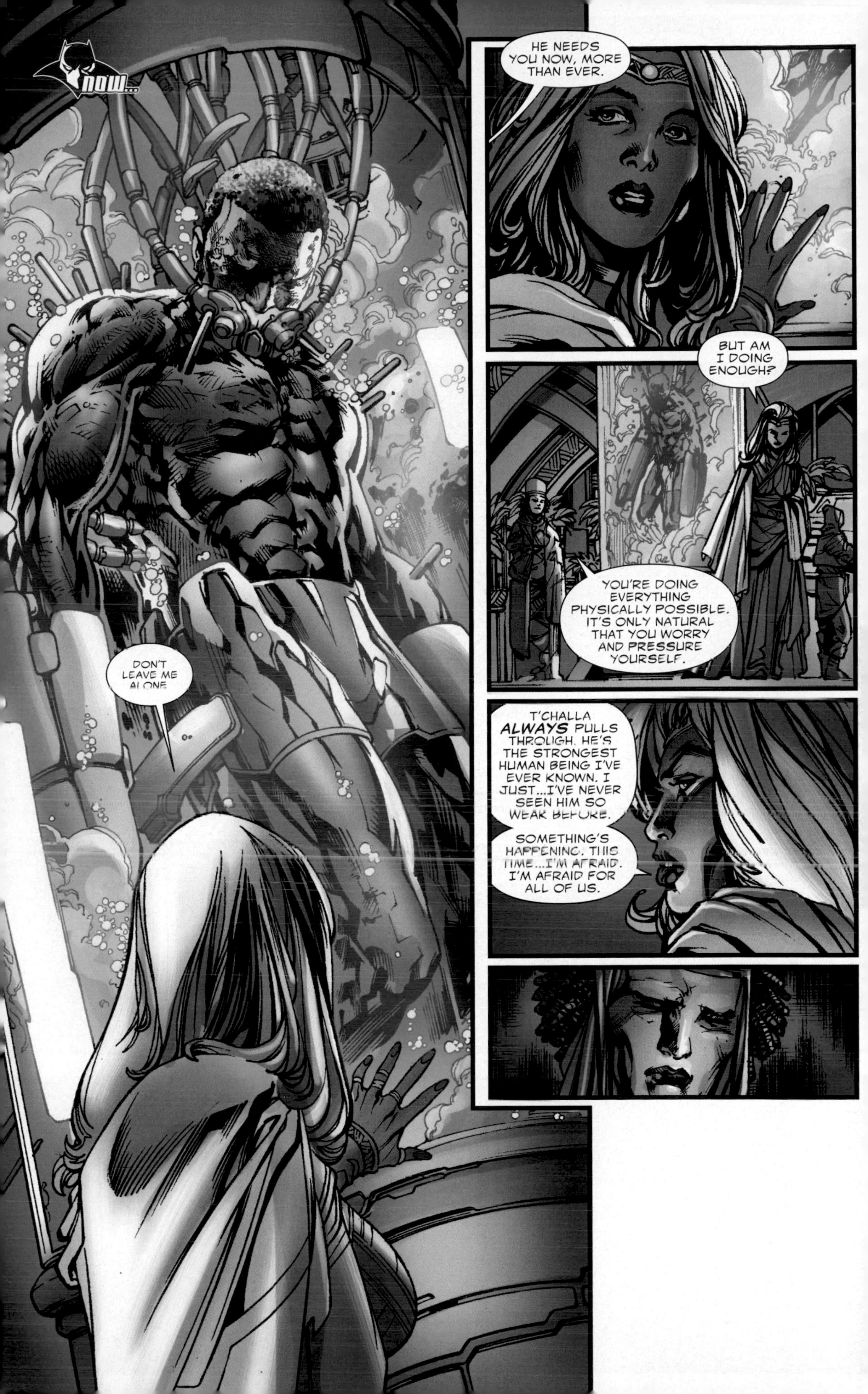
NOW...
DON'T LEAVE ME ALONE
HE NEEDS YOU NOW, MORE THAN EVER.
BUT AM I DOING ENOUGH?
YOU'RE DOING EVERYTHING PHYSICALLY POSSIBLE. IT'S ONLY NATURAL THAT YOU WORRY AND PRESSURE YOURSELF.
T'CHALLA ALWAYS PULLS THROUGH. HE'S THE STRONGEST HUMAN BEING I'VE EVER KNOWN. I JUST...I'VE NEVER SEEN HIM SO WEAK BEFORE.
SOMETHING'S HAPPENING. THIS TIME...I'M AFRAID. I'M AFRAID FOR ALL OF US.

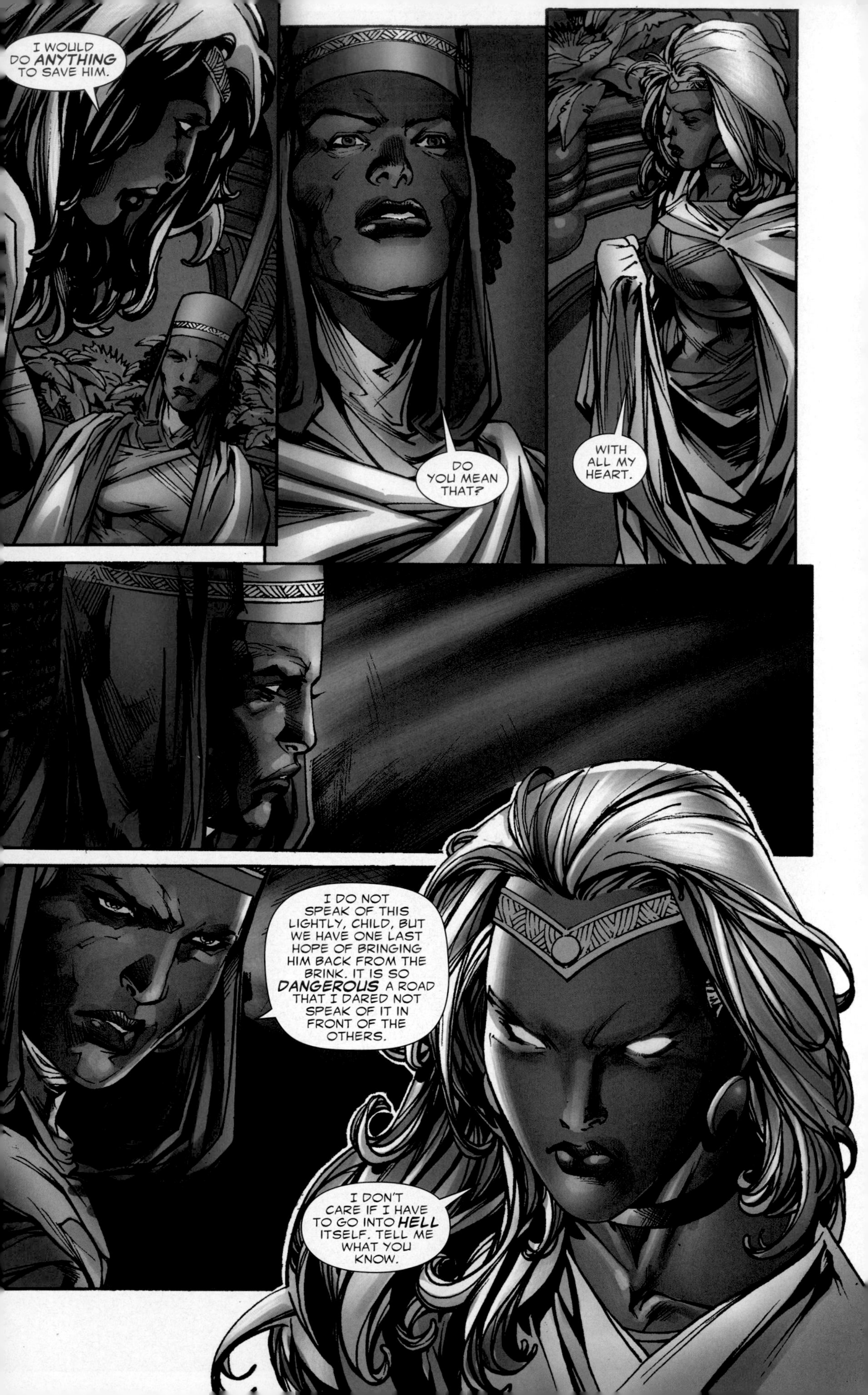
I WOULD DO ANYTHING TO SAVE HIM.
DO YOU MEAN THAT?
WITH ALL MY HEART.
I DO NOT SPEAK OF THIS LIGHTLY, CHILD, BUT WE HAVE ONE LAST HOPE OF BRINGING HIM BACK FROM THE BRINK. IT IS SO DANGEROUS A ROAD THAT I DARED NOT SPEAK OF IT IN FRONT OF THE OTHERS.
I DON'T CARE IF I HAVE TO GO INTO HELL ITSELF. TELL ME WHAT YOU KNOW.

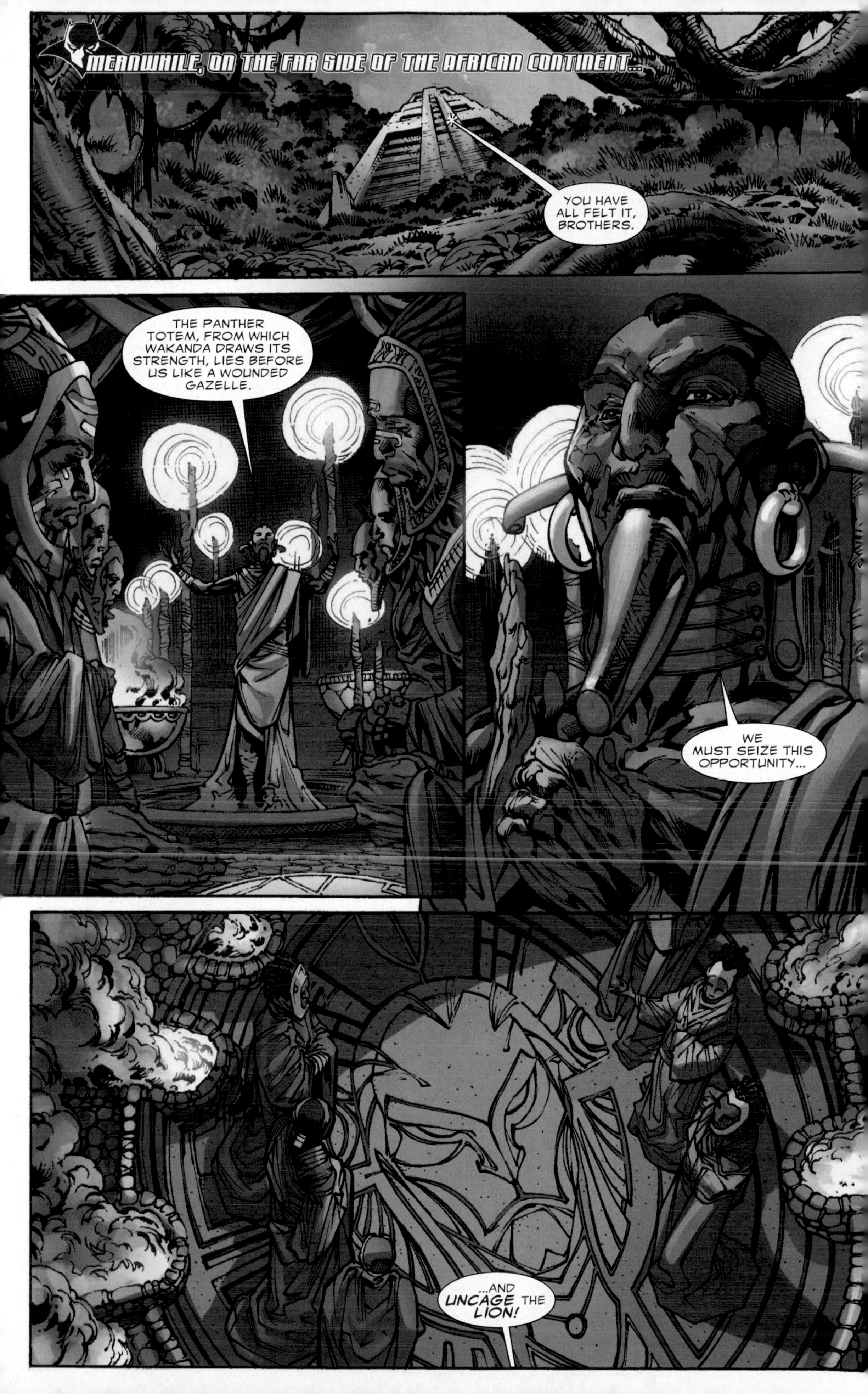
MEANWHILE, ON THE FAR SIDE OF THE AFRICAN CONTINENT...
YOU HAVE ALL FELT IT, BROTHERS.
THE PANTHER TOTEM, FROM WHICH WAKANDA DRAWS ITS STRENGTH, LIES BEFORE US LIKE A WOUNDED GAZELLE.
WE MUST SEIZE THIS OPPORTUNITY...
...AND *UNCAGE* THE *LION!*

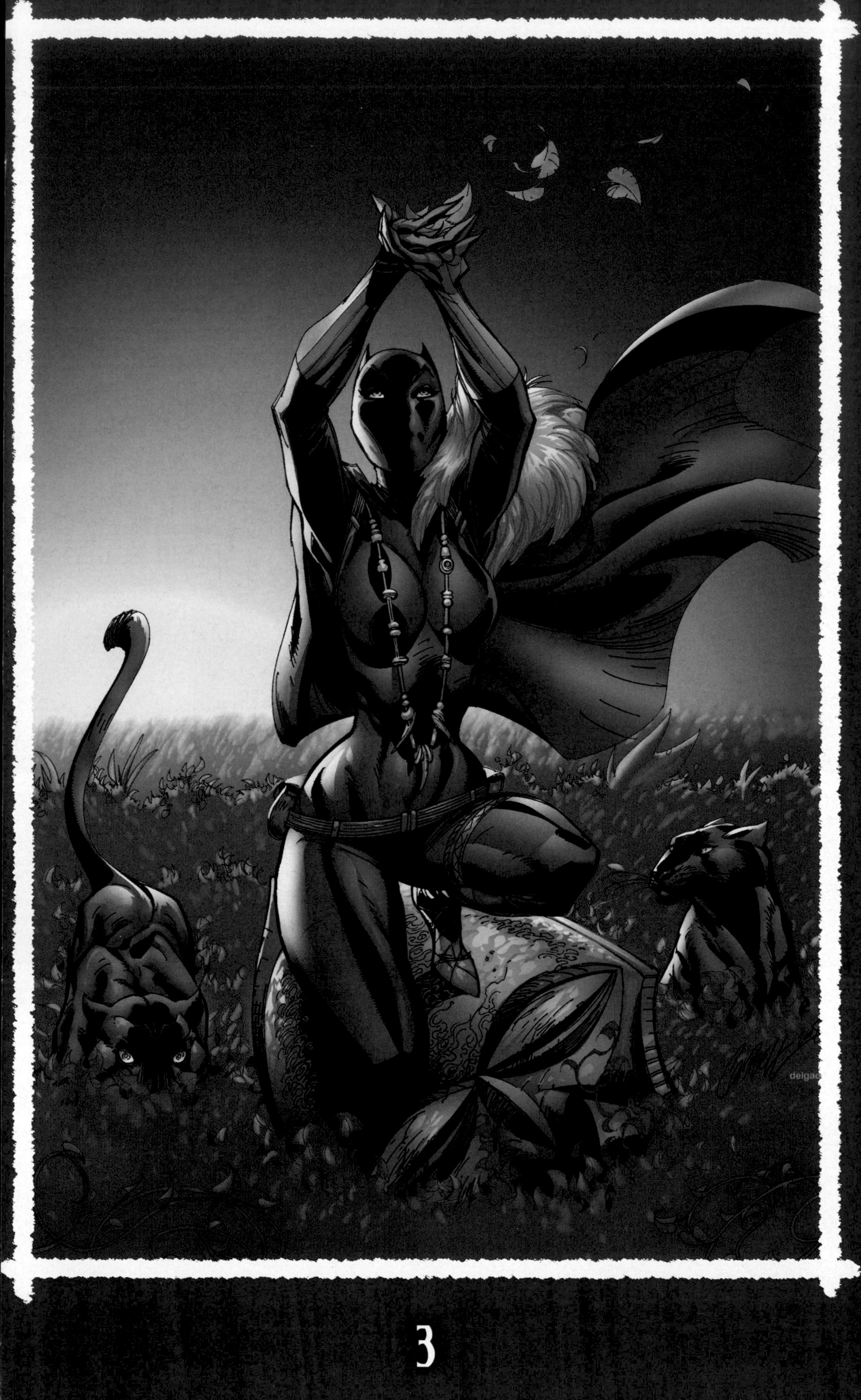

3

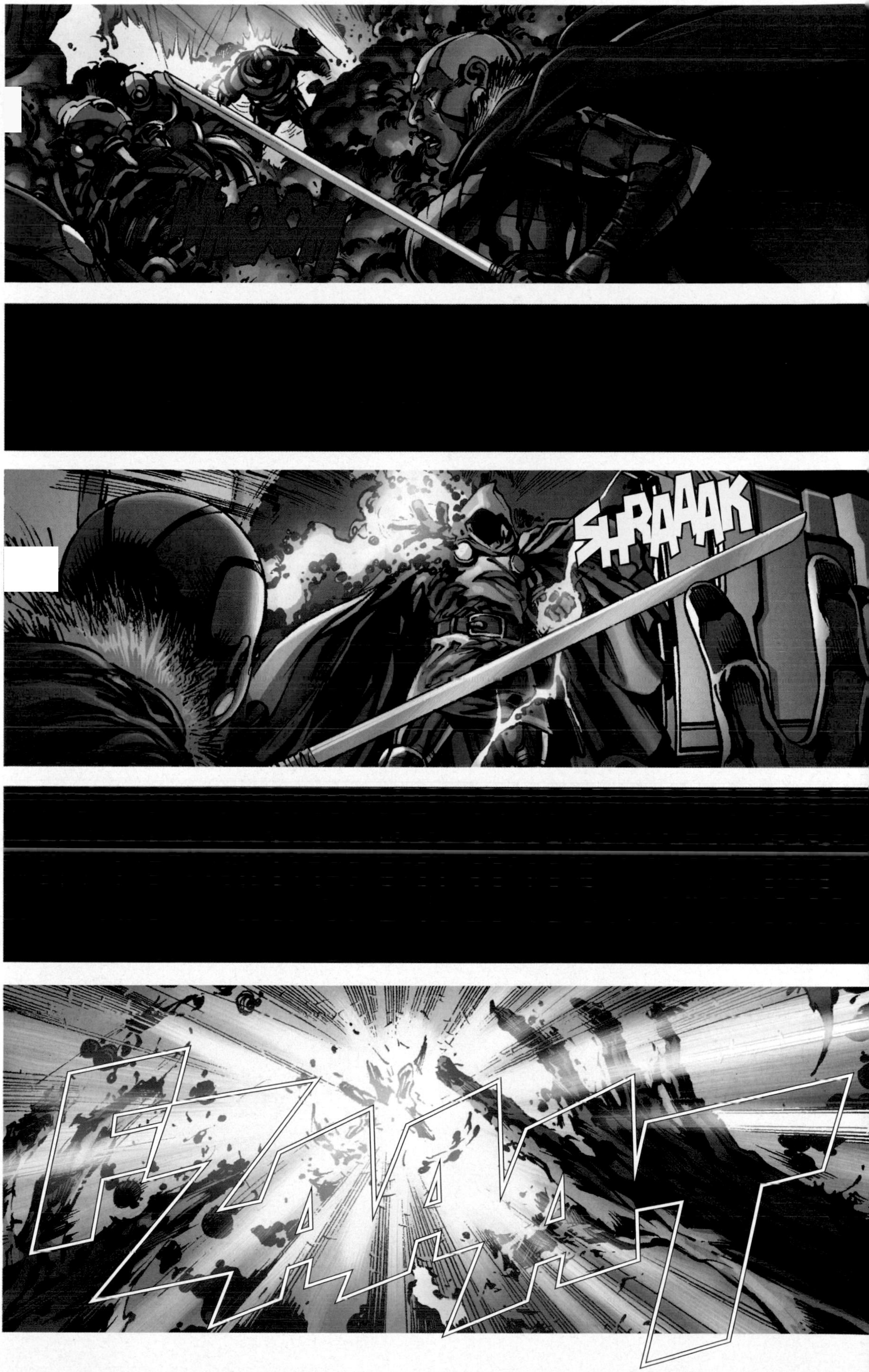
SHRAAAK

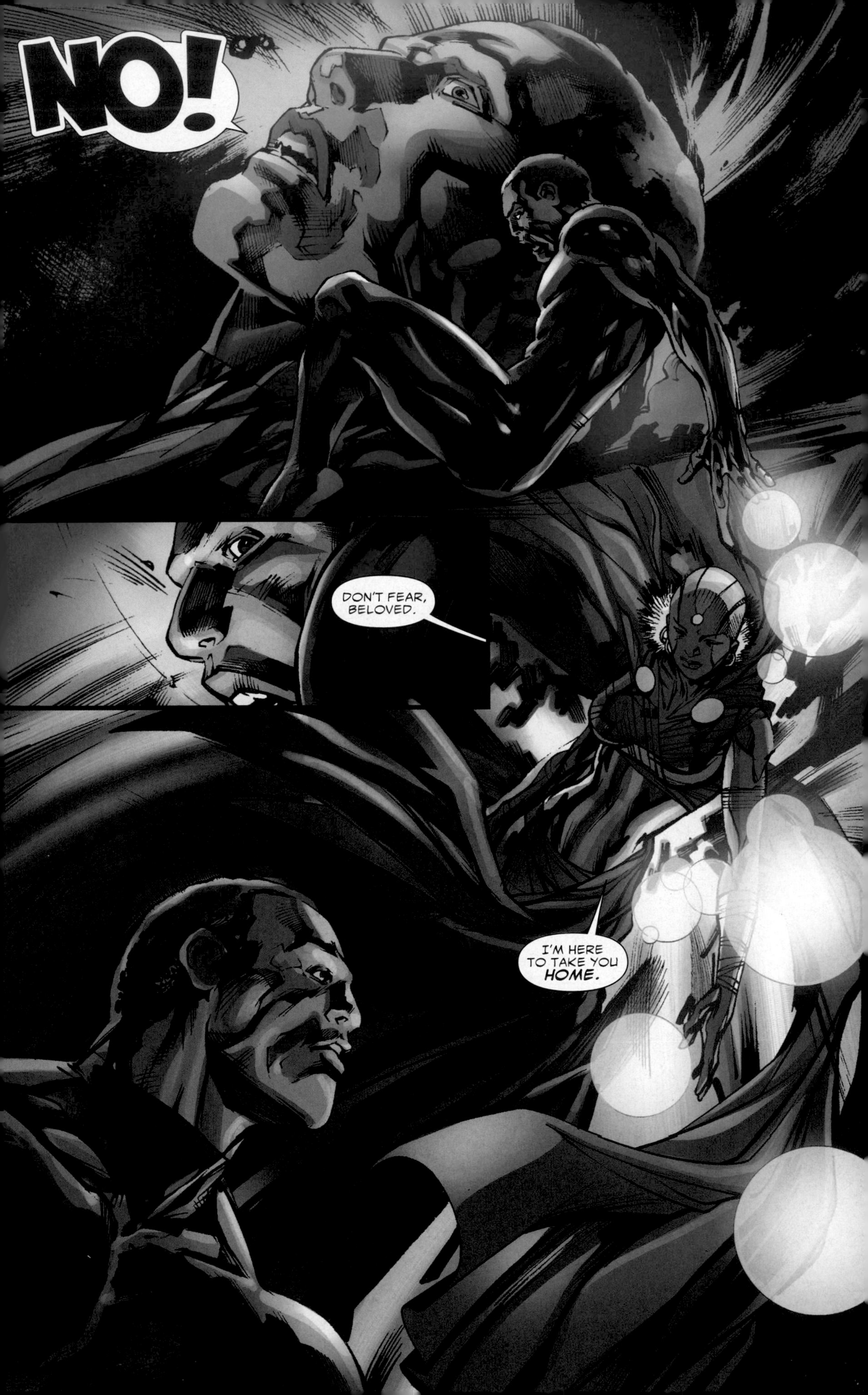
NO!
DON'T FEAR, BELOVED.
I'M HERE TO TAKE YOU HOME.

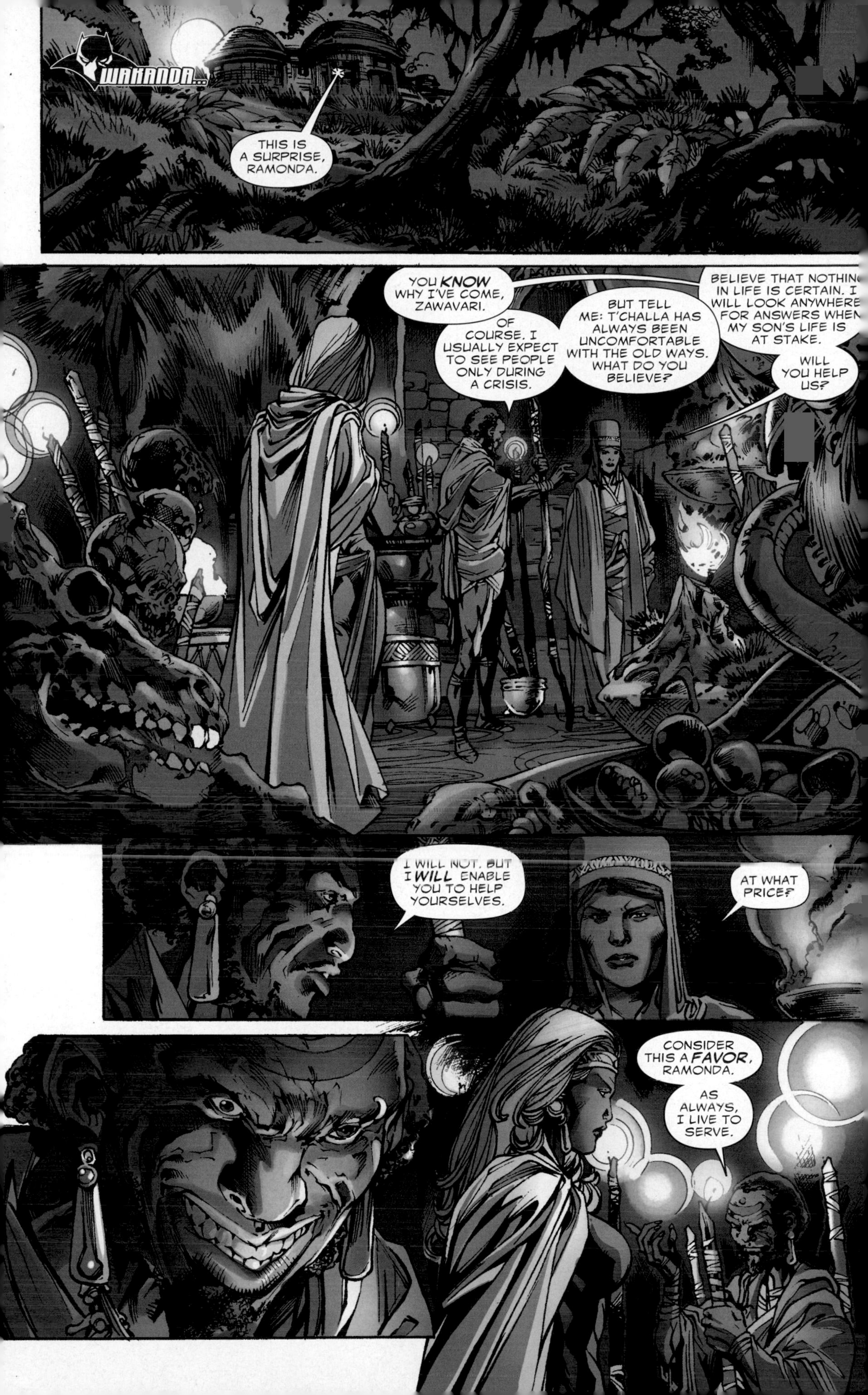
WAKANDA...
THIS IS A SURPRISE, RAMONDA.
YOU KNOW WHY I'VE COME, ZAWAVARI.
OF COURSE. I USUALLY EXPECT TO SEE PEOPLE ONLY DURING A CRISIS.
BUT TELL ME: T'CHALLA HAS ALWAYS BEEN UNCOMFORTABLE WITH THE OLD WAYS. WHAT DO YOU BELIEVE?
BELIEVE THAT NOTHING IN LIFE IS CERTAIN. I WILL LOOK ANYWHERE FOR ANSWERS WHEN MY SON'S LIFE IS AT STAKE.
WILL YOU HELP US?
I WILL NOT. BUT I WILL ENABLE YOU TO HELP YOURSELVES.
AT WHAT PRICE?
CONSIDER THIS A FAVOR, RAMONDA.
AS ALWAYS, I LIVE TO SERVE.

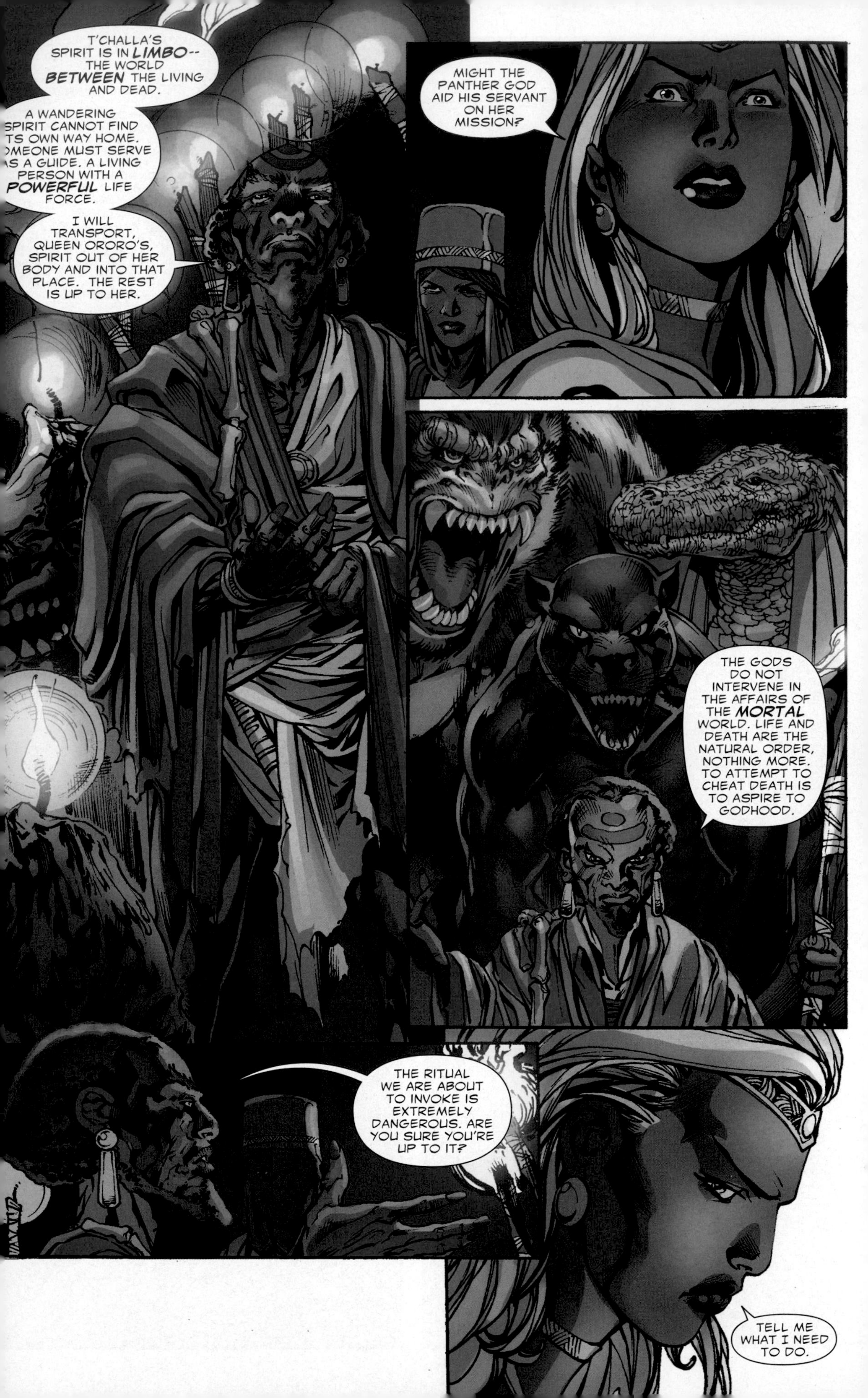
T'CHALLA'S SPIRIT IS IN LIMBO-- THE WORLD BETWEEN THE LIVING AND DEAD.
A WANDERING SPIRIT CANNOT FIND ITS OWN WAY HOME. SOMEONE MUST SERVE AS A GUIDE. A LIVING PERSON WITH A POWERFUL LIFE FORCE.
I WILL TRANSPORT, QUEEN ORORO'S, SPIRIT OUT OF HER BODY AND INTO THAT PLACE. THE REST IS UP TO HER.
MIGHT THE PANTHER GOD AID HIS SERVANT ON HER MISSION?
THE GODS DO NOT INTERVENE IN THE AFFAIRS OF THE MORTAL WORLD. LIFE AND DEATH ARE THE NATURAL ORDER, NOTHING MORE. TO ATTEMPT TO CHEAT DEATH IS TO ASPIRE TO GODHOOD.
THE RITUAL WE ARE ABOUT TO INVOKE IS EXTREMELY DANGEROUS. ARE YOU SURE YOU'RE UP TO IT?
TELL ME WHAT I NEED TO DO.

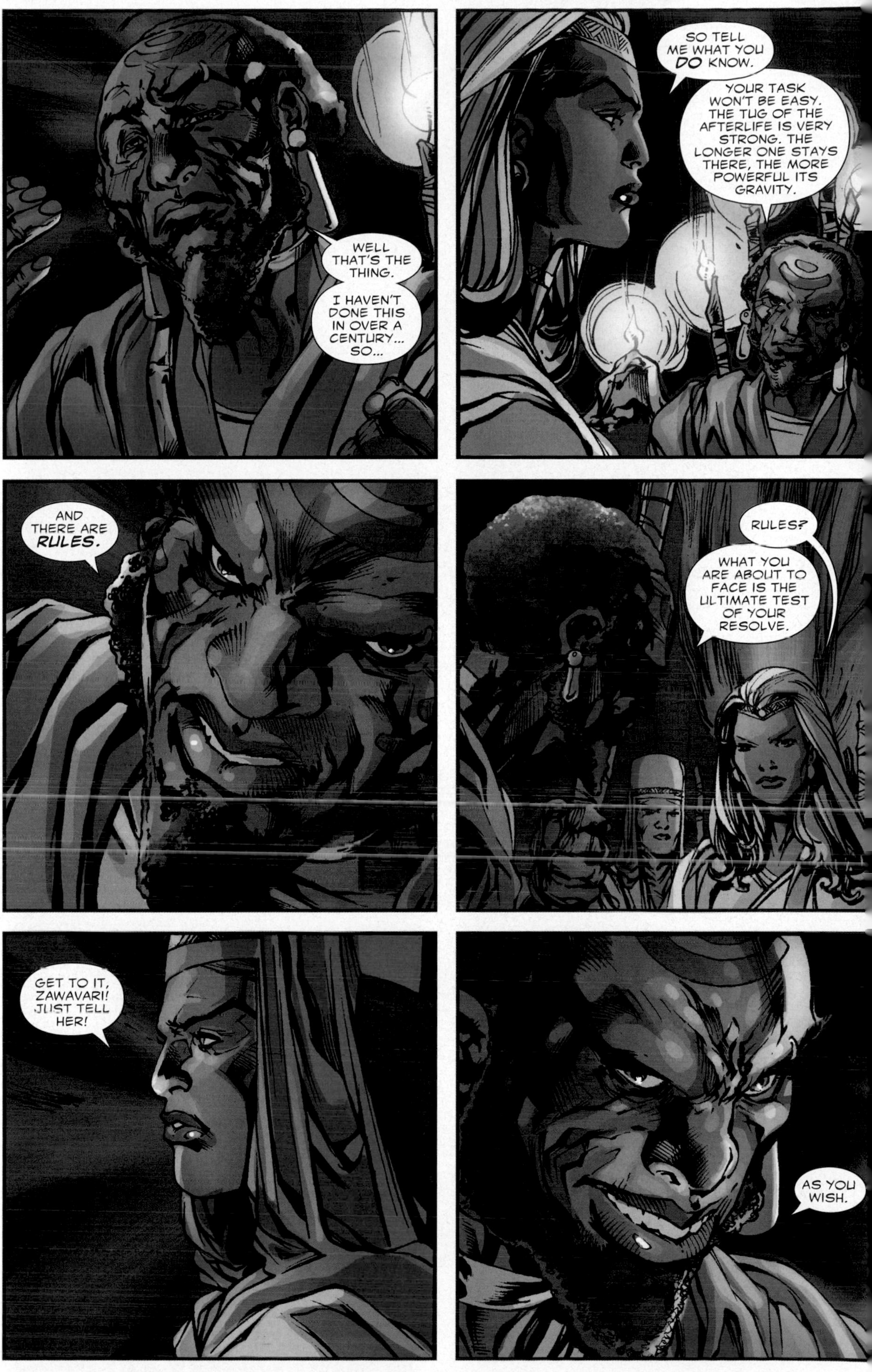
WELL THAT'S THE THING.
I HAVEN'T DONE THIS IN OVER A CENTURY... SO...
SO TELL ME WHAT YOU DO KNOW.
YOUR TASK WON'T BE EASY. THE TUG OF THE AFTERLIFE IS VERY STRONG. THE LONGER ONE STAYS THERE, THE MORE POWERFUL ITS GRAVITY.
AND THERE ARE RULES.
RULES?
WHAT YOU ARE ABOUT TO FACE IS THE ULTIMATE TEST OF YOUR RESOLVE.
GET TO IT, ZAWAVARI! JUST TELL HER!
AS YOU WISH.

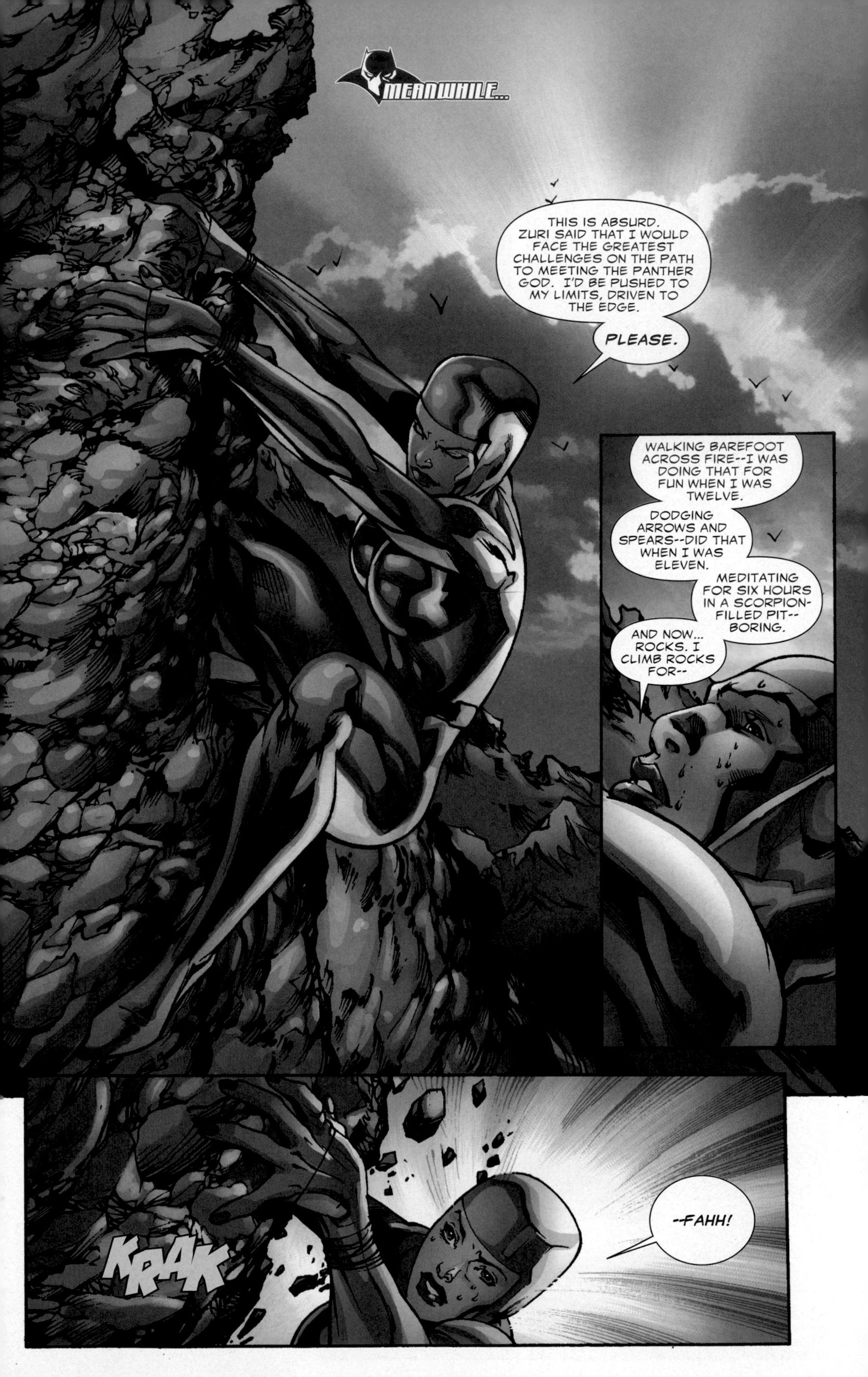
MEANWHILE...
THIS IS ABSURD. ZURI SAID THAT I WOULD FACE THE GREATEST CHALLENGES ON THE PATH TO MEETING THE PANTHER GOD. I'D BE PUSHED TO MY LIMITS, DRIVEN TO THE EDGE.
PLEASE.
WALKING BAREFOOT ACROSS FIRE--I WAS DOING THAT FOR FUN WHEN I WAS TWELVE.
DODGING ARROWS AND SPEARS--DID THAT WHEN I WAS ELEVEN.
MEDITATING FOR SIX HOURS IN A SCORPION-FILLED PIT--BORING.
AND NOW... ROCKS. I CLIMB ROCKS FOR--
KRAK
--FAHH!

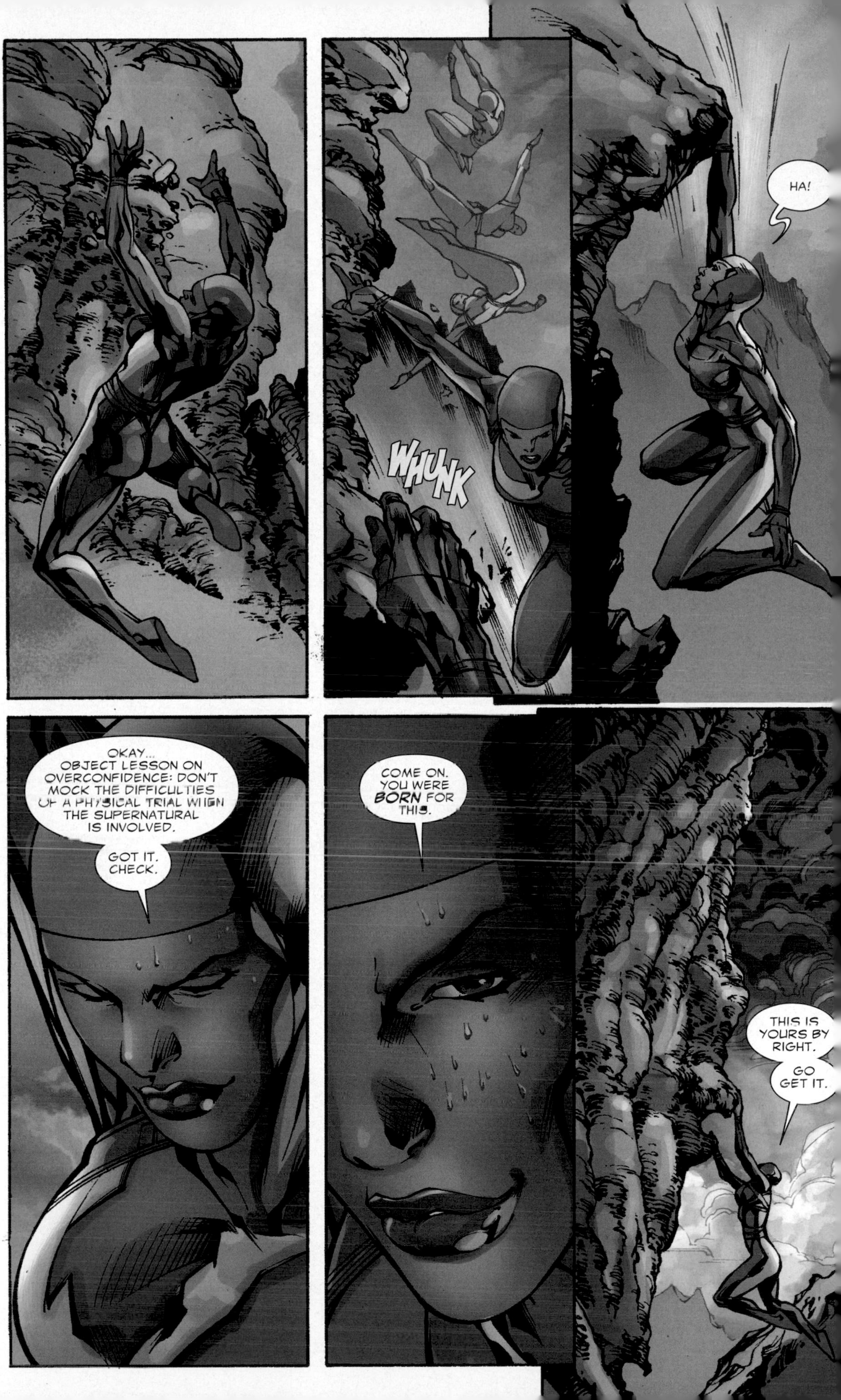
WHUNK
HA!
OKAY... OBJECT LESSON ON OVERCONFIDENCE: DON'T MOCK THE DIFFICULTIES OF A PHYSICAL TRIAL WHEN THE SUPERNATURAL IS INVOLVED.
GOT IT. CHECK.
COME ON. YOU WERE BORN FOR THIS.
THIS IS YOURS BY RIGHT.
GO GET IT.

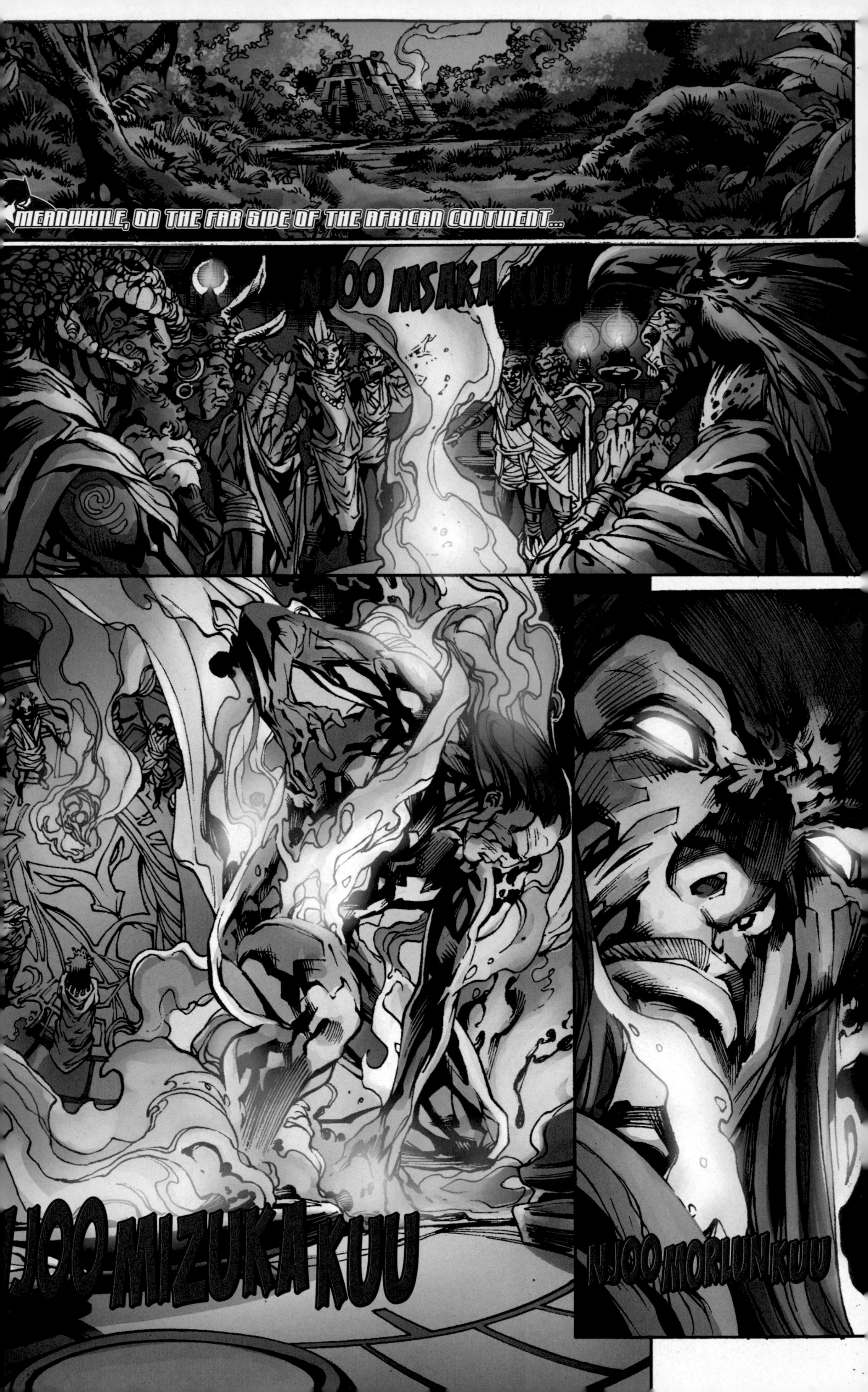
MEANWHILE, ON THE FAR SIDE OF THE AFRICAN CONTINENT...
NJOO MSAKA KUU
NJOO MIZUKA KUU
NJOO MORLUN KUU

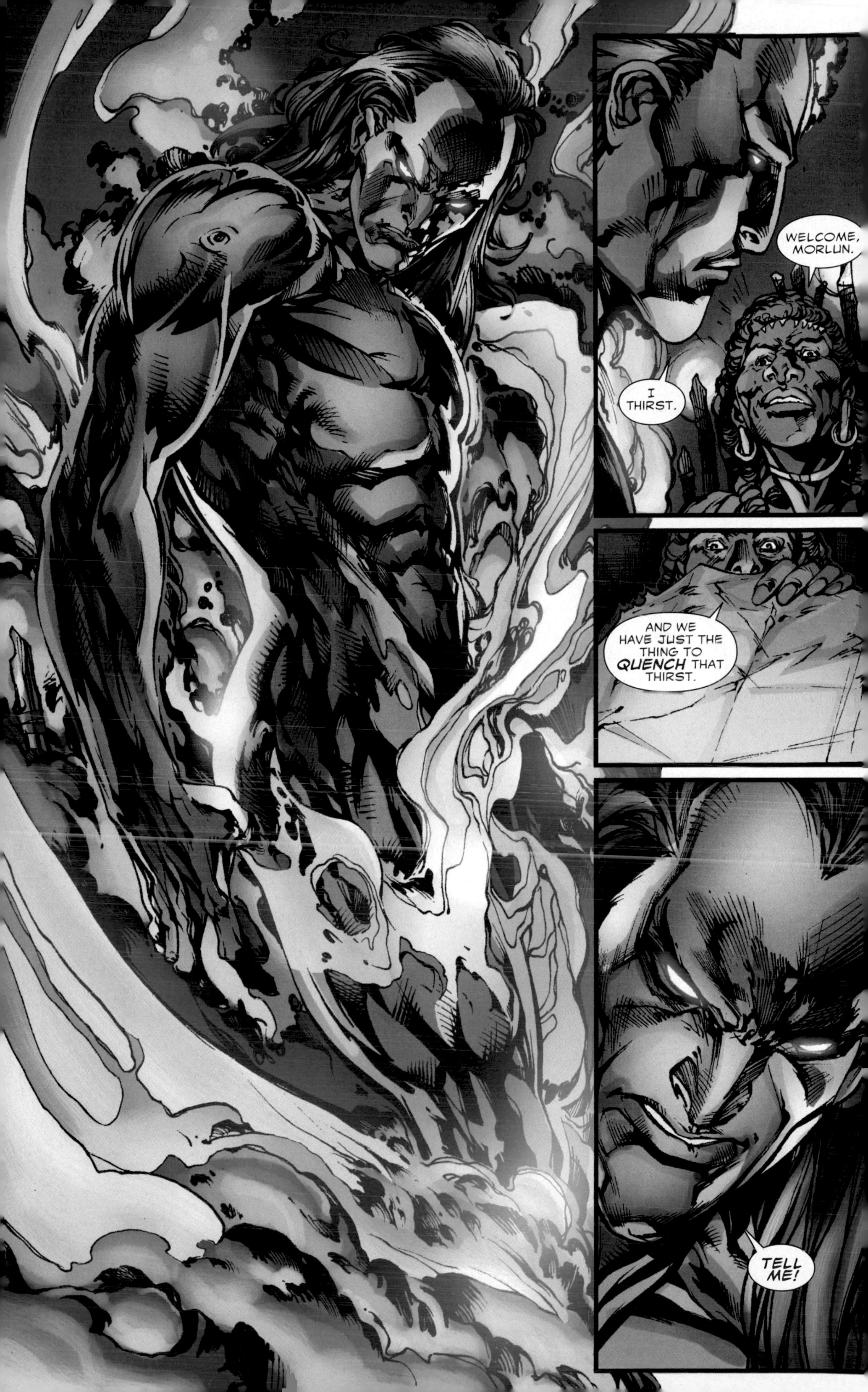
WELCOME, MORLUN.
I THIRST.
AND WE HAVE JUST THE THING TO QUENCH THAT THIRST.
TELL ME!

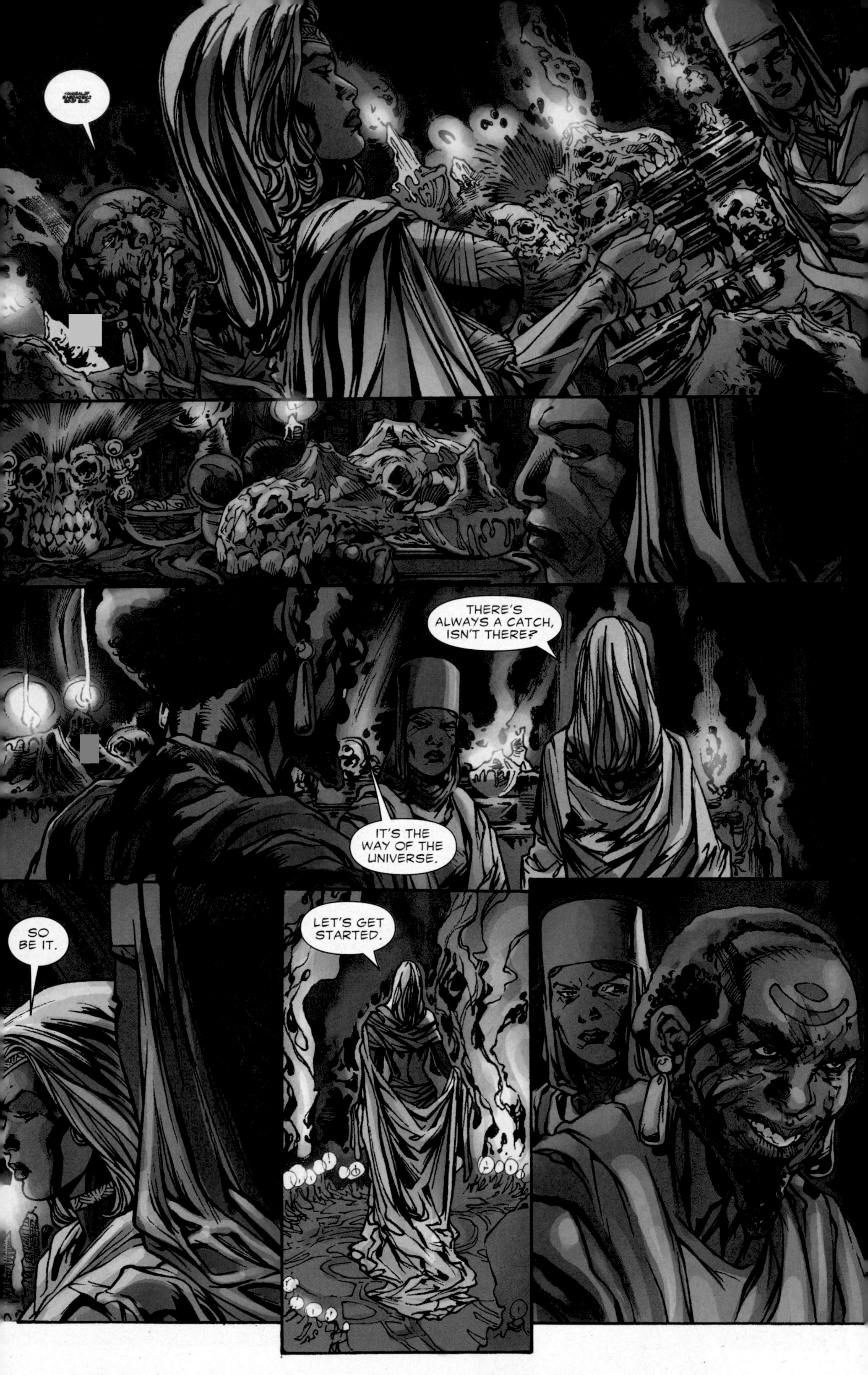
THERE'S ALWAYS A CATCH, ISN'T THERE?
IT'S THE WAY OF THE UNIVERSE.
SO BE IT.
LET'S GET STARTED.

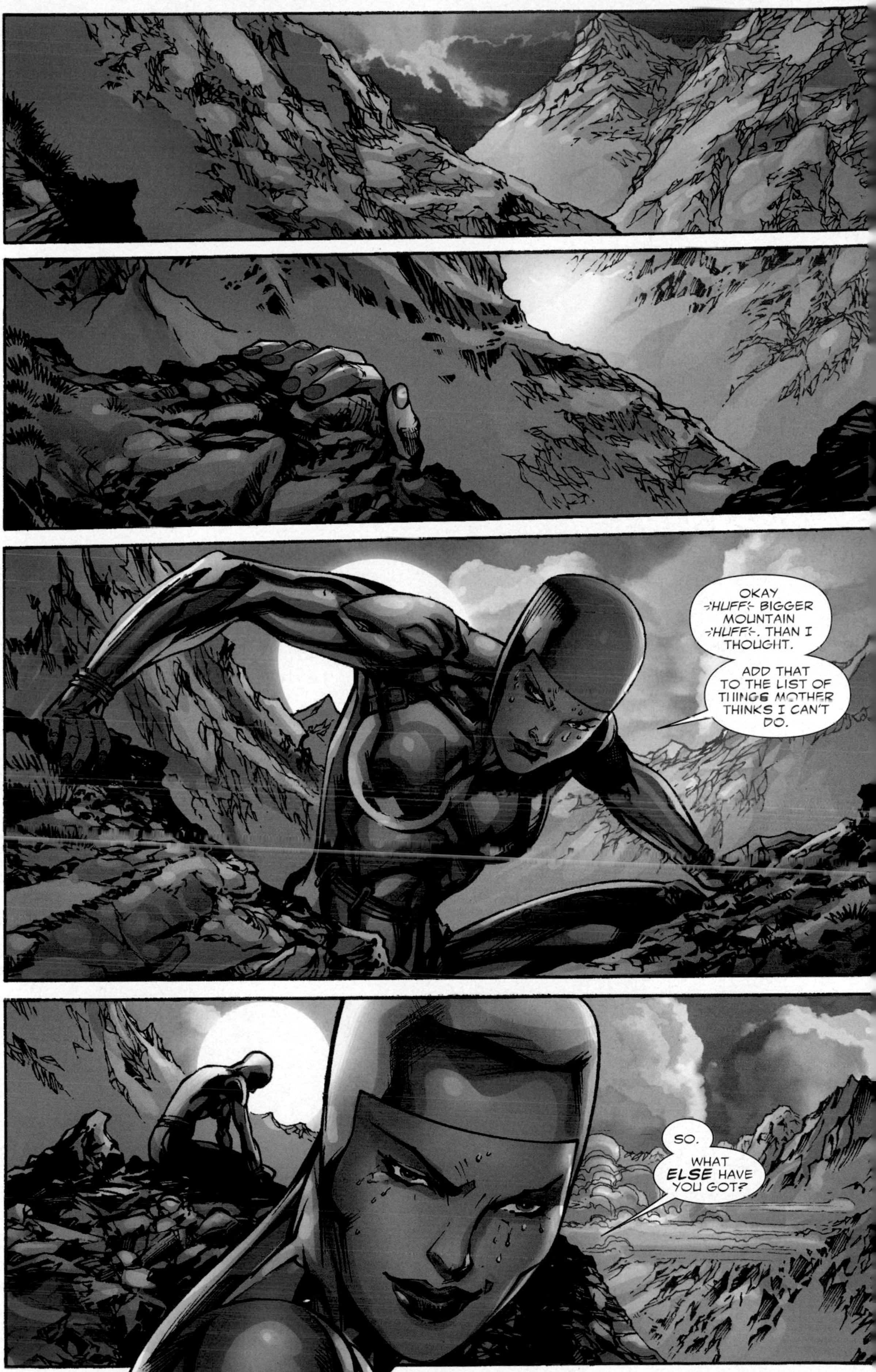
OKAY -HUFF- BIGGER MOUNTAIN -HUFF- THAN I THOUGHT.
ADD THAT TO THE LIST OF THINGS MOTHER THINKS I CAN'T DO.
SO.
WHAT ELSE HAVE YOU GOT?

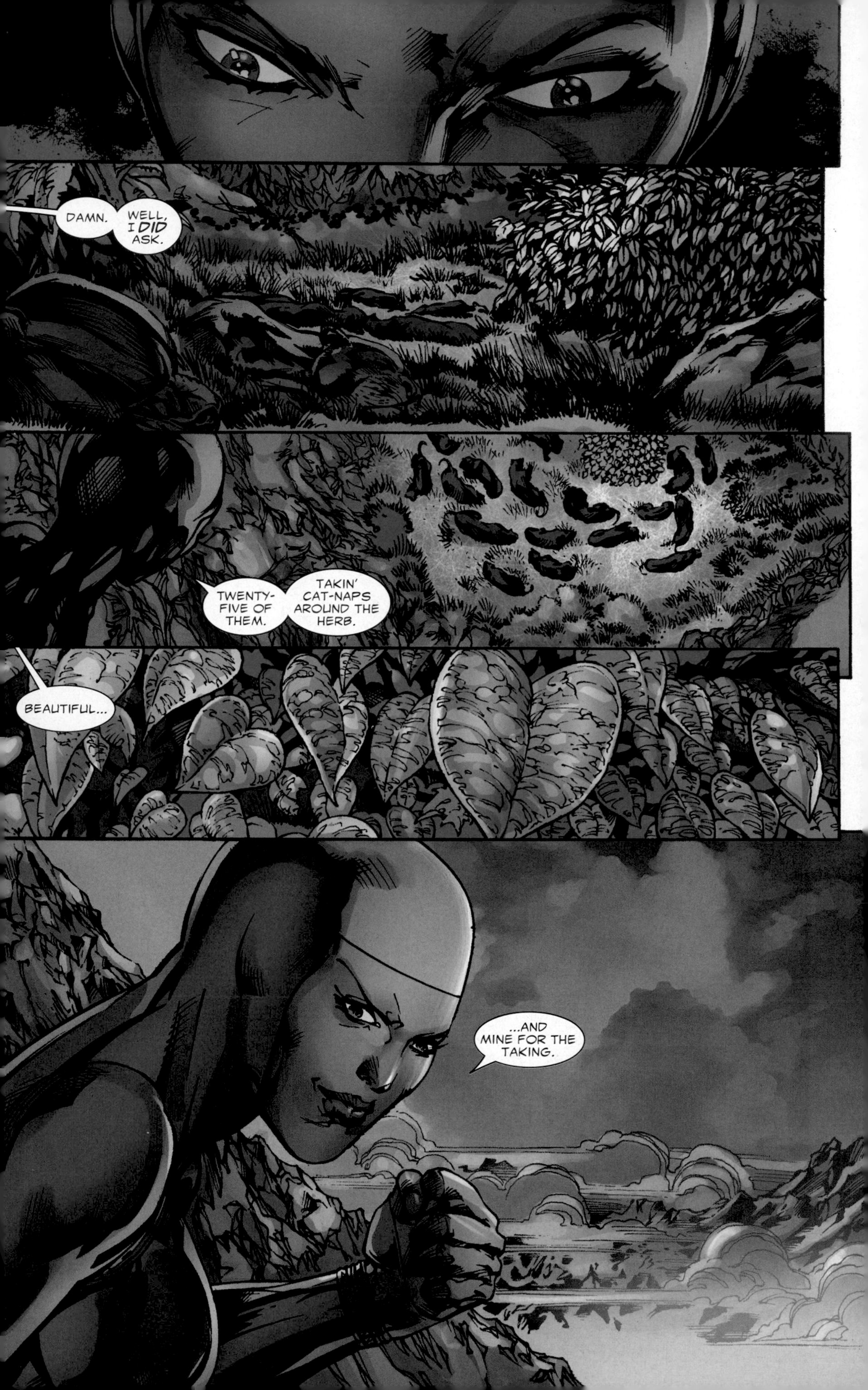
DAMN.
WELL, I DID ASK.
TWENTY-FIVE OF THEM.
TAKIN' CAT-NAPS AROUND THE HERB.
BEAUTIFUL...
...AND MINE FOR THE TAKING.

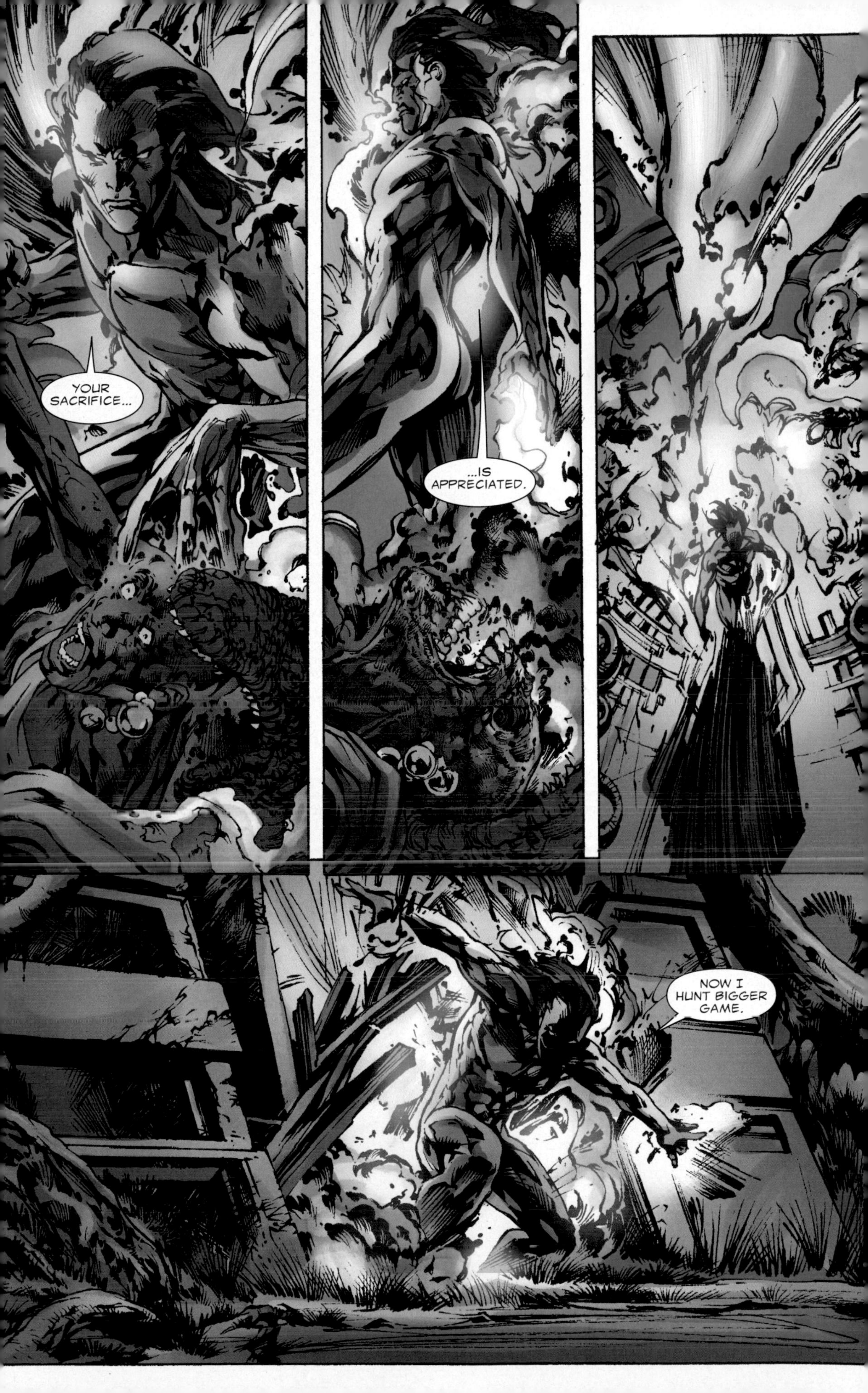
YOUR SACRIFICE...
...IS APPRECIATED.
NOW I HUNT BIGGER GAME.

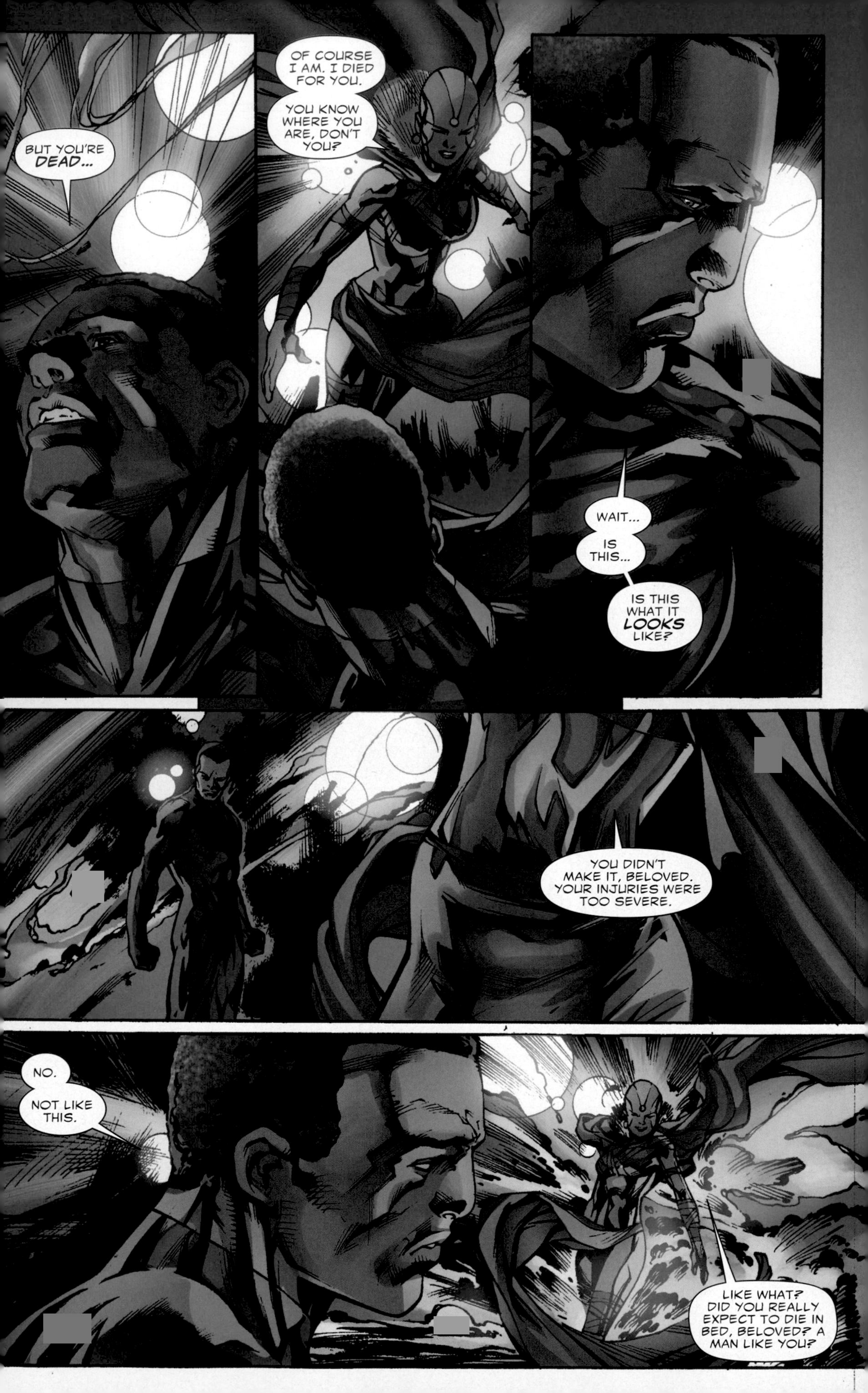
BUT YOU'RE DEAD...
OF COURSE I AM. I DIED FOR YOU.
YOU KNOW WHERE YOU ARE, DON'T YOU?
WAIT...
IS THIS...
IS THIS WHAT IT LOOKS LIKE?
YOU DIDN'T MAKE IT, BELOVED. YOUR INJURIES WERE TOO SEVERE.
NO.
NOT LIKE THIS.
LIKE WHAT? DID YOU REALLY EXPECT TO DIE IN BED, BELOVED? A MAN LIKE YOU?

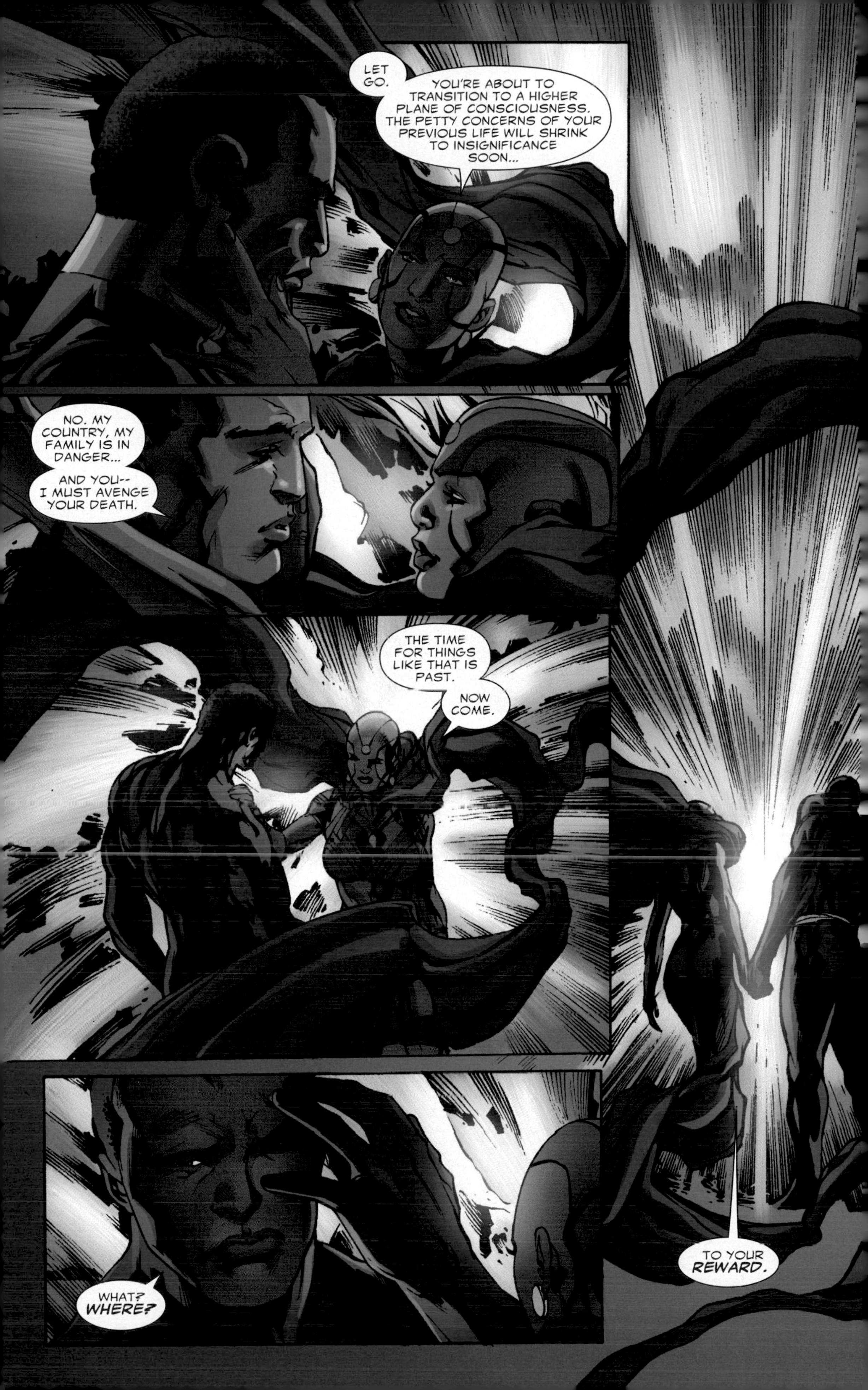

LET GO.
YOU'RE ABOUT TO TRANSITION TO A HIGHER PLANE OF CONSCIOUSNESS. THE PETTY CONCERNS OF YOUR PREVIOUS LIFE WILL SHRINK TO INSIGNIFICANCE SOON...
NO. MY COUNTRY, MY FAMILY IS IN DANGER...
AND YOU-- I MUST AVENGE YOUR DEATH.
THE TIME FOR THINGS LIKE THAT IS PAST.
NOW COME.
WHAT? WHERE?
TO YOUR REWARD.

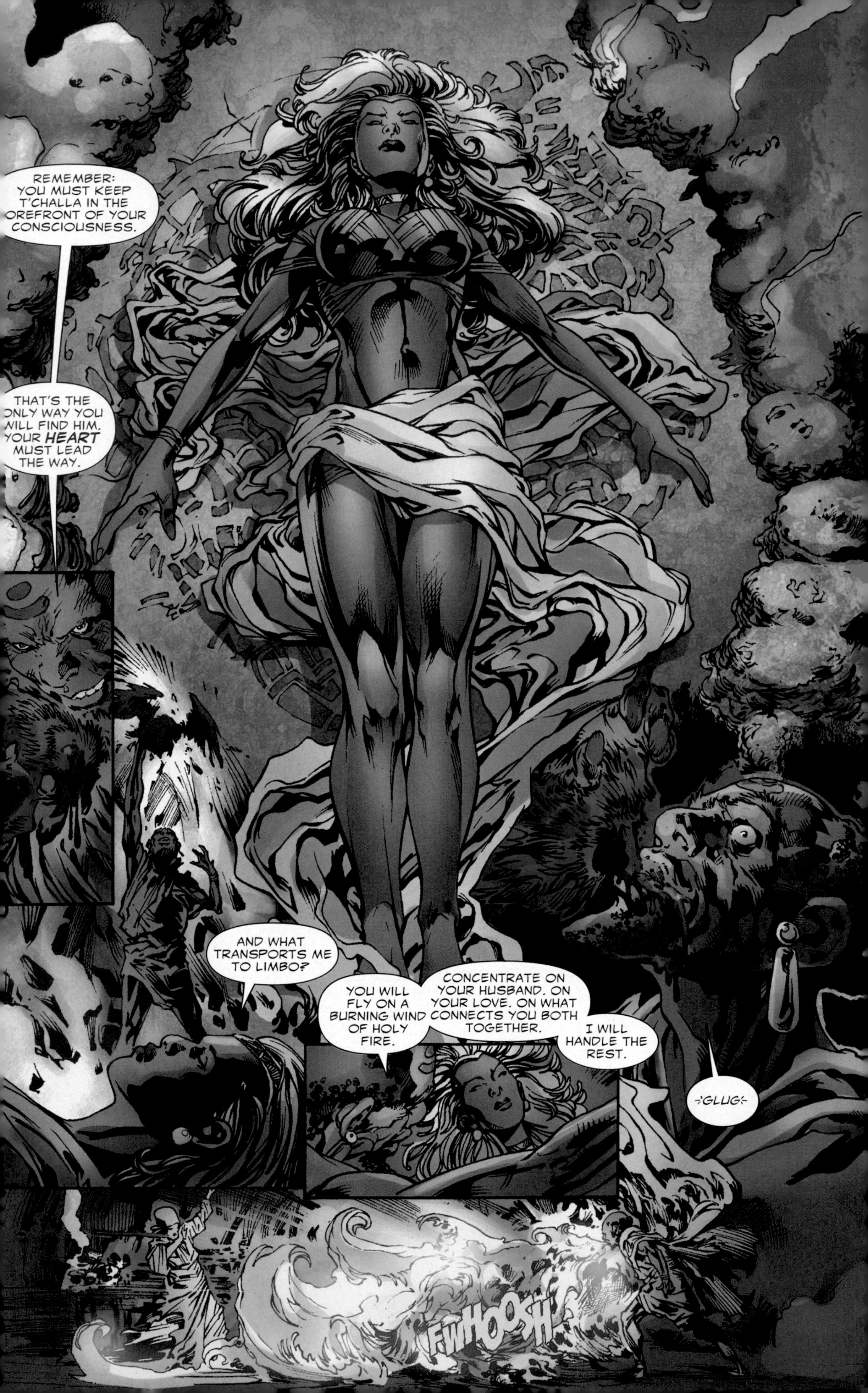
REMEMBER: YOU MUST KEEP T'CHALLA IN THE FOREFRONT OF YOUR CONSCIOUSNESS.
THAT'S THE ONLY WAY YOU WILL FIND HIM. YOUR **HEART** MUST LEAD THE WAY.
AND WHAT TRANSPORTS ME TO LIMBO?
YOU WILL FLY ON A BURNING WIND OF HOLY FIRE.
CONCENTRATE ON YOUR HUSBAND. ON YOUR LOVE. ON WHAT CONNECTS YOU BOTH TOGETHER.
I WILL HANDLE THE REST.
GLUG
FWHOOSH

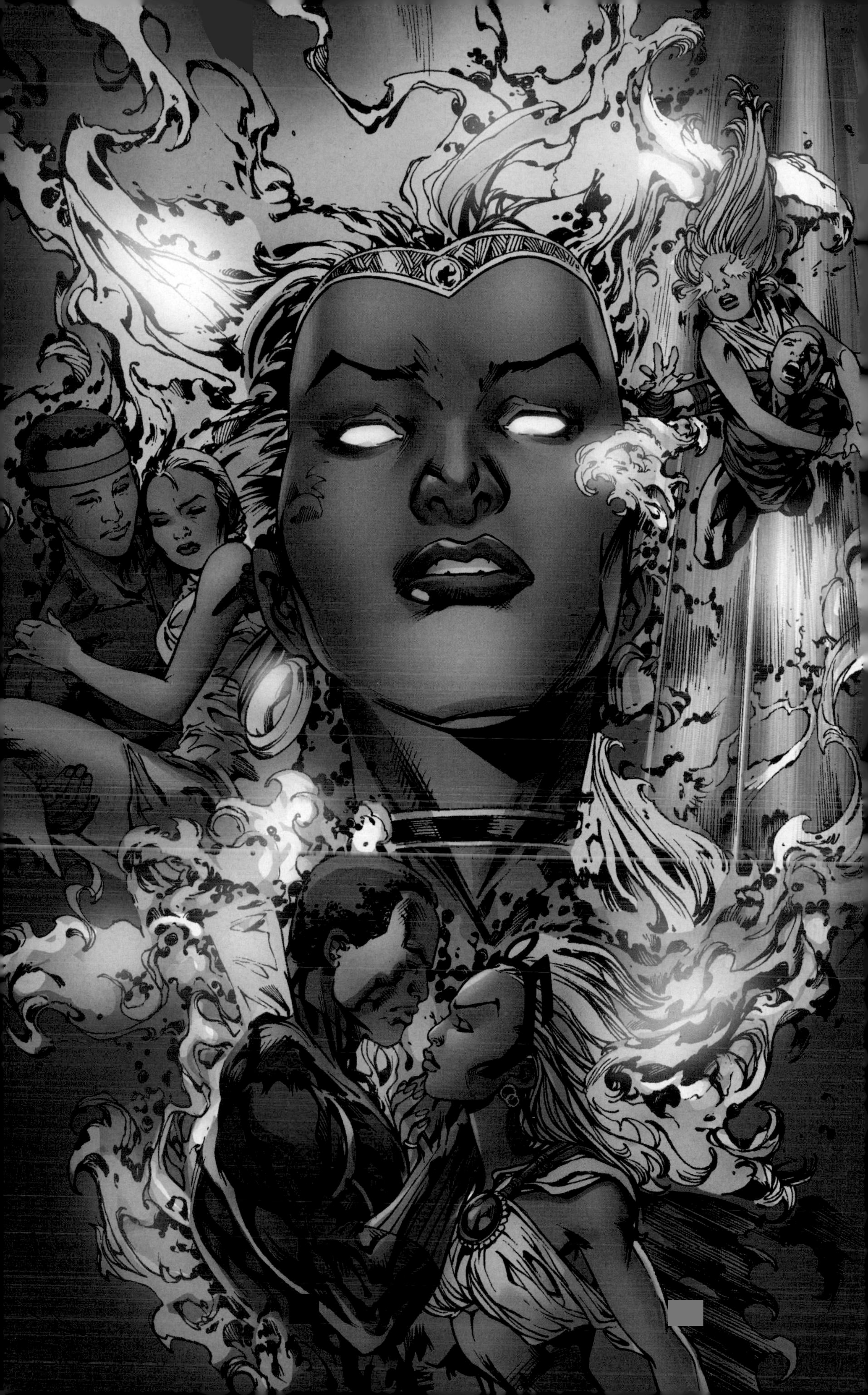

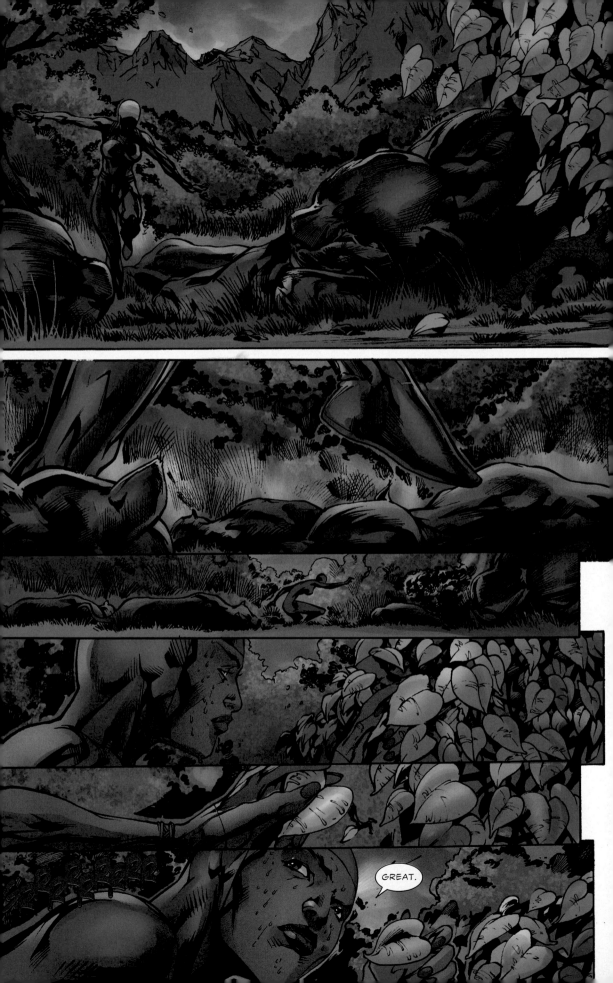

GREAT.

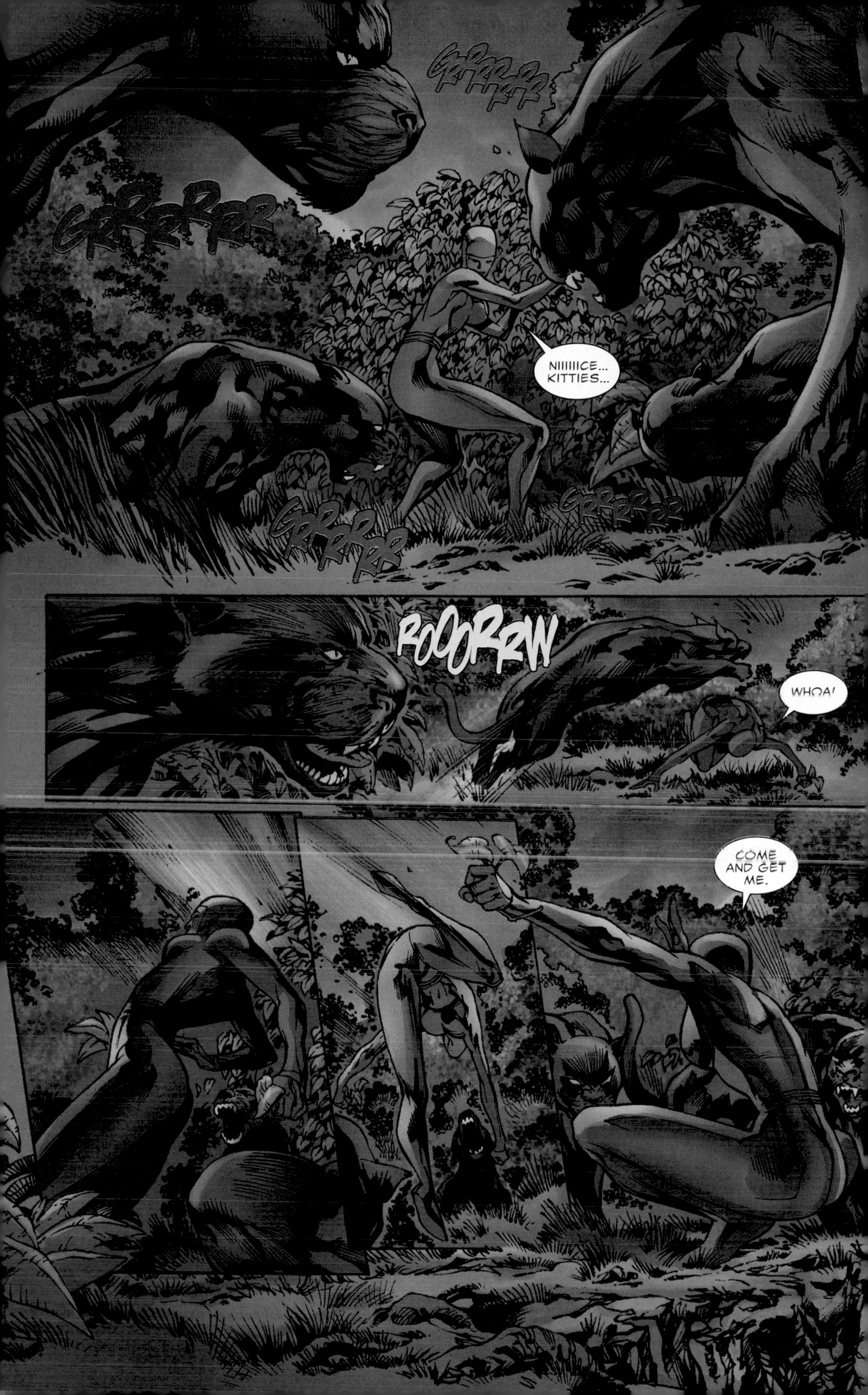
GRRRRRR
GRRRRR
NIIIIICE... KITTIES...
GRRRRRR
GRRRRR
ROOORRW
WHOA!
COME AND GET ME.

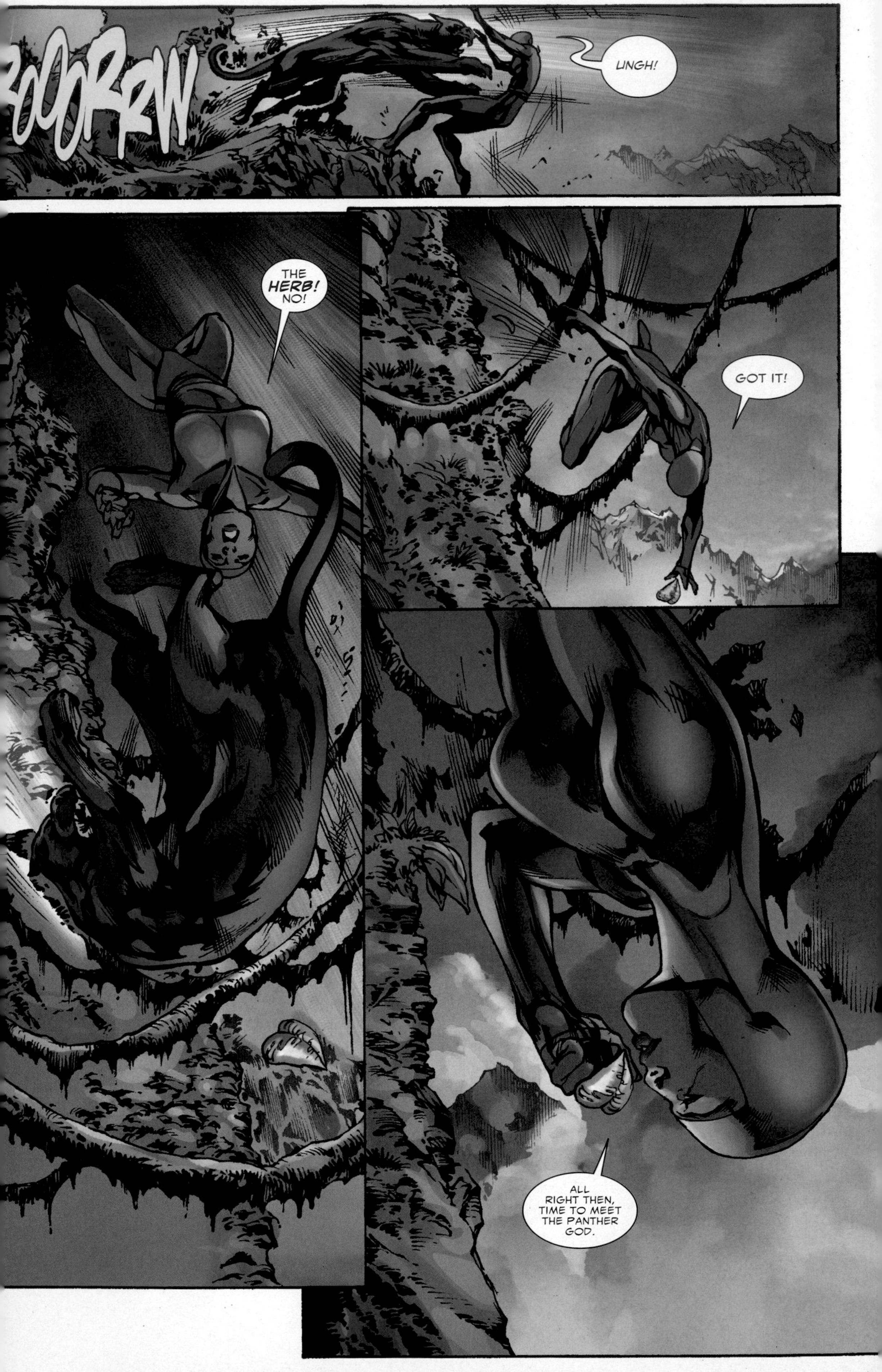
OORRW
UNGH!
THE HERB! NO!
GOT IT!
ALL RIGHT THEN, TIME TO MEET THE PANTHER GOD.

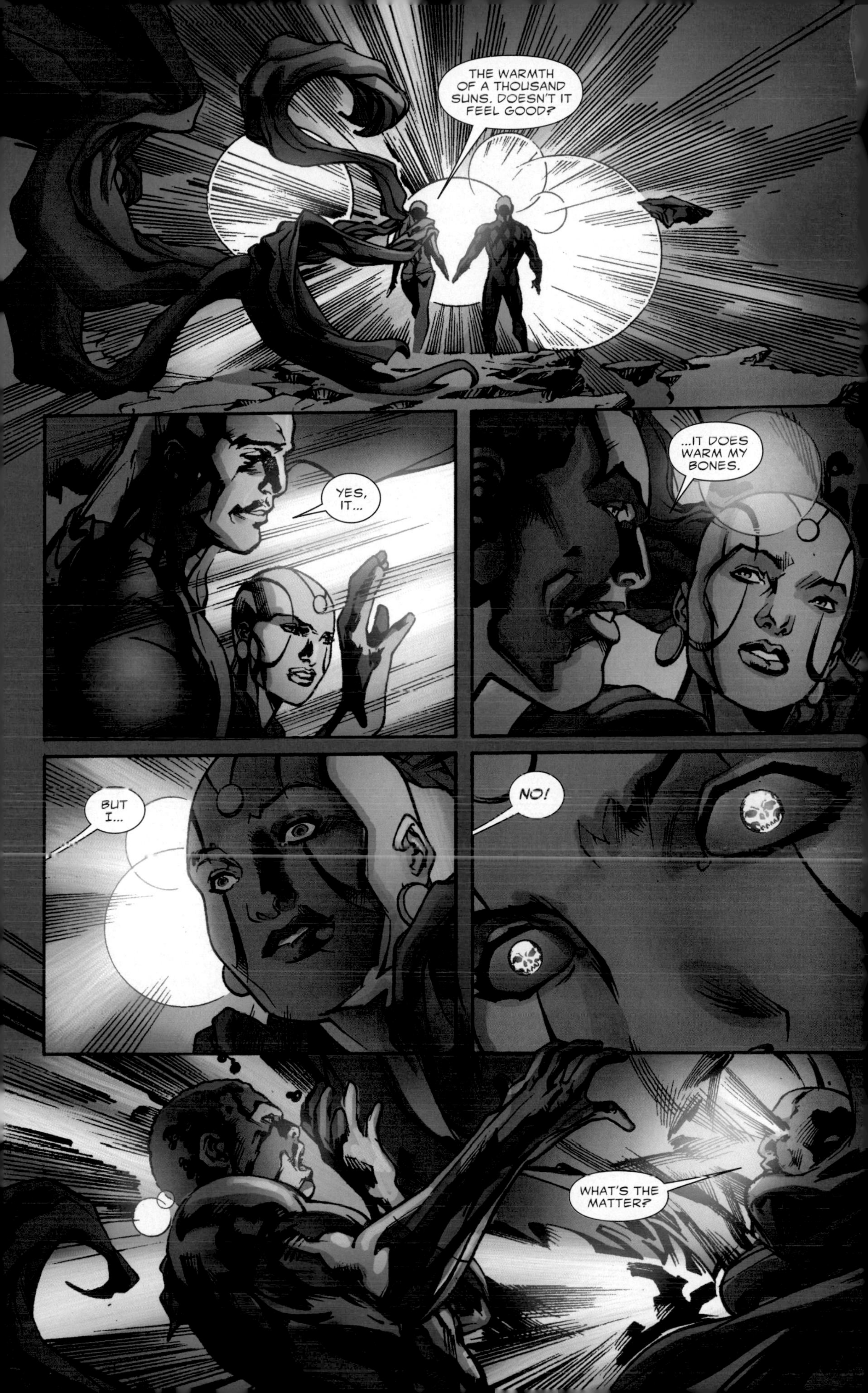
THE WARMTH OF A THOUSAND SUNS. DOESN'T IT FEEL GOOD?
YES, IT...
...IT DOES WARM MY BONES.
BUT I...
NO!
WHAT'S THE MATTER?

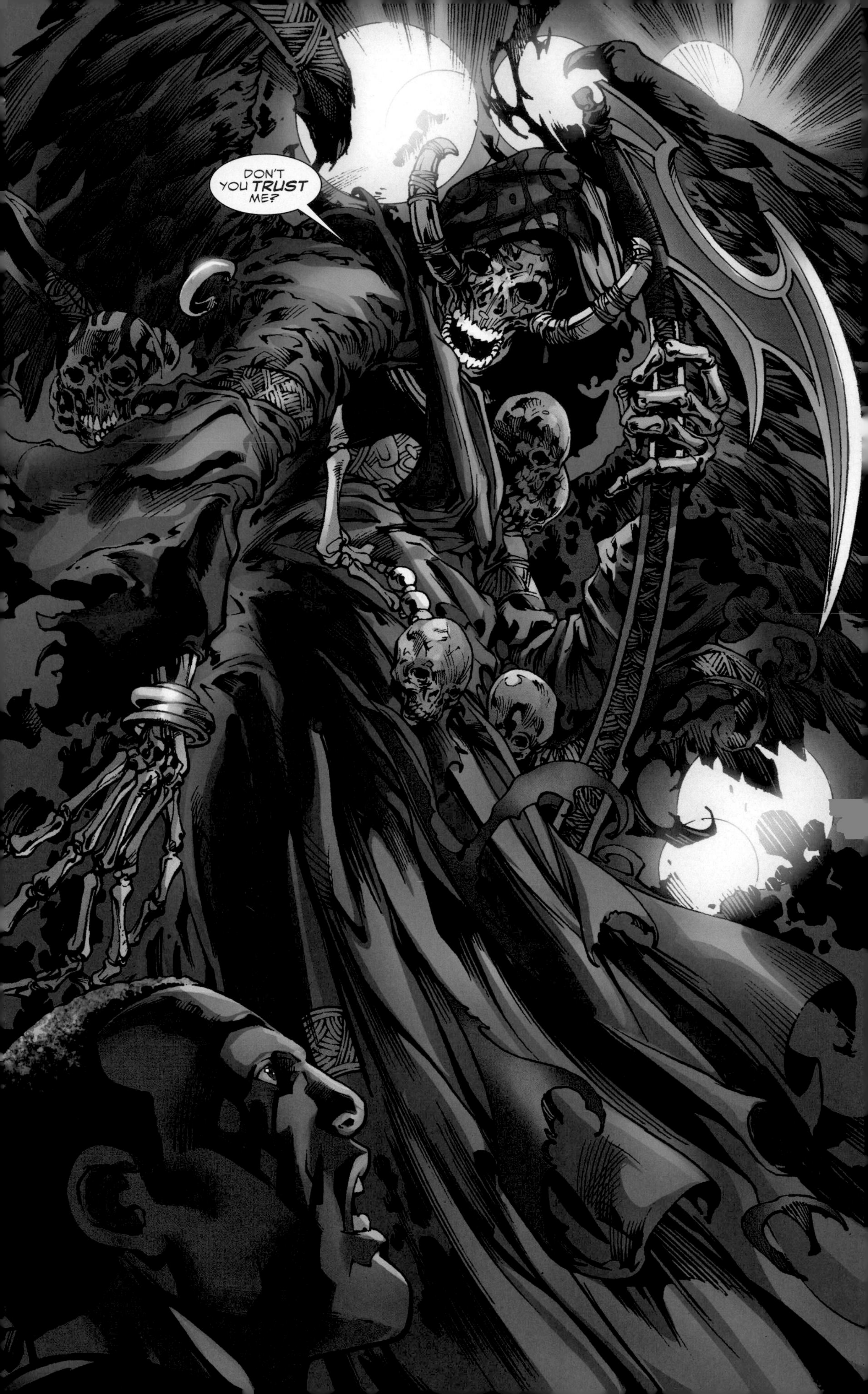
DON'T YOU TRUST ME?

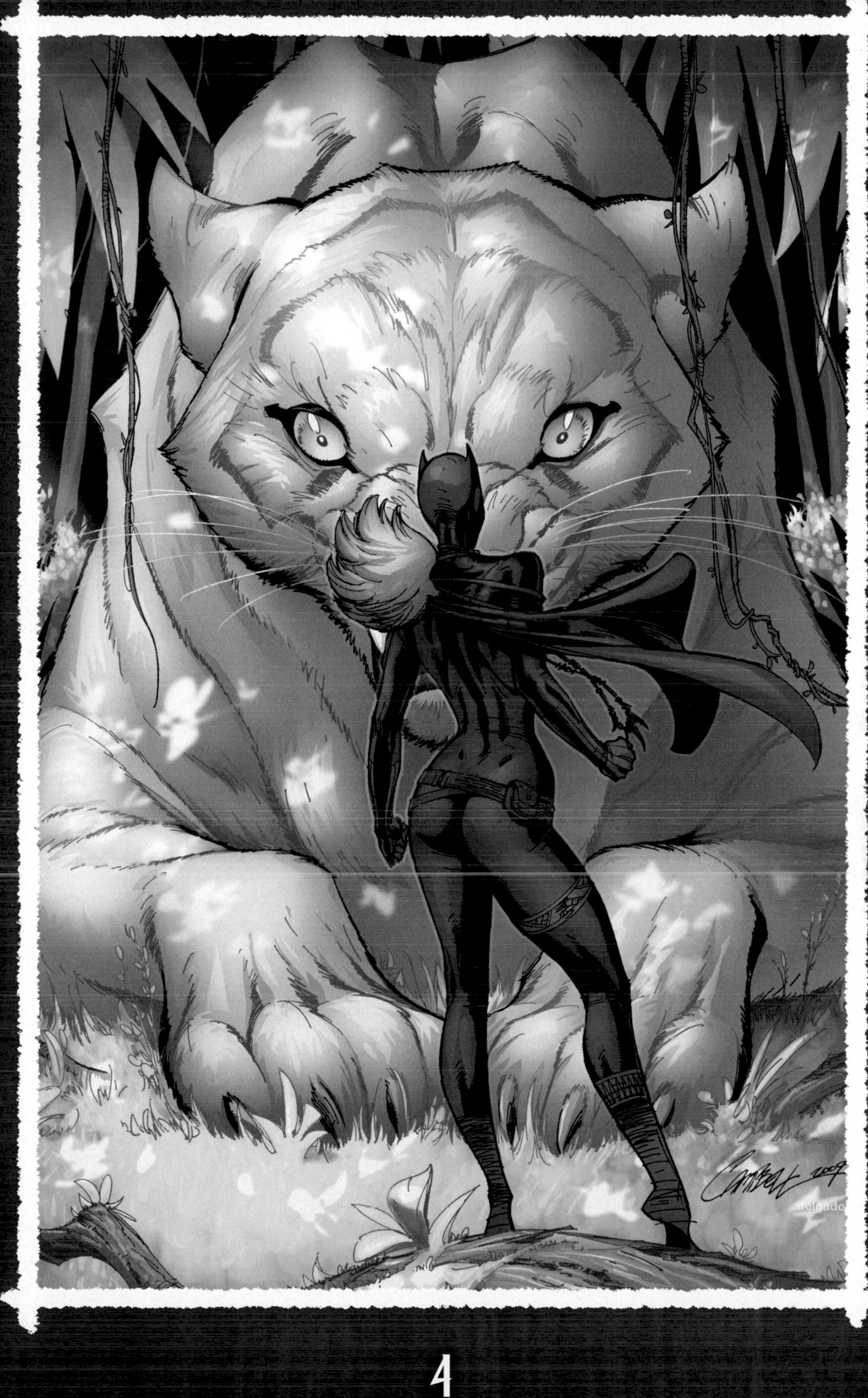

4

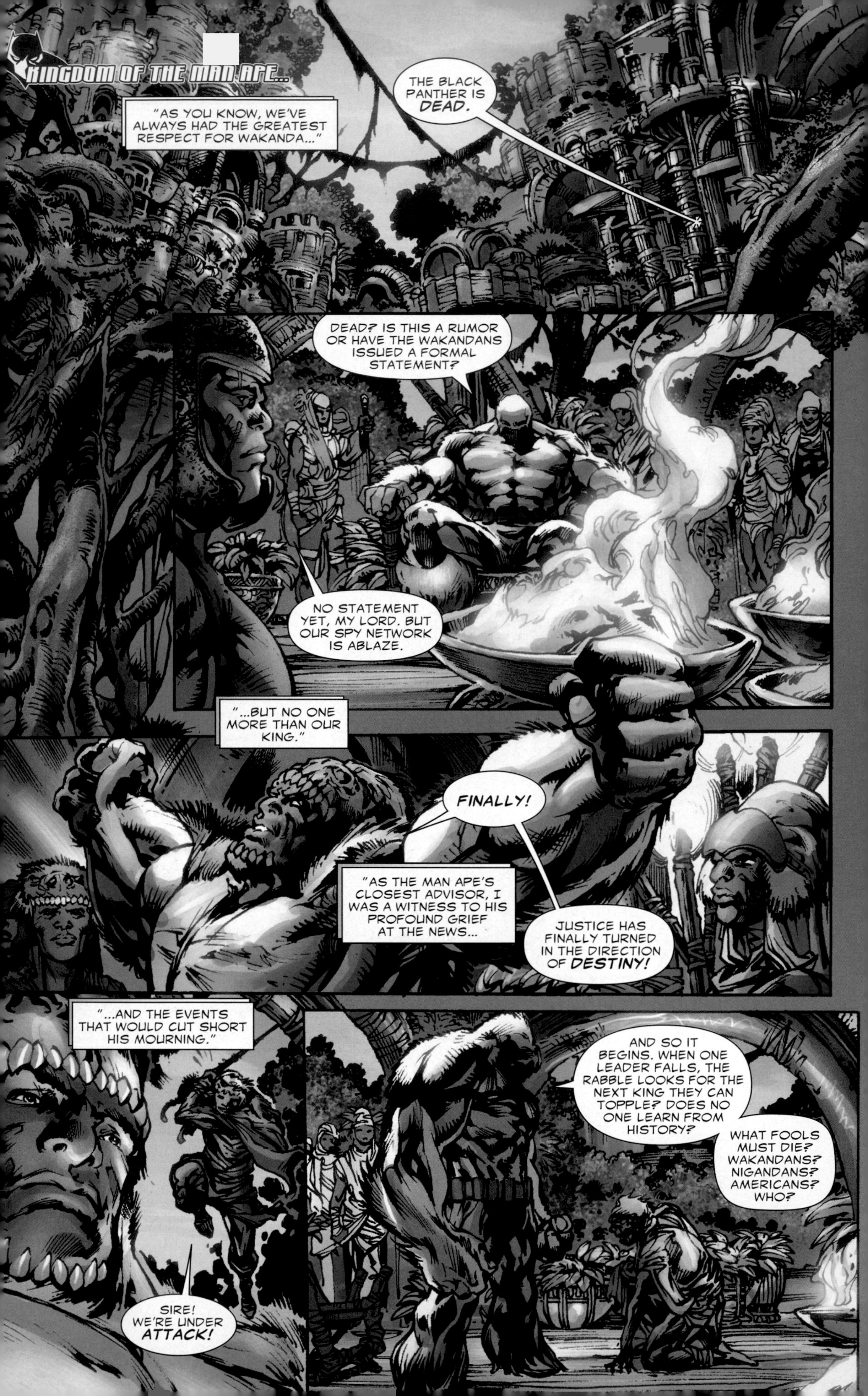

KINGDOM OF THE MAN APE...
"AS YOU KNOW, WE'VE ALWAYS HAD THE GREATEST RESPECT FOR WAKANDA..."
THE BLACK PANTHER IS DEAD.
DEAD? IS THIS A RUMOR OR HAVE THE WAKANDANS ISSUED A FORMAL STATEMENT?
NO STATEMENT YET, MY LORD. BUT OUR SPY NETWORK IS ABLAZE.
"...BUT NO ONE MORE THAN OUR KING."
FINALLY!
"AS THE MAN APE'S CLOSEST ADVISOR, I WAS A WITNESS TO HIS PROFOUND GRIEF AT THE NEWS...
JUSTICE HAS FINALLY TURNED IN THE DIRECTION OF DESTINY!
"...AND THE EVENTS THAT WOULD CUT SHORT HIS MOURNING."
SIRE! WE'RE UNDER ATTACK!
AND SO IT BEGINS. WHEN ONE LEADER FALLS, THE RABBLE LOOKS FOR THE NEXT KING THEY CAN TOPPLE? DOES NO ONE LEARN FROM HISTORY?
WHAT FOOLS MUST DIE? WAKANDANS? NIGANDANS? AMERICANS? WHO?

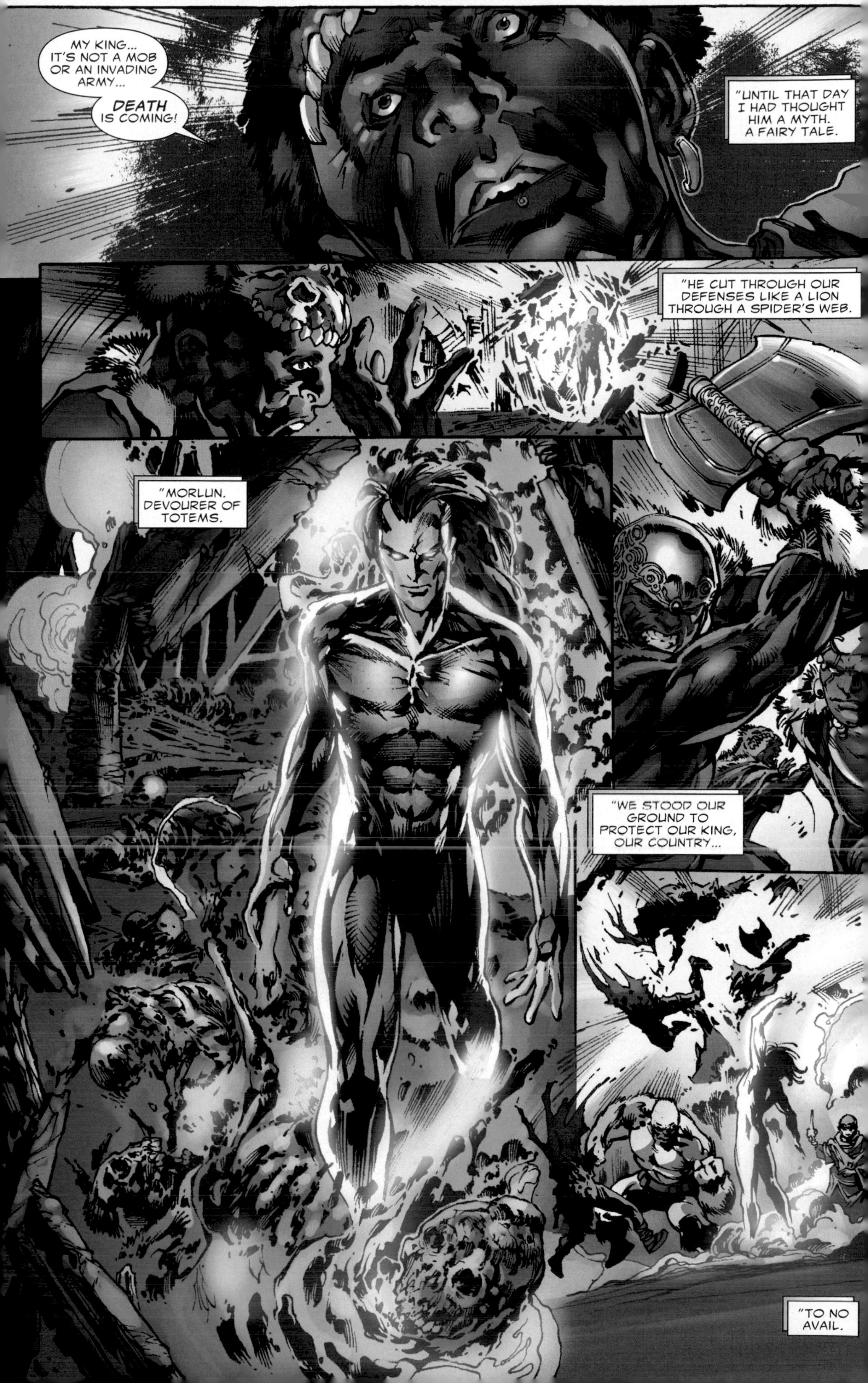
MY KING... IT'S NOT A MOB OR AN INVADING ARMY... DEATH IS COMING!
"UNTIL THAT DAY I HAD THOUGHT HIM A MYTH. A FAIRY TALE.
"HE CUT THROUGH OUR DEFENSES LIKE A LION THROUGH A SPIDER'S WEB.
"MORLUN. DEVOURER OF TOTEMS.
"WE STOOD OUR GROUND TO PROTECT OUR KING, OUR COUNTRY...
"TO NO AVAIL.

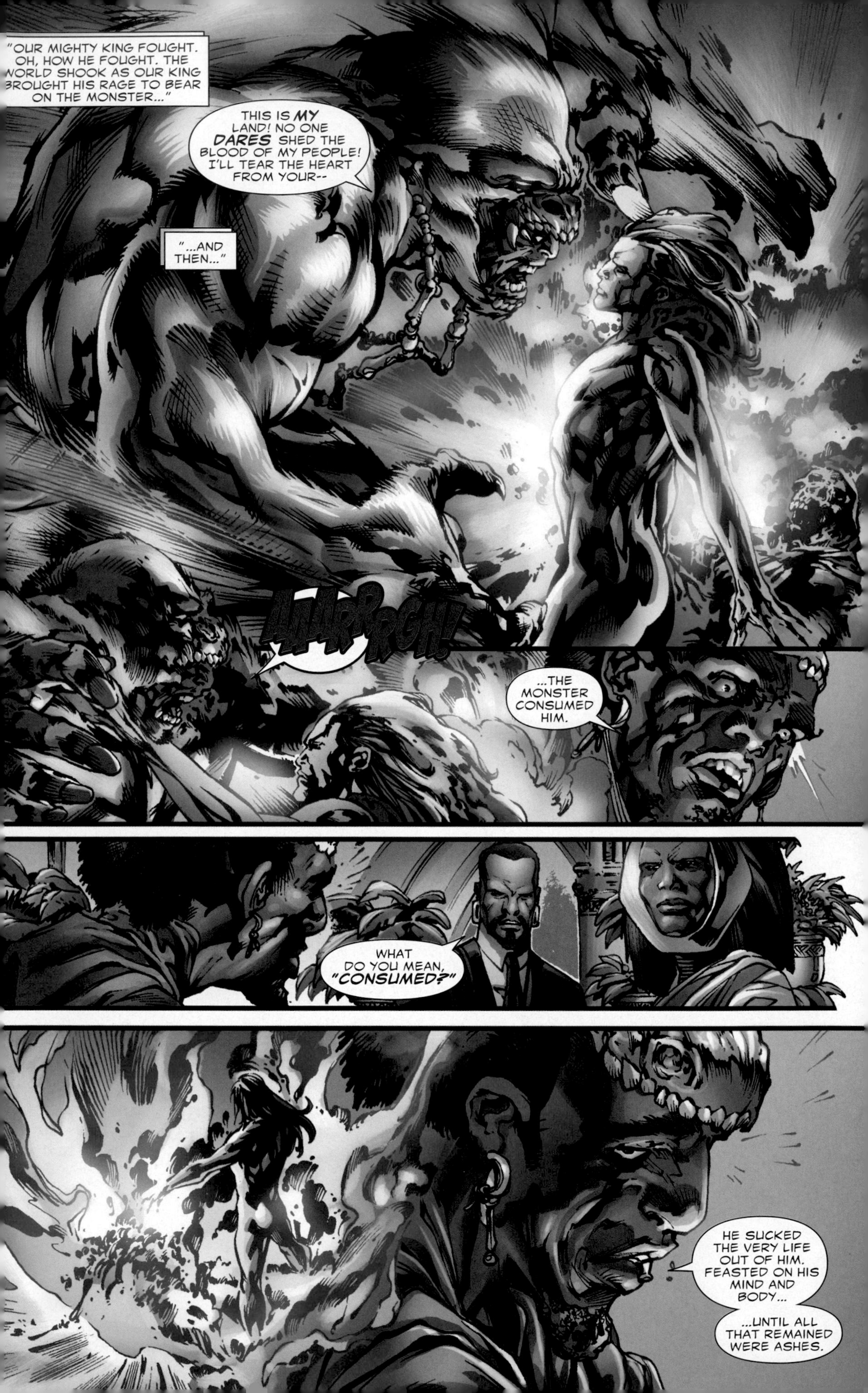
"OUR MIGHTY KING FOUGHT. OH, HOW HE FOUGHT. THE WORLD SHOOK AS OUR KING BROUGHT HIS RAGE TO BEAR ON THE MONSTER..."
THIS IS MY LAND! NO ONE DARES SHED THE BLOOD OF MY PEOPLE! I'LL TEAR THE HEART FROM YOUR--
"...AND THEN..."
AAAHRRGH!
...THE MONSTER CONSUMED HIM.
WHAT DO YOU MEAN, "CONSUMED?"
HE SUCKED THE VERY LIFE OUT OF HIM. FEASTED ON HIS MIND AND BODY...
...UNTIL ALL THAT REMAINED WERE ASHES.

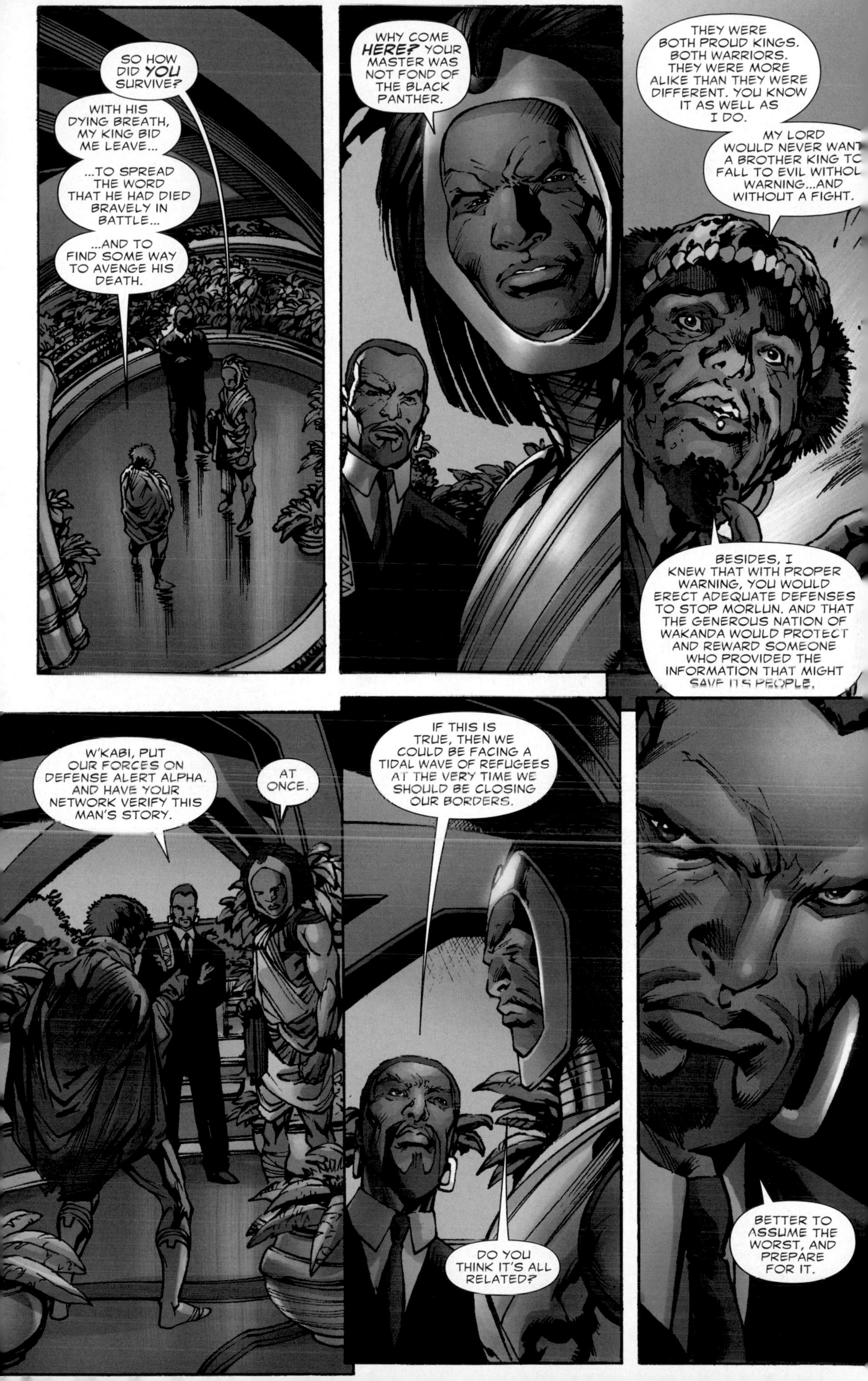
SO HOW DID *YOU* SURVIVE?
WITH HIS DYING BREATH, MY KING BID ME LEAVE...
...TO SPREAD THE WORD THAT HE HAD DIED BRAVELY IN BATTLE...
...AND TO FIND SOME WAY TO AVENGE HIS DEATH.
WHY COME ***HERE?*** YOUR MASTER WAS NOT FOND OF THE BLACK PANTHER.
THEY WERE BOTH PROUD KINGS. BOTH WARRIORS. THEY WERE MORE ALIKE THAN THEY WERE DIFFERENT. YOU KNOW IT AS WELL AS I DO.
MY LORD WOULD NEVER WANT A BROTHER KING TO FALL TO EVIL WITHOUT WARNING...AND WITHOUT A FIGHT.
BESIDES, I KNEW THAT WITH PROPER WARNING, YOU WOULD ERECT ADEQUATE DEFENSES TO STOP MORLUN. AND THAT THE GENEROUS NATION OF WAKANDA WOULD PROTECT AND REWARD SOMEONE WHO PROVIDED THE INFORMATION THAT MIGHT SAVE ITS PEOPLE.
W'KABI, PUT OUR FORCES ON DEFENSE ALERT ALPHA. AND HAVE YOUR NETWORK VERIFY THIS MAN'S STORY.
AT ONCE.
IF THIS IS TRUE, THEN WE COULD BE FACING A TIDAL WAVE OF REFUGEES AT THE VERY TIME WE SHOULD BE CLOSING OUR BORDERS.
DO YOU THINK IT'S ALL RELATED?
BETTER TO ASSUME THE WORST, AND PREPARE FOR IT.

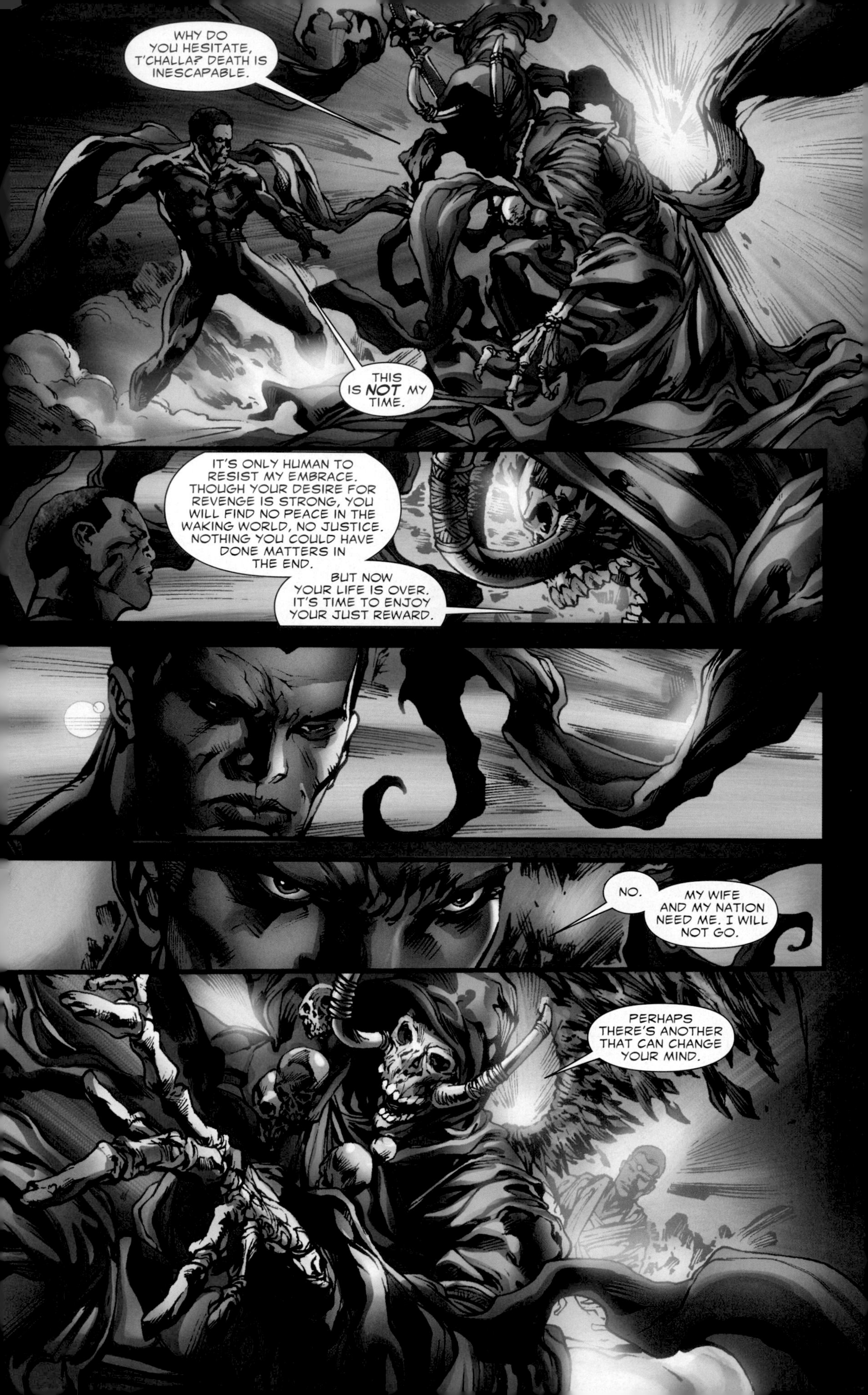
WHY DO YOU HESITATE, T'CHALLA? DEATH IS INESCAPABLE.
THIS IS **NOT** MY TIME.
IT'S ONLY HUMAN TO RESIST MY EMBRACE. THOUGH YOUR DESIRE FOR REVENGE IS STRONG, YOU WILL FIND NO PEACE IN THE WAKING WORLD, NO JUSTICE. NOTHING YOU COULD HAVE DONE MATTERS IN THE END.
BUT NOW YOUR LIFE IS OVER. IT'S TIME TO ENJOY YOUR JUST REWARD.
NO.
MY WIFE AND MY NATION NEED ME. I WILL NOT GO.
PERHAPS THERE'S ANOTHER THAT CAN CHANGE YOUR MIND.

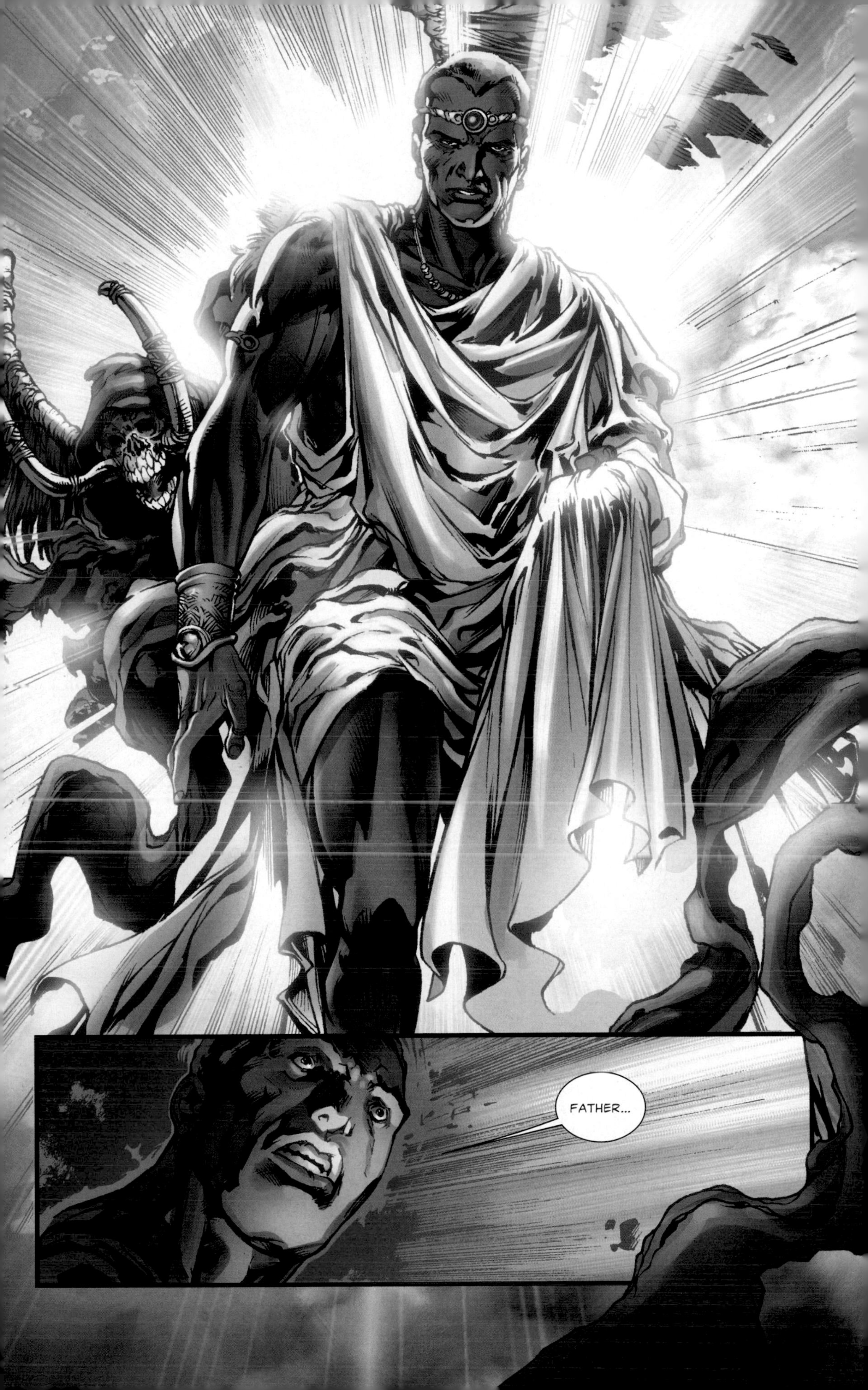
FATHER...

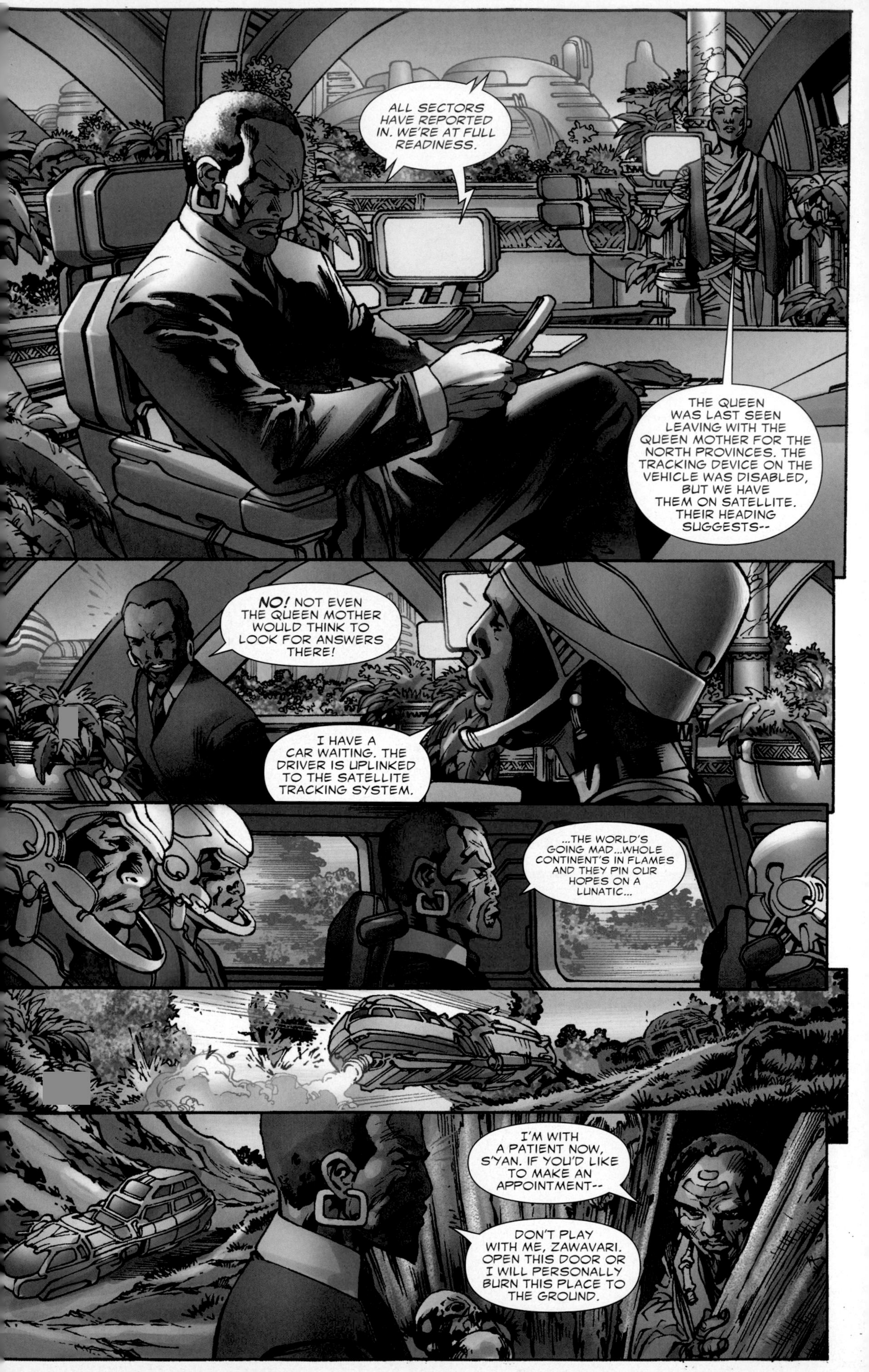
ALL SECTORS HAVE REPORTED IN. WE'RE AT FULL READINESS.
THE QUEEN WAS LAST SEEN LEAVING WITH THE QUEEN MOTHER FOR THE NORTH PROVINCES. THE TRACKING DEVICE ON THE VEHICLE WAS DISABLED, BUT WE HAVE THEM ON SATELLITE. THEIR HEADING SUGGESTS--
NO! NOT EVEN THE QUEEN MOTHER WOULD THINK TO LOOK FOR ANSWERS THERE!
I HAVE A CAR WAITING. THE DRIVER IS UPLINKED TO THE SATELLITE TRACKING SYSTEM.
...THE WORLD'S GOING MAD...WHOLE CONTINENT'S IN FLAMES AND THEY PIN OUR HOPES ON A LUNATIC...
I'M WITH A PATIENT NOW, S'YAN. IF YOU'D LIKE TO MAKE AN APPOINTMENT--
DON'T PLAY WITH ME, ZAWAVARI. OPEN THIS DOOR OR I WILL PERSONALLY BURN THIS PLACE TO THE GROUND.

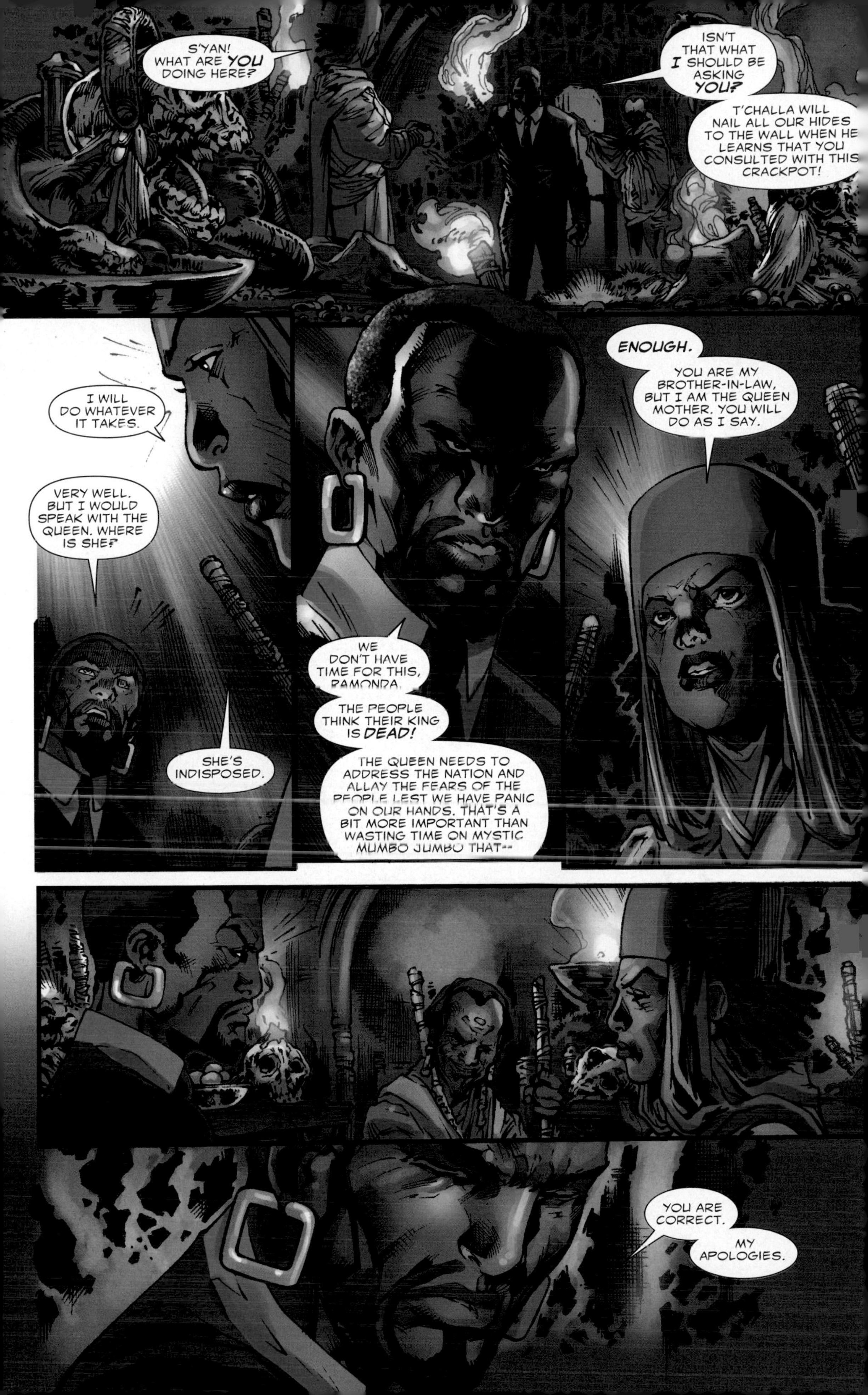
S'YAN! WHAT ARE YOU DOING HERE?
ISN'T THAT WHAT I SHOULD BE ASKING YOU?
T'CHALLA WILL NAIL ALL OUR HIDES TO THE WALL WHEN HE LEARNS THAT YOU CONSULTED WITH THIS CRACKPOT!
I WILL DO WHATEVER IT TAKES.
VERY WELL. BUT I WOULD SPEAK WITH THE QUEEN. WHERE IS SHE?
SHE'S INDISPOSED.
WE DON'T HAVE TIME FOR THIS, RAMONDA.
THE PEOPLE THINK THEIR KING IS DEAD!
THE QUEEN NEEDS TO ADDRESS THE NATION AND ALLAY THE FEARS OF THE PEOPLE LEST WE HAVE PANIC ON OUR HANDS. THAT'S A BIT MORE IMPORTANT THAN WASTING TIME ON MYSTIC MUMBO JUMBO THAT--
ENOUGH.
YOU ARE MY BROTHER-IN-LAW, BUT I AM THE QUEEN MOTHER. YOU WILL DO AS I SAY.
YOU ARE CORRECT.
MY APOLOGIES.

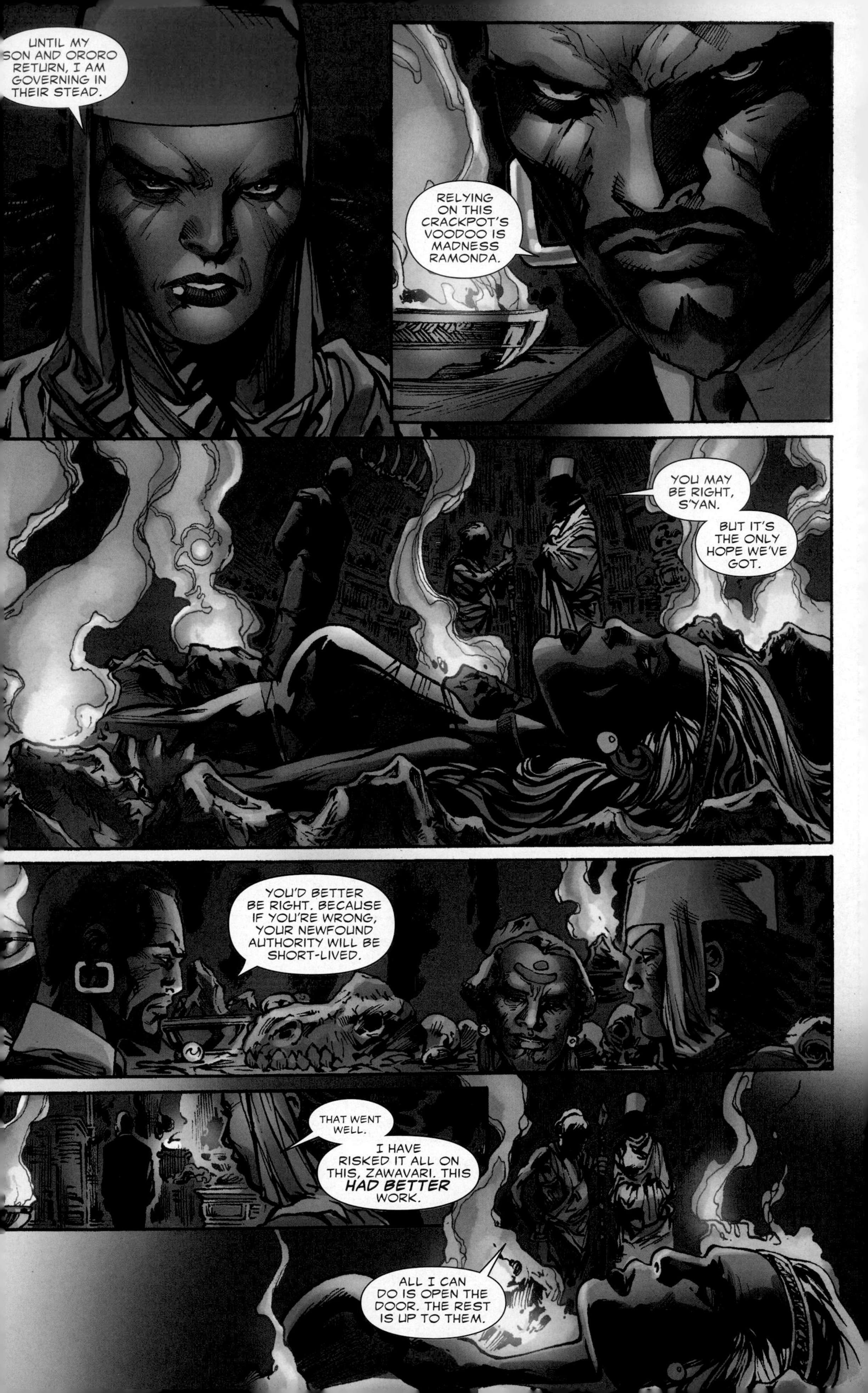
UNTIL MY SON AND ORORO RETURN, I AM GOVERNING IN THEIR STEAD.
RELYING ON THIS CRACKPOT'S VOODOO IS MADNESS RAMONDA.
YOU MAY BE RIGHT, S'YAN.
BUT IT'S THE ONLY HOPE WE'VE GOT.
YOU'D BETTER BE RIGHT. BECAUSE IF YOU'RE WRONG, YOUR NEWFOUND AUTHORITY WILL BE SHORT-LIVED.
THAT WENT WELL.
I HAVE RISKED IT ALL ON THIS, ZAWAVARI. THIS ***HAD BETTER*** WORK.
ALL I CAN DO IS OPEN THE DOOR. THE REST IS UP TO THEM.

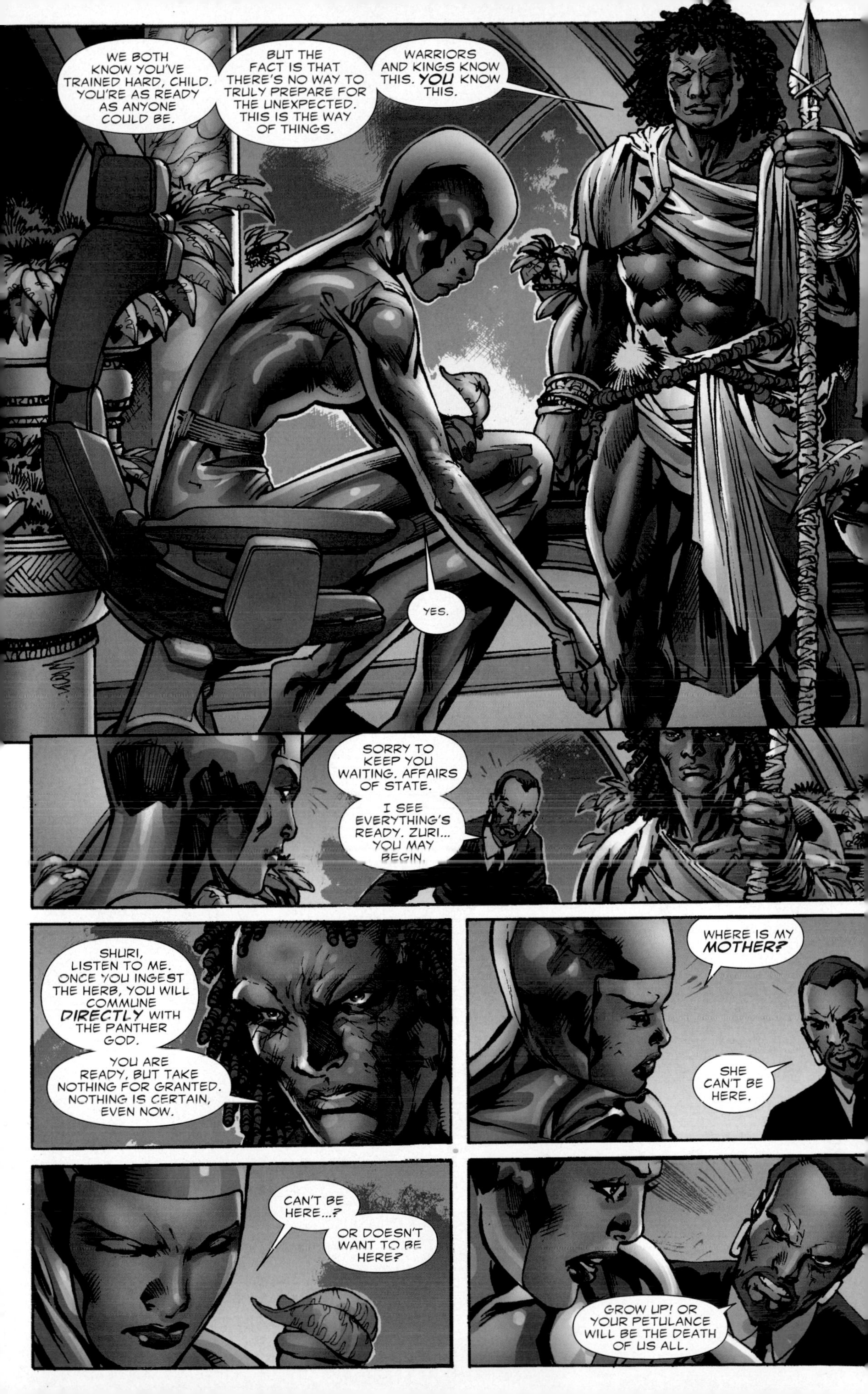
WE BOTH KNOW YOU'VE TRAINED HARD, CHILD. YOU'RE AS READY AS ANYONE COULD BE.
BUT THE FACT IS THAT THERE'S NO WAY TO TRULY PREPARE FOR THE UNEXPECTED. THIS IS THE WAY OF THINGS.
WARRIORS AND KINGS KNOW THIS. *YOU* KNOW THIS.
YES.
SORRY TO KEEP YOU WAITING. AFFAIRS OF STATE.
I SEE EVERYTHING'S READY. ZURI... YOU MAY BEGIN.
SHURI, LISTEN TO ME. ONCE YOU INGEST THE HERB, YOU WILL COMMUNE *DIRECTLY* WITH THE PANTHER GOD.
YOU ARE READY, BUT TAKE NOTHING FOR GRANTED. NOTHING IS CERTAIN, EVEN NOW.
WHERE IS MY *MOTHER?*
SHE CAN'T BE HERE.
CAN'T BE HERE...?
OR DOESN'T WANT TO BE HERE?
GROW UP! OR YOUR PETULANCE WILL BE THE DEATH OF US ALL.

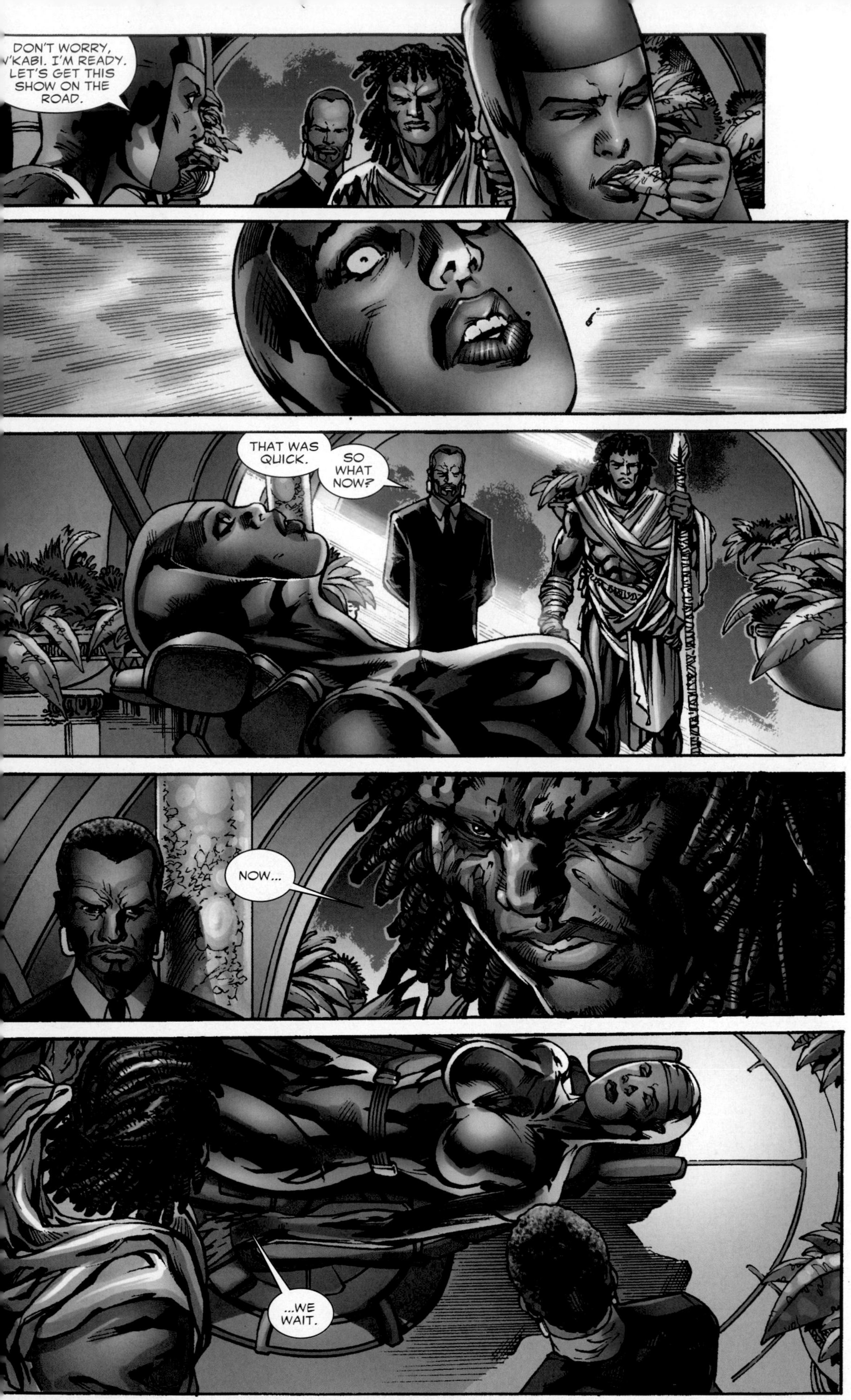
DON'T WORRY, W'KABI. I'M READY. LET'S GET THIS SHOW ON THE ROAD.
THAT WAS QUICK.
SO WHAT NOW?
NOW...
...WE WAIT.

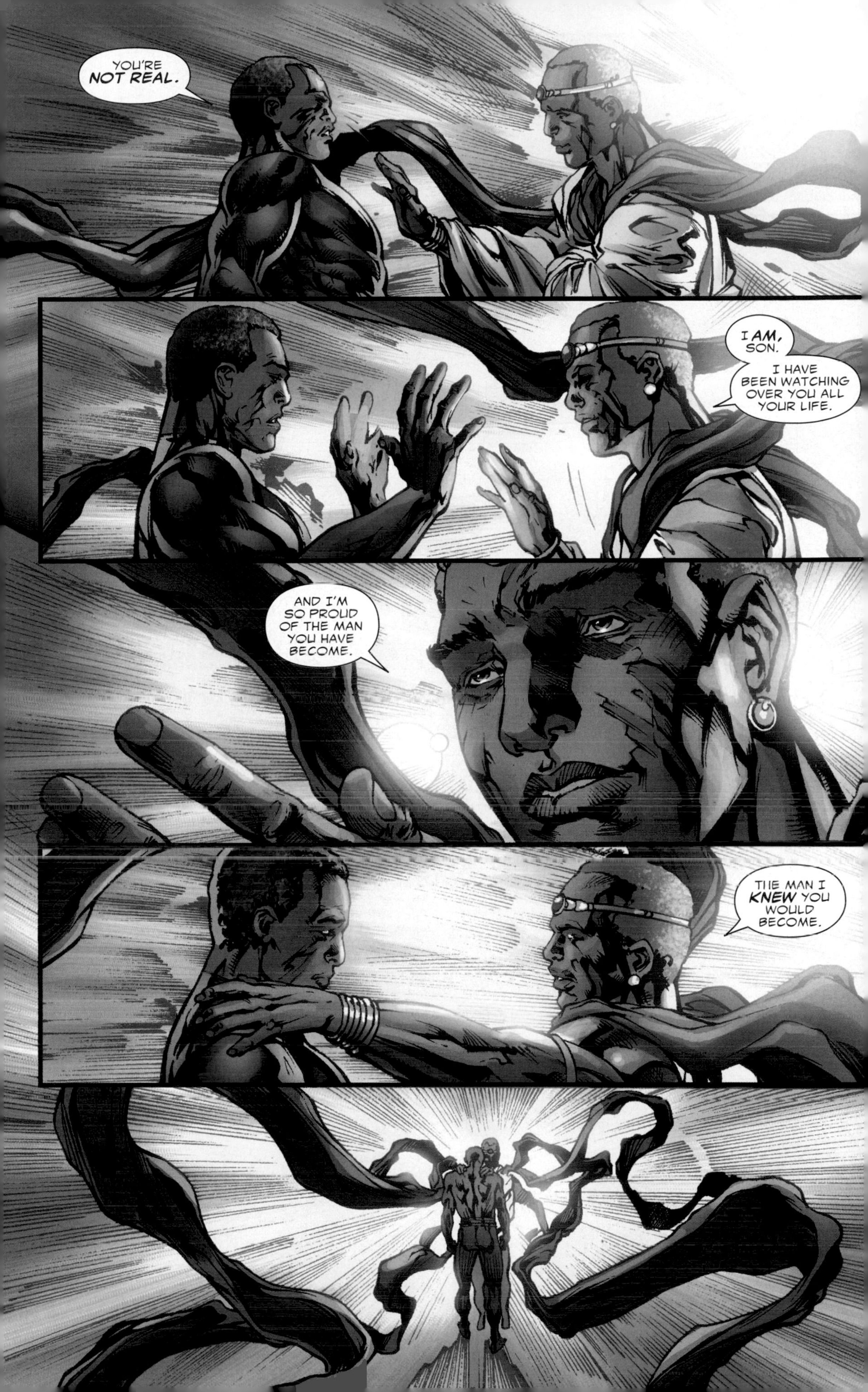

YOU'RE NOT REAL.
I AM, SON.
I HAVE BEEN WATCHING OVER YOU ALL YOUR LIFE.
AND I'M SO PROUD OF THE MAN YOU HAVE BECOME.
THE MAN I KNEW YOU WOULD BECOME.

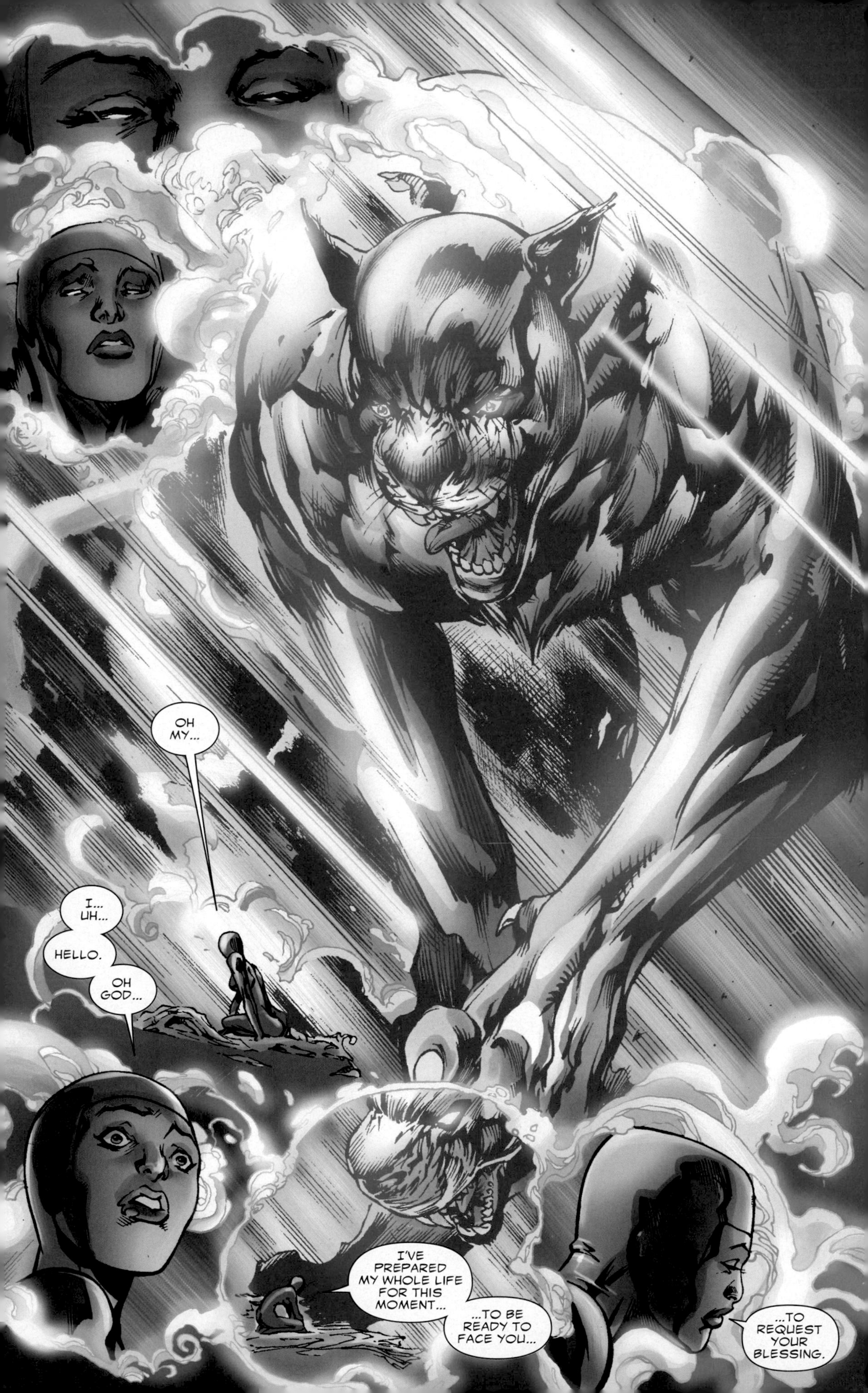
OH MY...
I... UH...
HELLO.
OH GOD...
I'VE PREPARED MY WHOLE LIFE FOR THIS MOMENT...
...TO BE READY TO FACE YOU...
...TO REQUEST YOUR BLESSING.

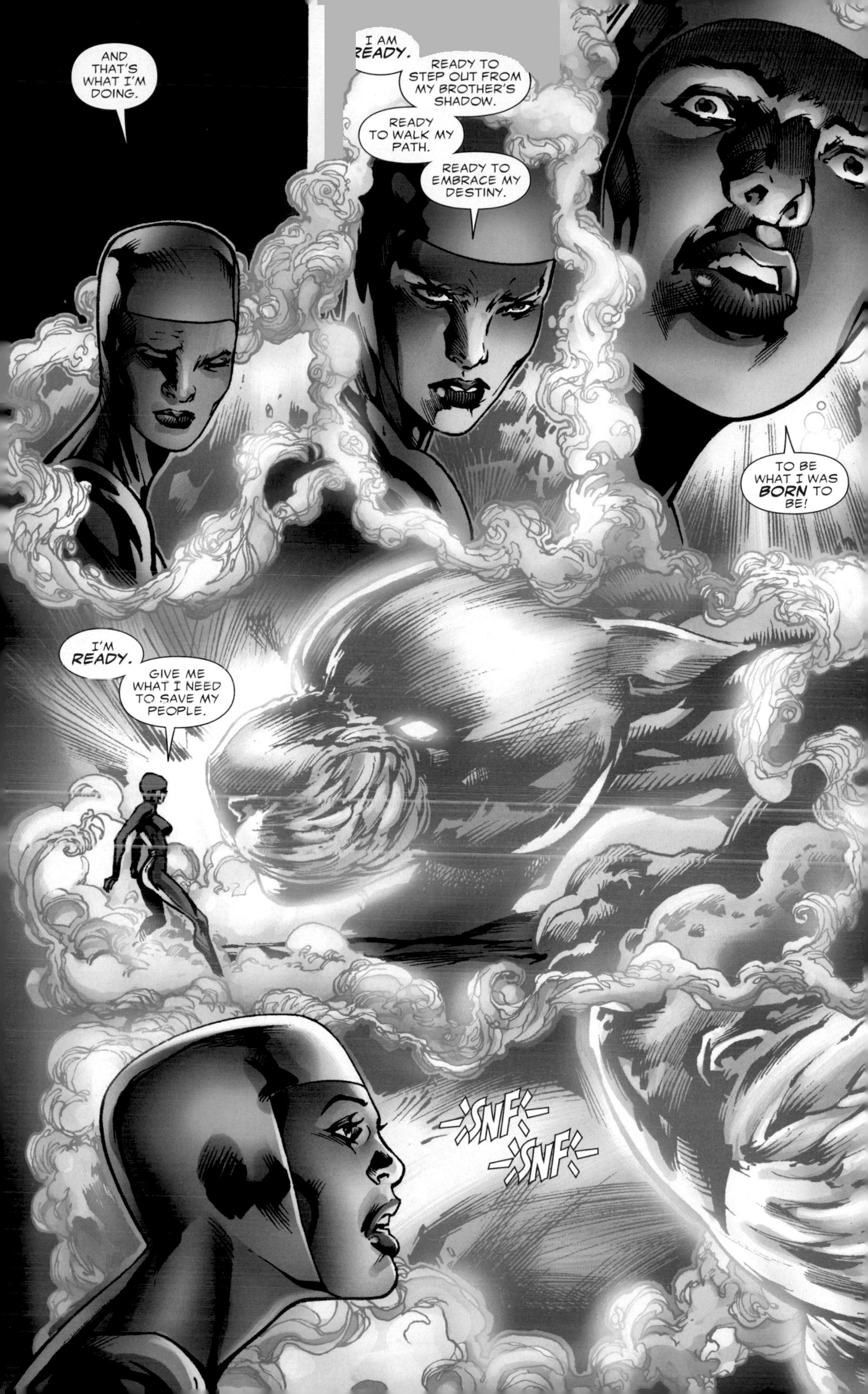
AND THAT'S WHAT I'M DOING.
I AM READY.
READY TO STEP OUT FROM MY BROTHER'S SHADOW.
READY TO WALK MY PATH.
READY TO EMBRACE MY DESTINY.
TO BE WHAT I WAS BORN TO BE!
I'M READY.
GIVE ME WHAT I NEED TO SAVE MY PEOPLE.
SNF
SNF

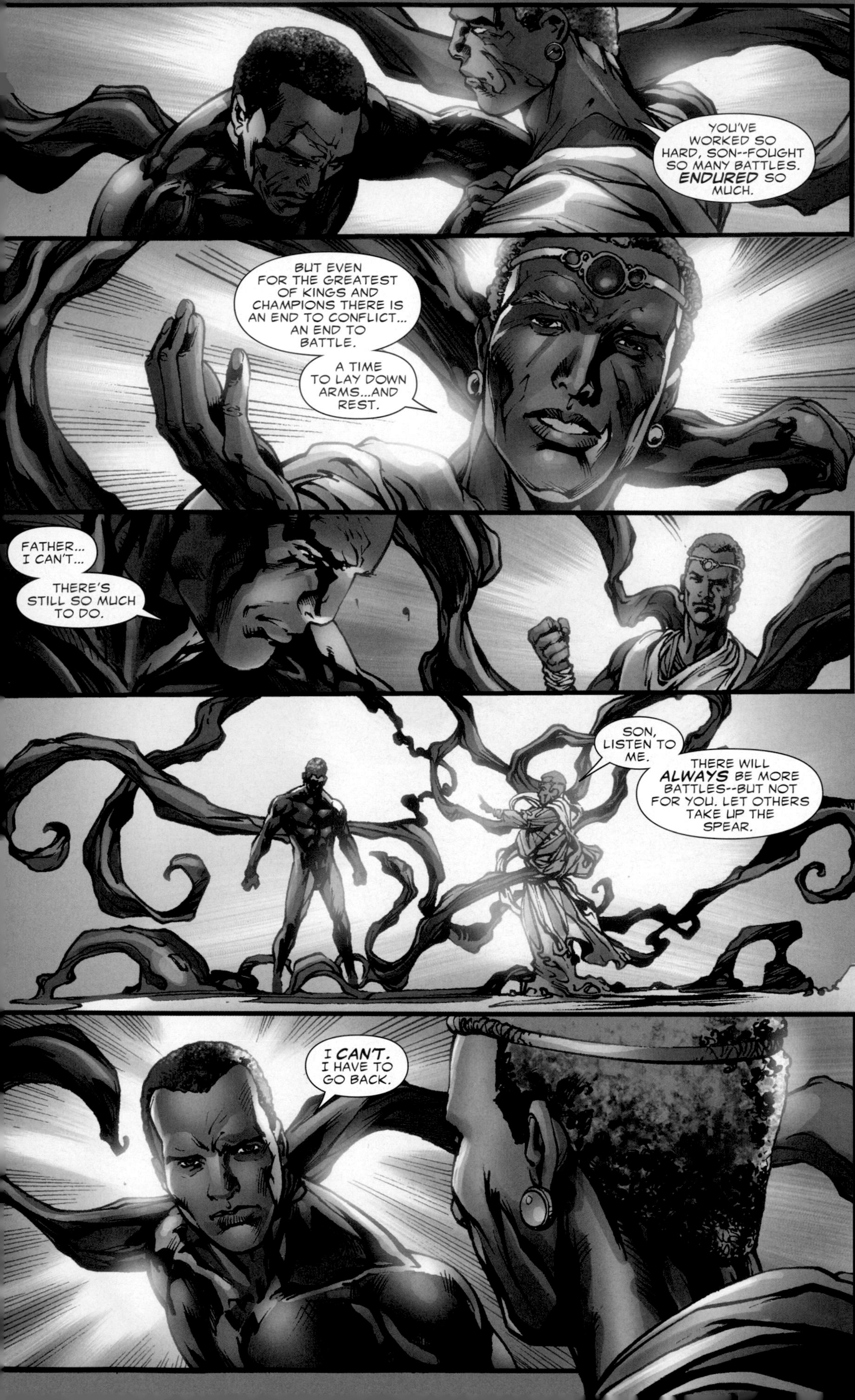
YOU'VE WORKED SO HARD, SON--FOUGHT SO MANY BATTLES. ENDURED SO MUCH.
BUT EVEN FOR THE GREATEST OF KINGS AND CHAMPIONS THERE IS AN END TO CONFLICT... AN END TO BATTLE.
A TIME TO LAY DOWN ARMS...AND REST.
FATHER... I CAN'T...
THERE'S STILL SO MUCH TO DO.
SON, LISTEN TO ME.
THERE WILL ALWAYS BE MORE BATTLES--BUT NOT FOR YOU. LET OTHERS TAKE UP THE SPEAR.
I CAN'T. I HAVE TO GO BACK.

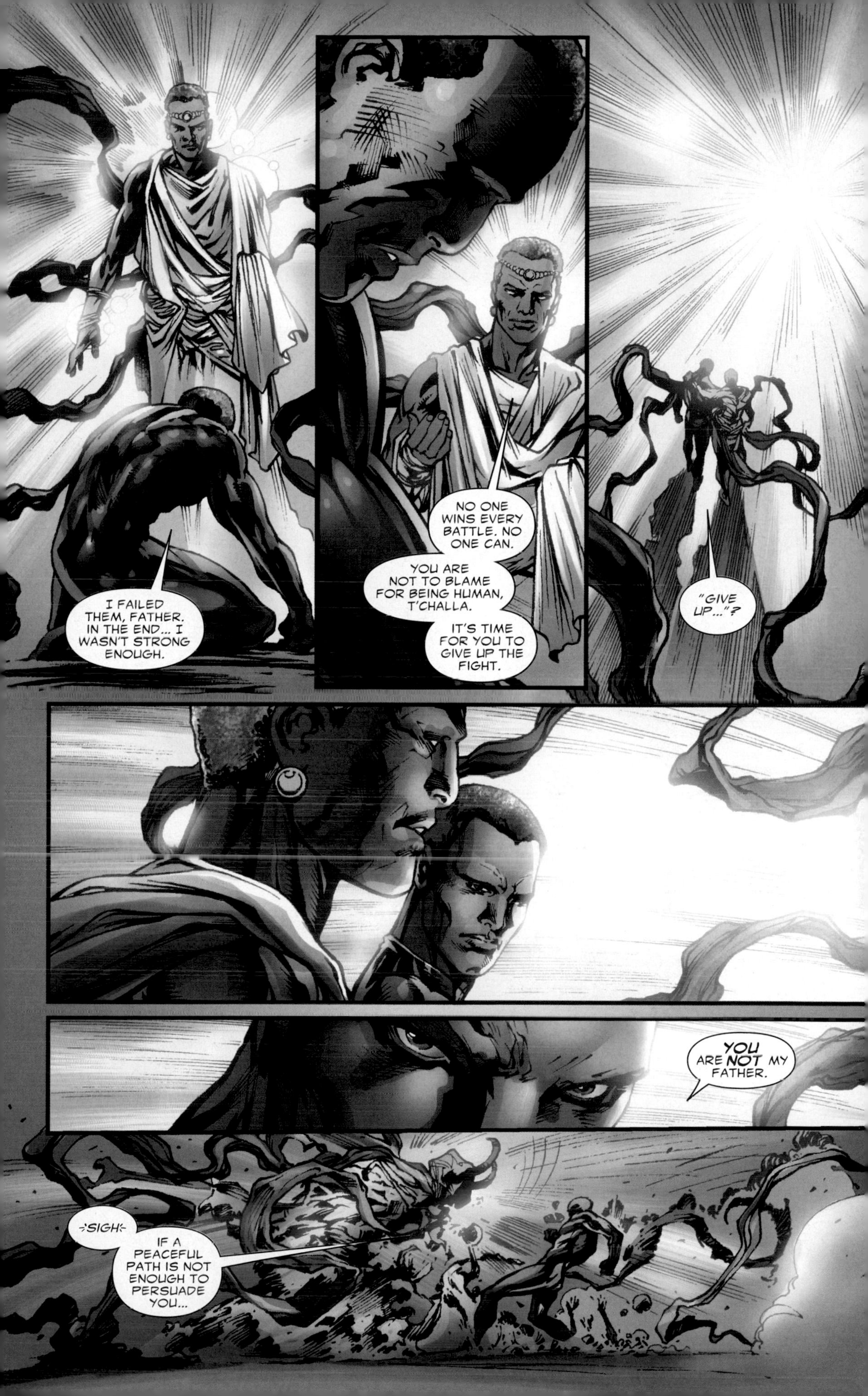
I FAILED THEM, FATHER. IN THE END... I WASN'T STRONG ENOUGH.
NO ONE WINS EVERY BATTLE. NO ONE CAN.
YOU ARE NOT TO BLAME FOR BEING HUMAN, T'CHALLA.
IT'S TIME FOR YOU TO GIVE UP THE FIGHT.
"GIVE UP..."?
YOU ARE NOT MY FATHER.
SIGH
IF A PEACEFUL PATH IS NOT ENOUGH TO PERSUADE YOU...

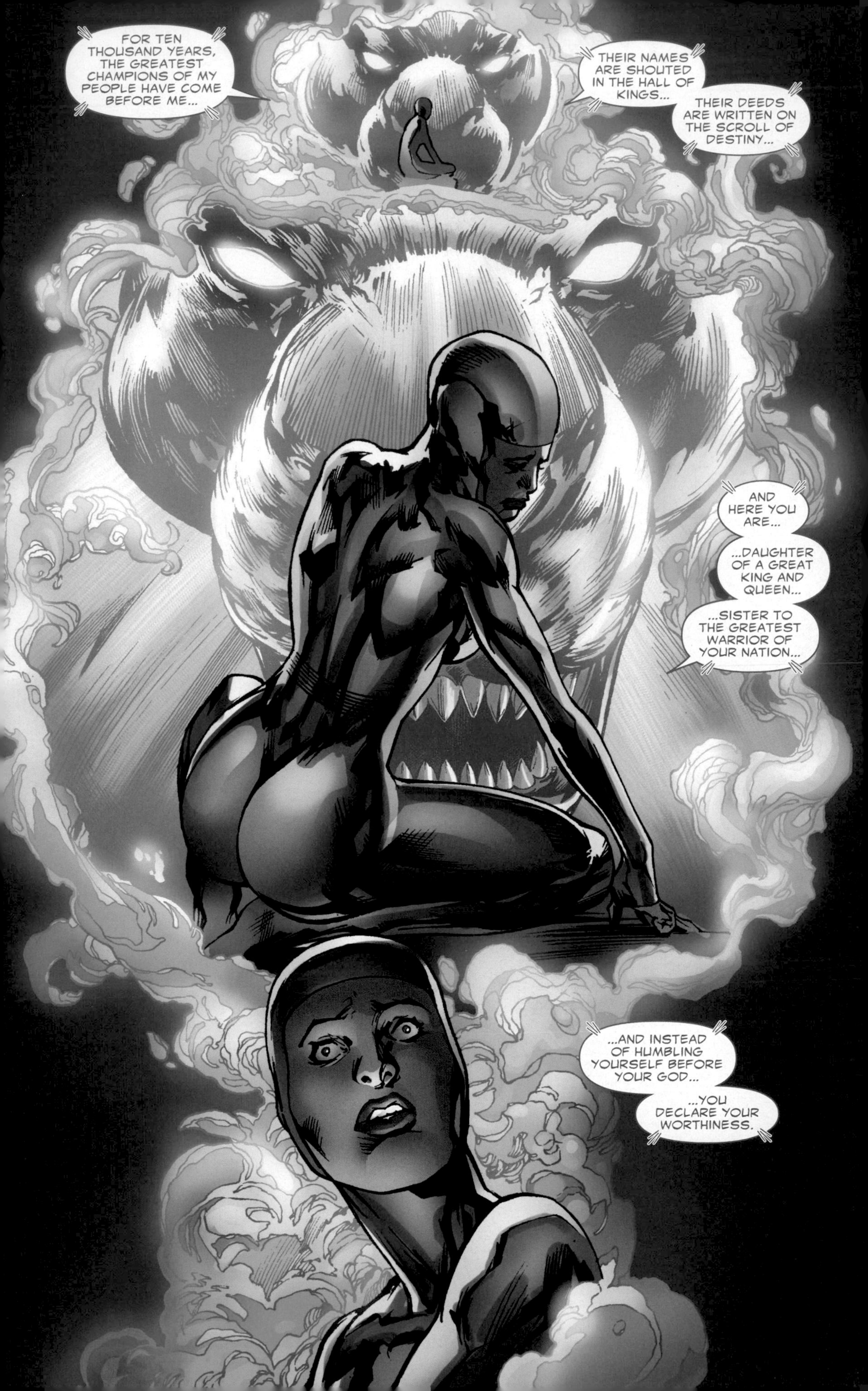
FOR TEN THOUSAND YEARS, THE GREATEST CHAMPIONS OF MY PEOPLE HAVE COME BEFORE ME...
THEIR NAMES ARE SHOUTED IN THE HALL OF KINGS...
THEIR DEEDS ARE WRITTEN ON THE SCROLL OF DESTINY...
AND HERE YOU ARE...
...DAUGHTER OF A GREAT KING AND QUEEN...
...SISTER TO THE GREATEST WARRIOR OF YOUR NATION...
...AND INSTEAD OF HUMBLING YOURSELF BEFORE YOUR GOD...
...YOU DECLARE YOUR WORTHINESS.

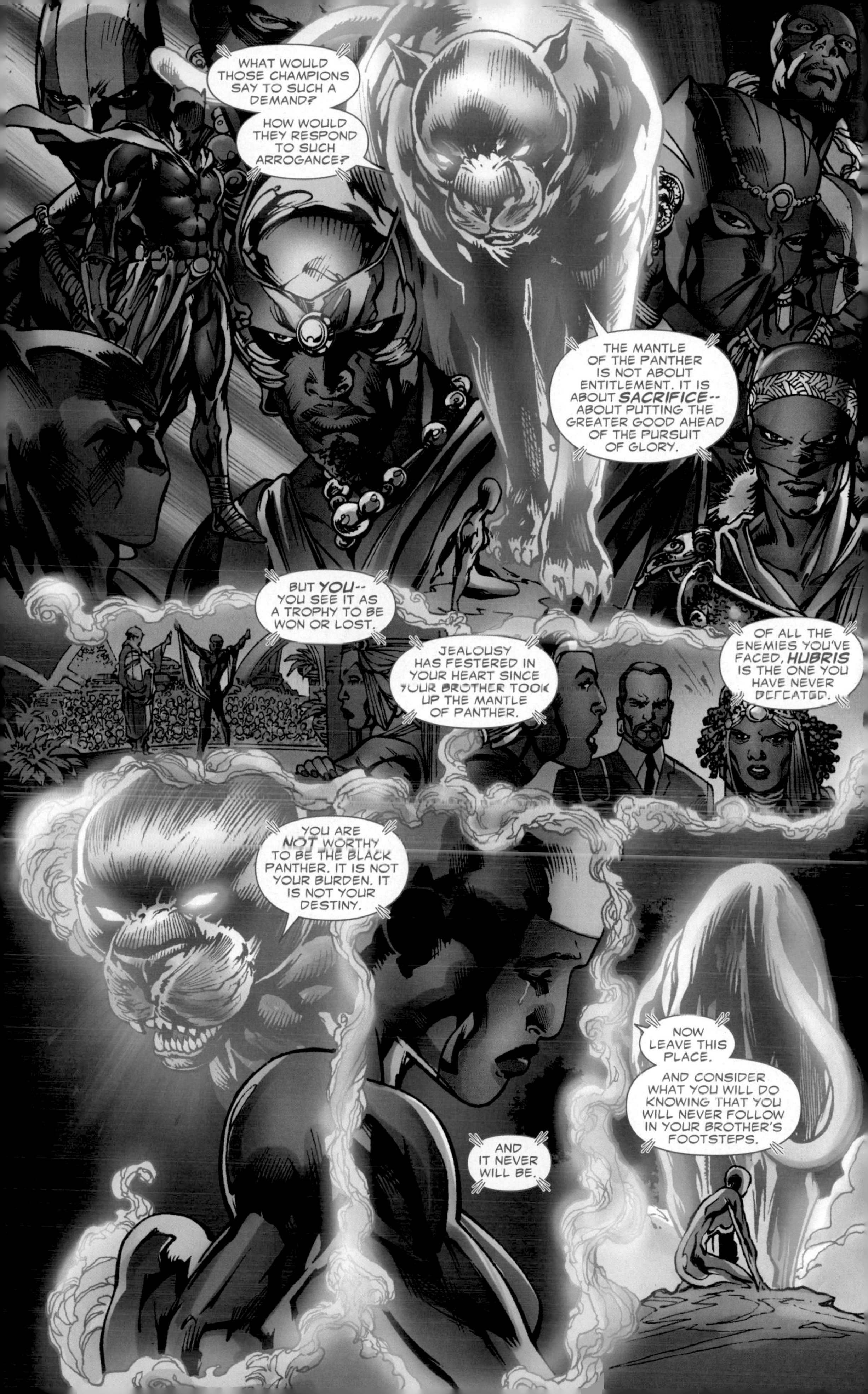
WHAT WOULD THOSE CHAMPIONS SAY TO SUCH A DEMAND?
HOW WOULD THEY RESPOND TO SUCH ARROGANCE?
THE MANTLE OF THE PANTHER IS NOT ABOUT ENTITLEMENT. IT IS ABOUT SACRIFICE-- ABOUT PUTTING THE GREATER GOOD AHEAD OF THE PURSUIT OF GLORY.
BUT YOU-- YOU SEE IT AS A TROPHY TO BE WON OR LOST.
JEALOUSY HAS FESTERED IN YOUR HEART SINCE YOUR BROTHER TOOK UP THE MANTLE OF PANTHER.
OF ALL THE ENEMIES YOU'VE FACED, HUBRIS IS THE ONE YOU HAVE NEVER DEFEATED.
YOU ARE NOT WORTHY TO BE THE BLACK PANTHER. IT IS NOT YOUR BURDEN. IT IS NOT YOUR DESTINY.
AND IT NEVER WILL BE.
NOW LEAVE THIS PLACE.
AND CONSIDER WHAT YOU WILL DO KNOWING THAT YOU WILL NEVER FOLLOW IN YOUR BROTHER'S FOOTSTEPS.

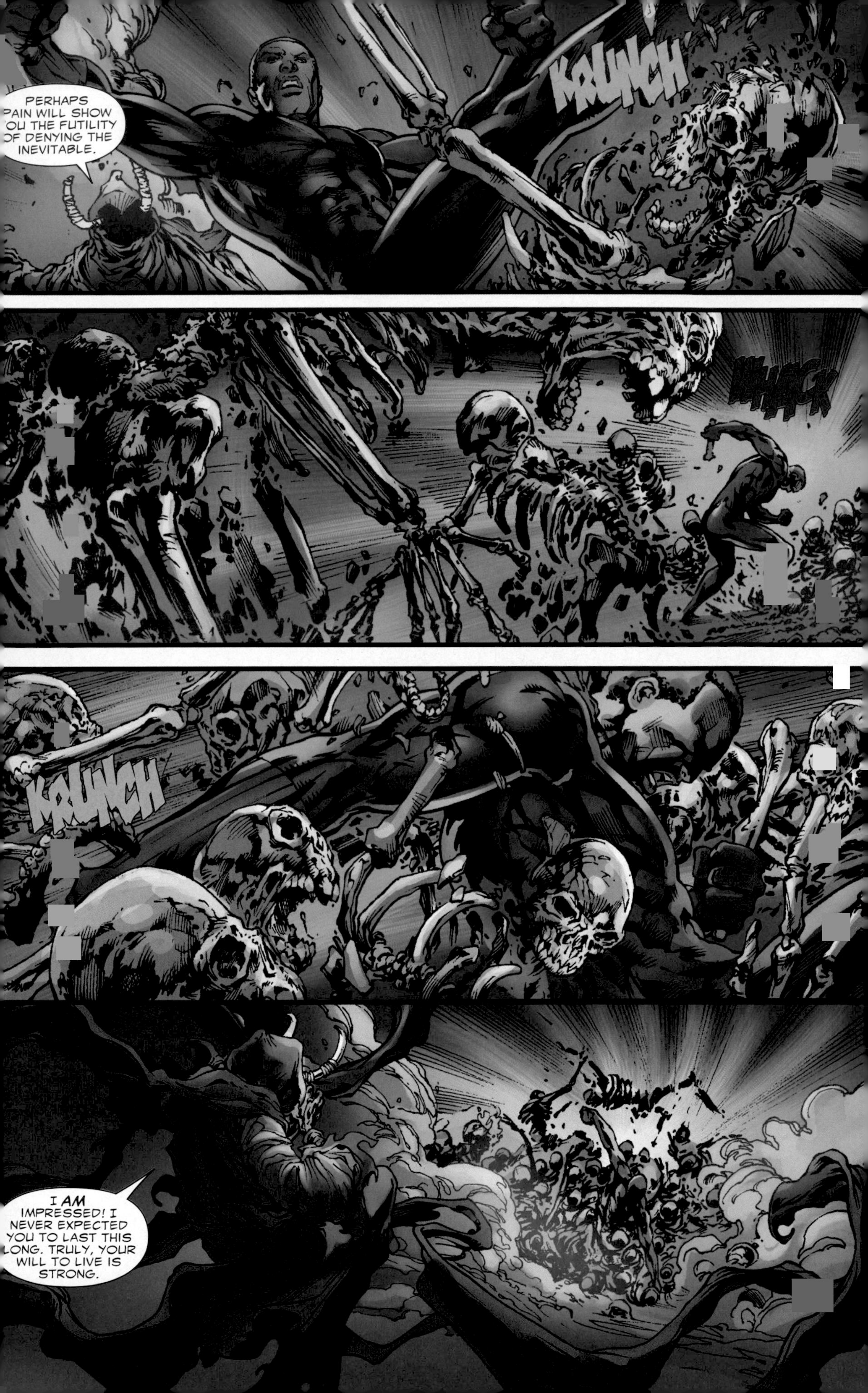
PERHAPS PAIN WILL SHOW YOU THE FUTILITY OF DENYING THE INEVITABLE.
KRUNCH
WHACK
KRUNCH
I AM IMPRESSED! I NEVER EXPECTED YOU TO LAST THIS LONG. TRULY, YOUR WILL TO LIVE IS STRONG.

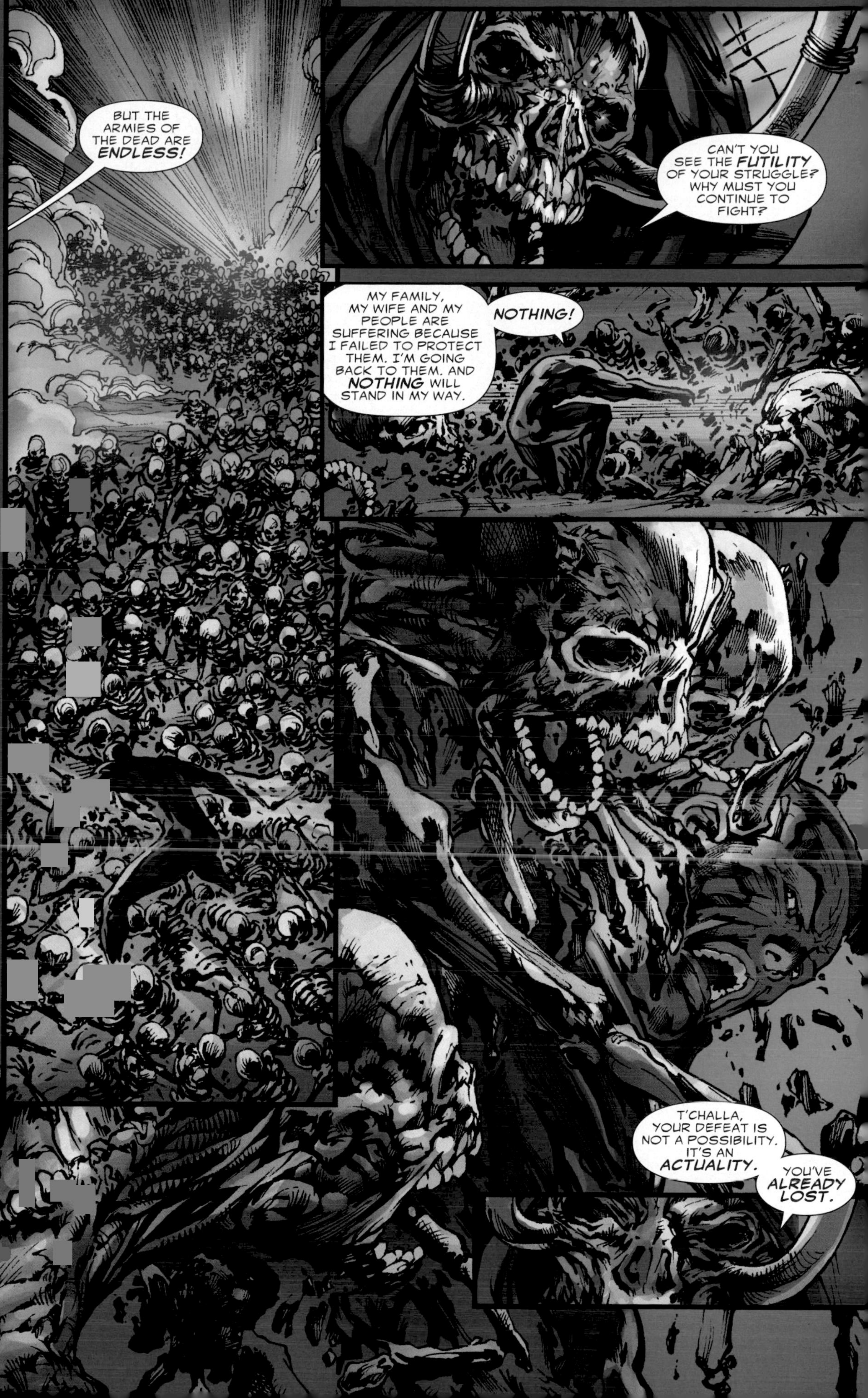
BUT THE ARMIES OF THE DEAD ARE ENDLESS!
CAN'T YOU SEE THE FUTILITY OF YOUR STRUGGLE? WHY MUST YOU CONTINUE TO FIGHT?
MY FAMILY, MY WIFE AND MY PEOPLE ARE SUFFERING BECAUSE I FAILED TO PROTECT THEM. I'M GOING BACK TO THEM. AND NOTHING WILL STAND IN MY WAY.
NOTHING!
T'CHALLA, YOUR DEFEAT IS NOT A POSSIBILITY. IT'S AN ACTUALITY.
YOU'VE ALREADY LOST.

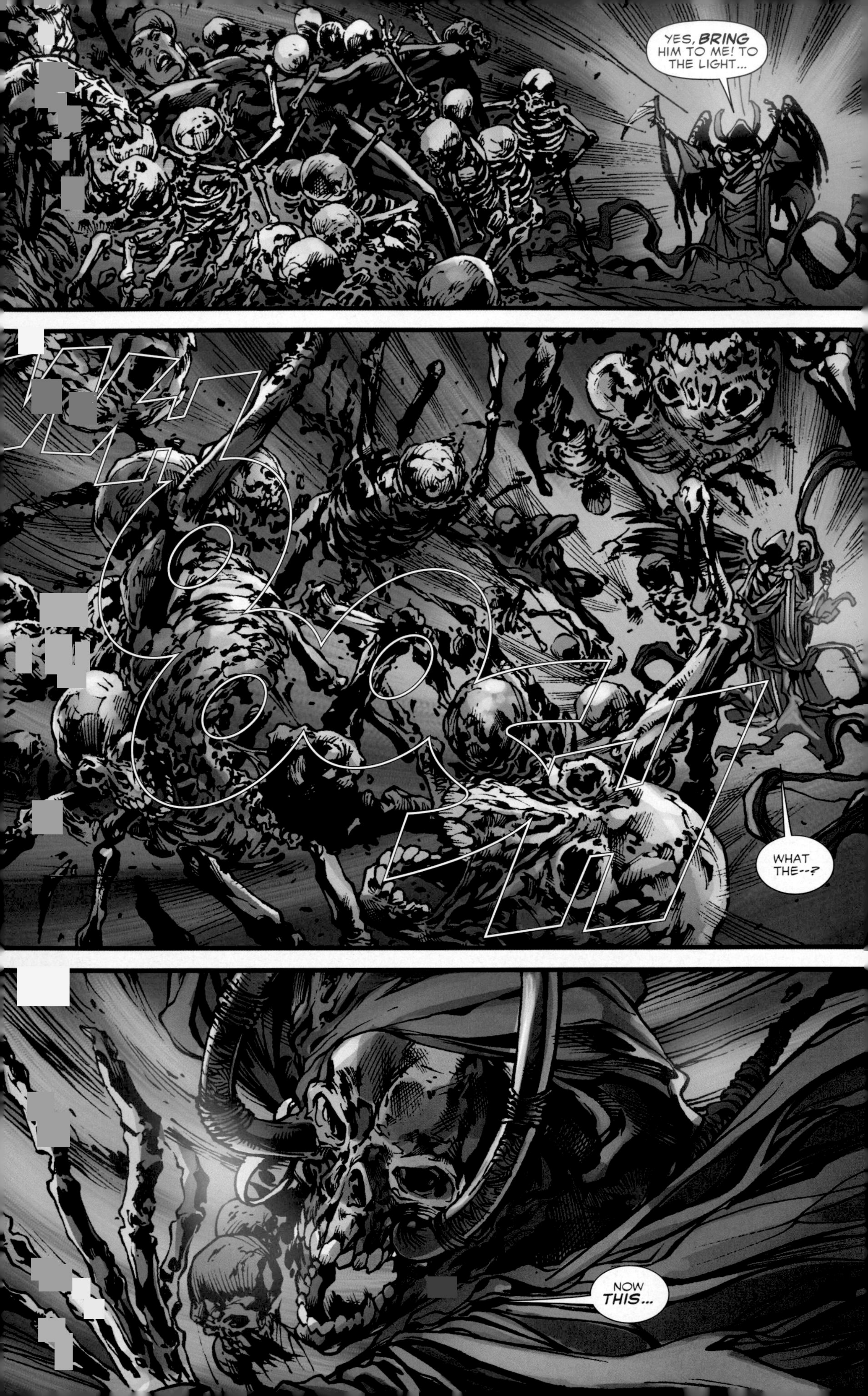
YES, **BRING** HIM TO ME! TO THE LIGHT...
WHAT THE--?
NOW **THIS**...

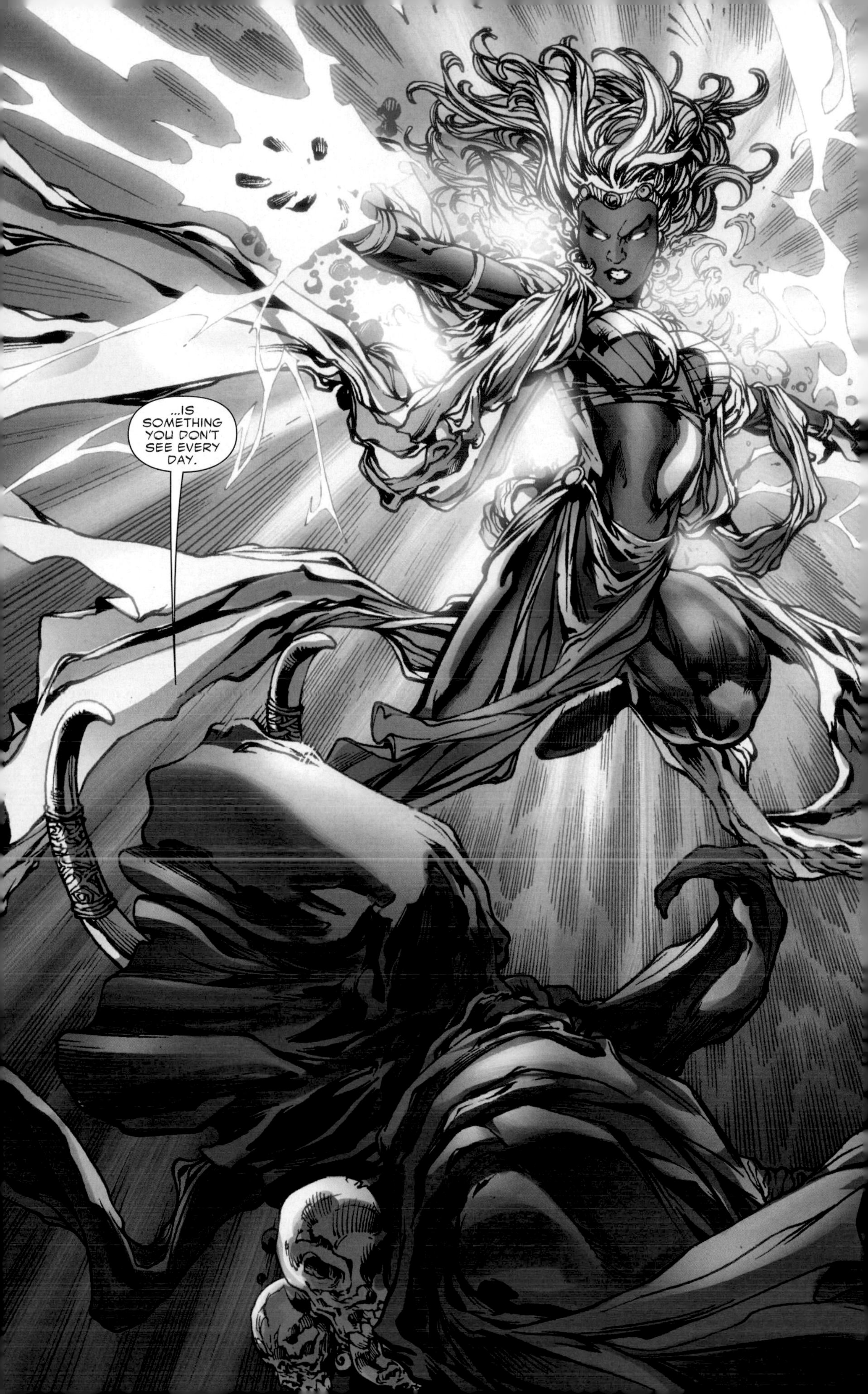
...IS SOMETHING YOU DON'T SEE EVERY DAY.

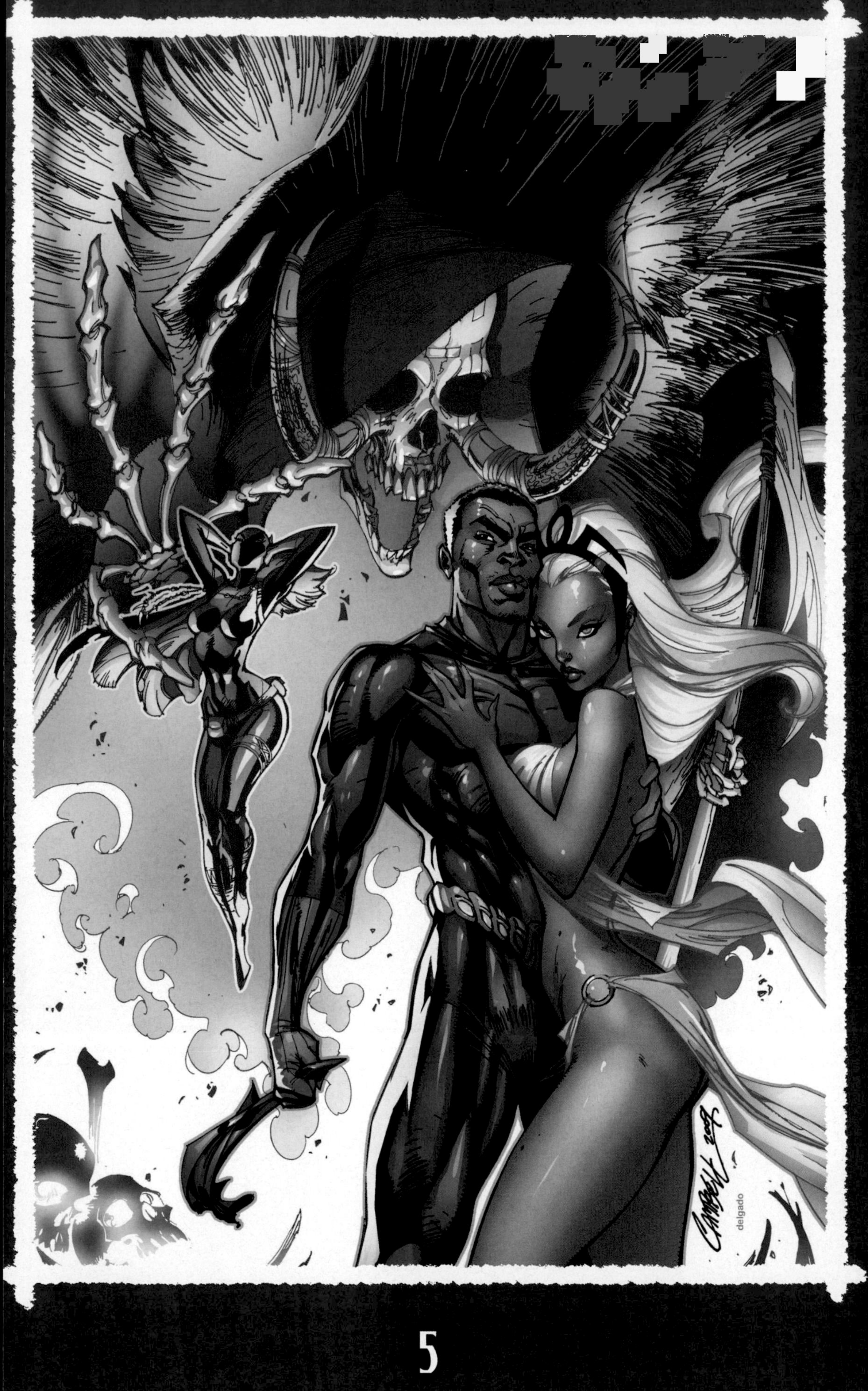
delgado

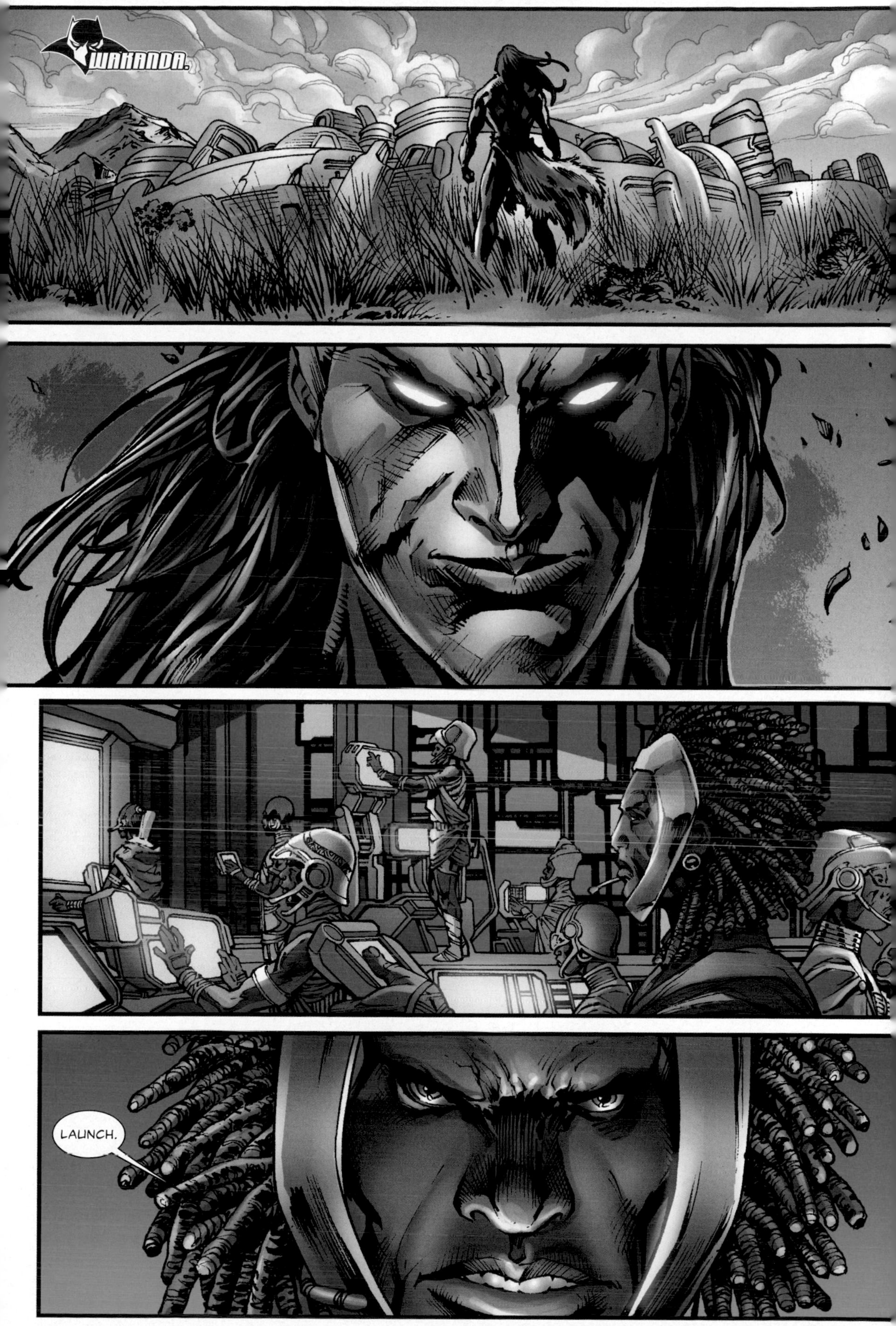
WAKANDA.
LAUNCH.

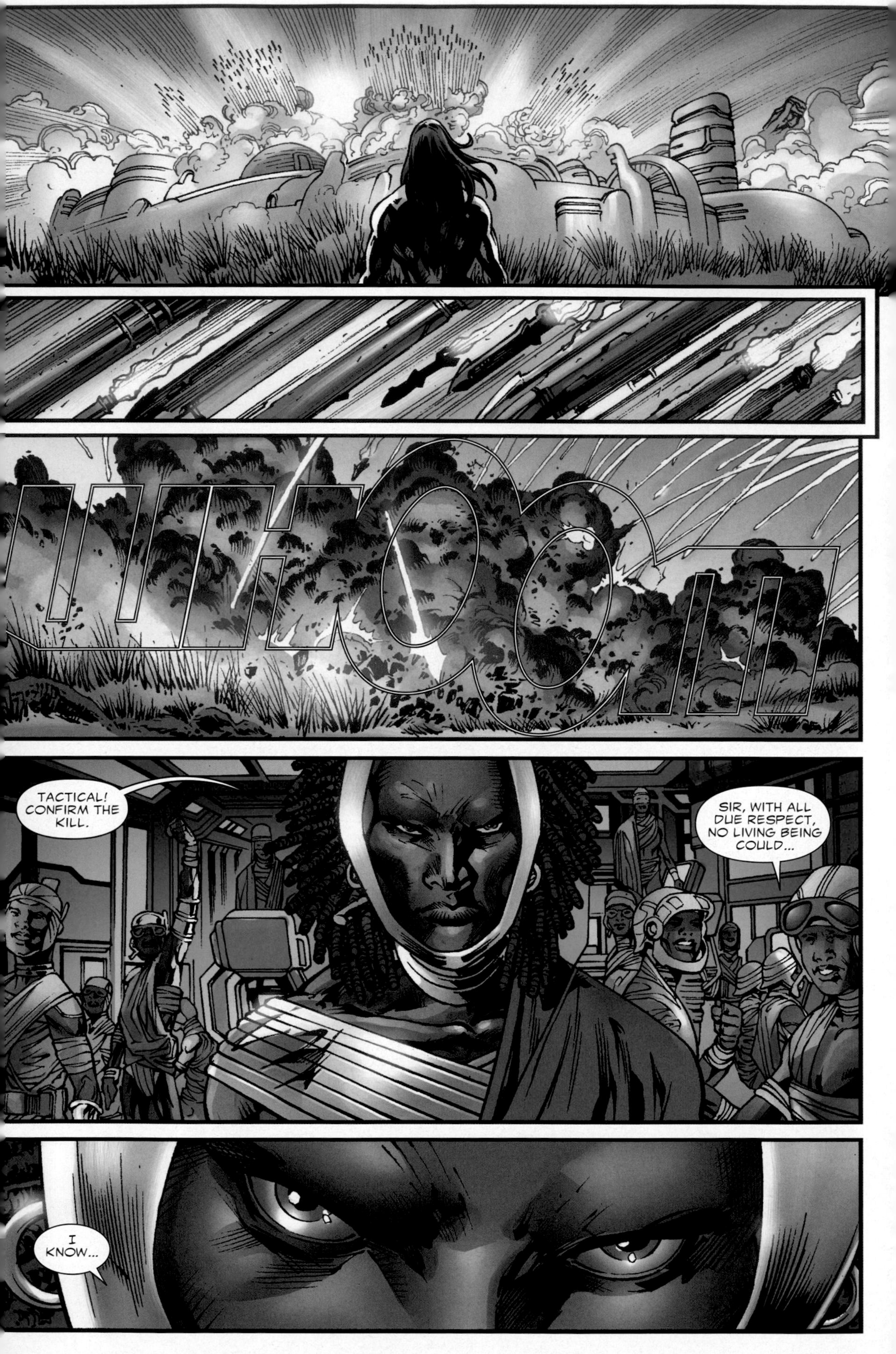
TACTICAL! CONFIRM THE KILL.
SIR, WITH ALL DUE RESPECT, NO LIVING BEING COULD...
I KNOW...

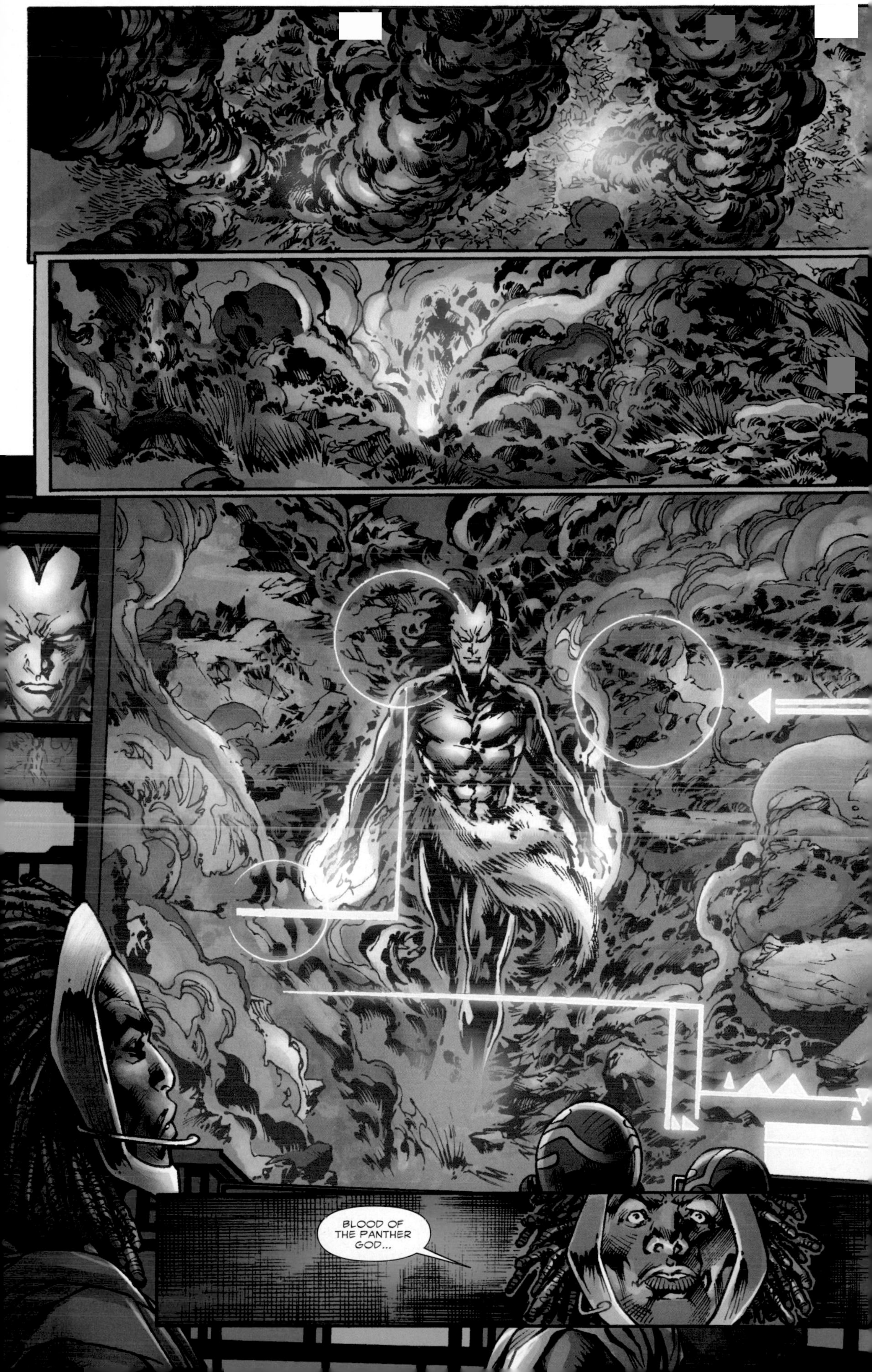
BLOOD OF THE PANTHER GOD...

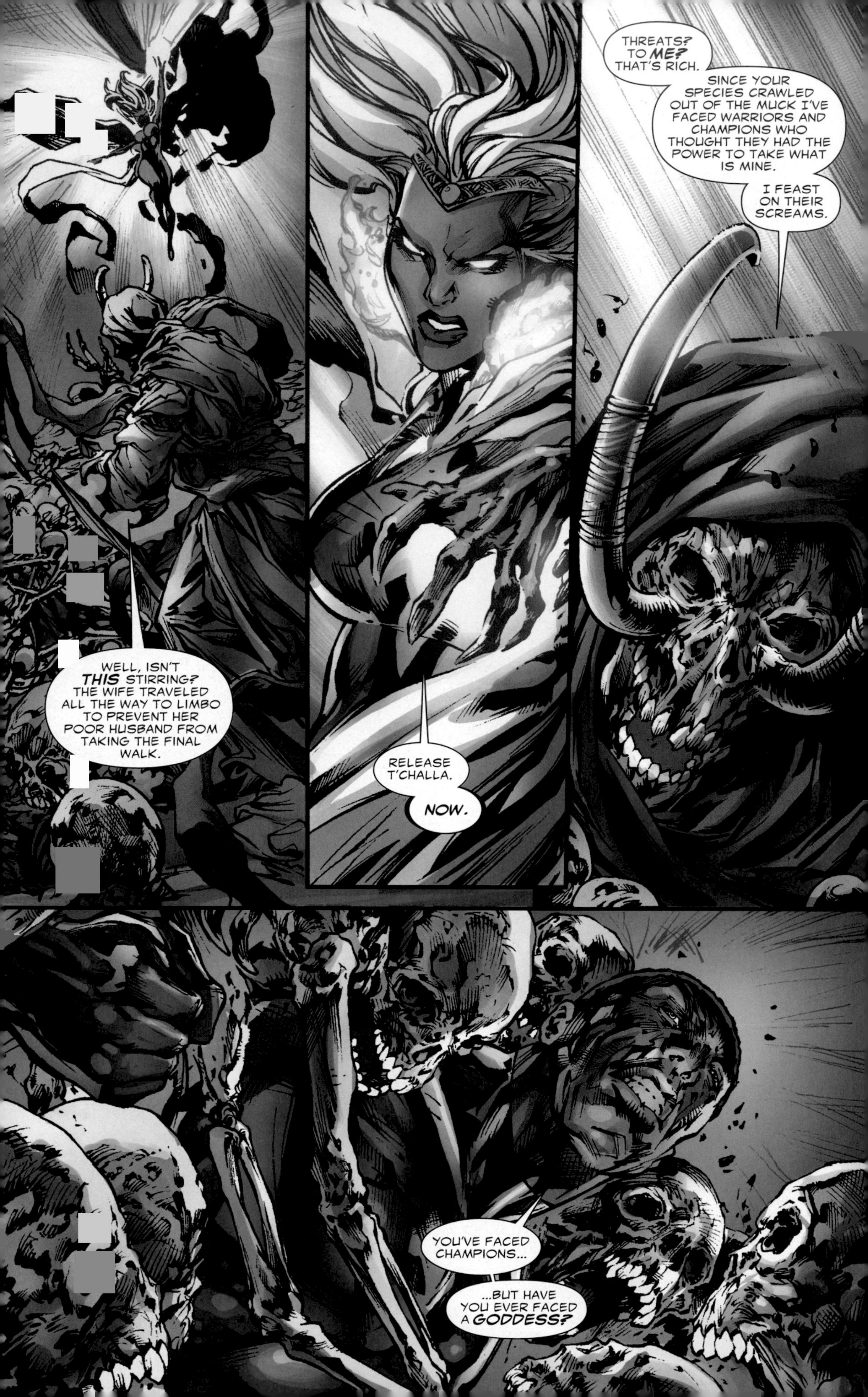
WELL, ISN'T THIS STIRRING? THE WIFE TRAVELED ALL THE WAY TO LIMBO TO PREVENT HER POOR HUSBAND FROM TAKING THE FINAL WALK.
RELEASE T'CHALLA.
NOW.
THREATS? TO ME? THAT'S RICH.
SINCE YOUR SPECIES CRAWLED OUT OF THE MUCK I'VE FACED WARRIORS AND CHAMPIONS WHO THOUGHT THEY HAD THE POWER TO TAKE WHAT IS MINE.
I FEAST ON THEIR SCREAMS.
YOU'VE FACED CHAMPIONS...
...BUT HAVE YOU EVER FACED A GODDESS?

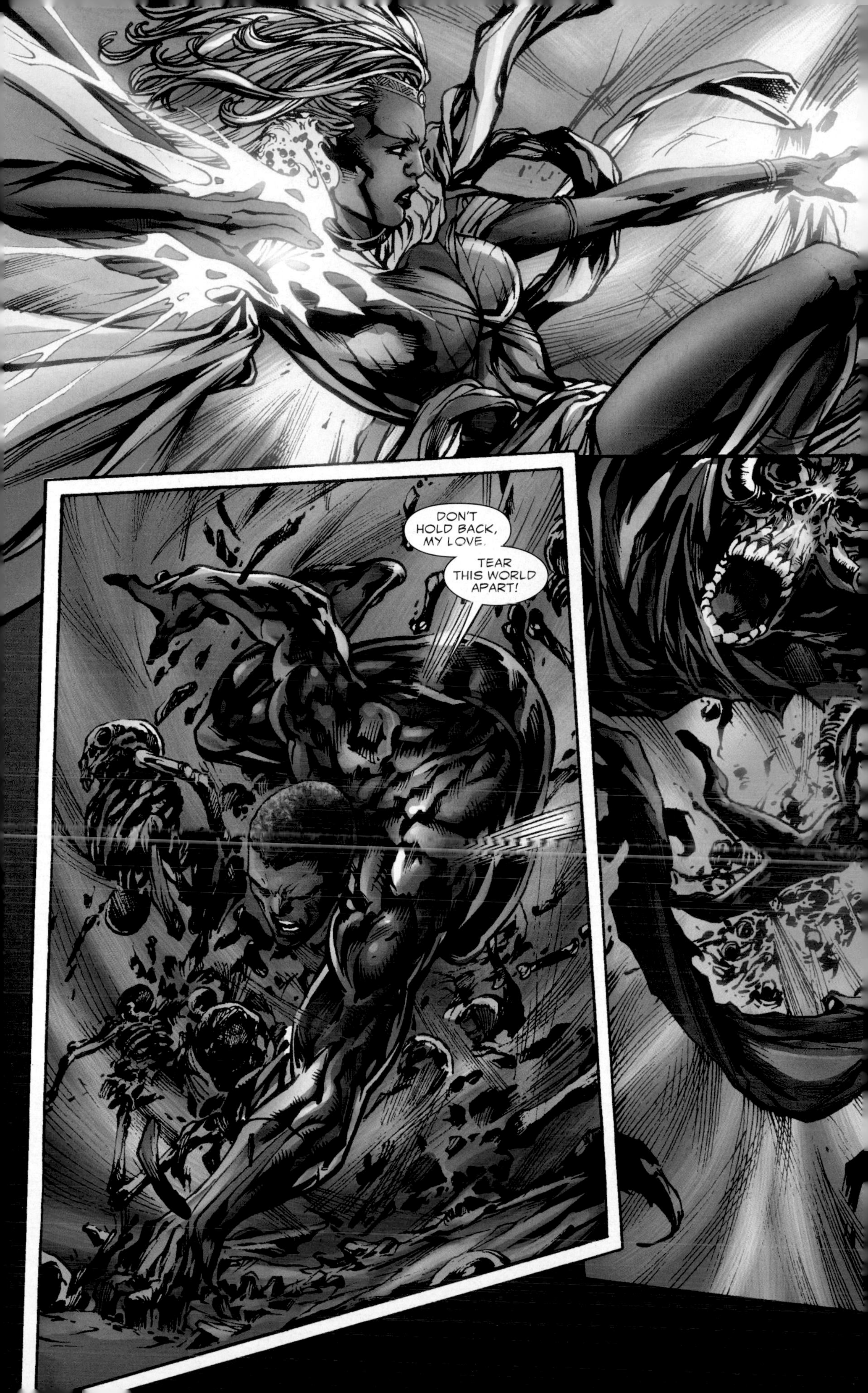
DON'T HOLD BACK, MY LOVE.
TEAR THIS WORLD APART!

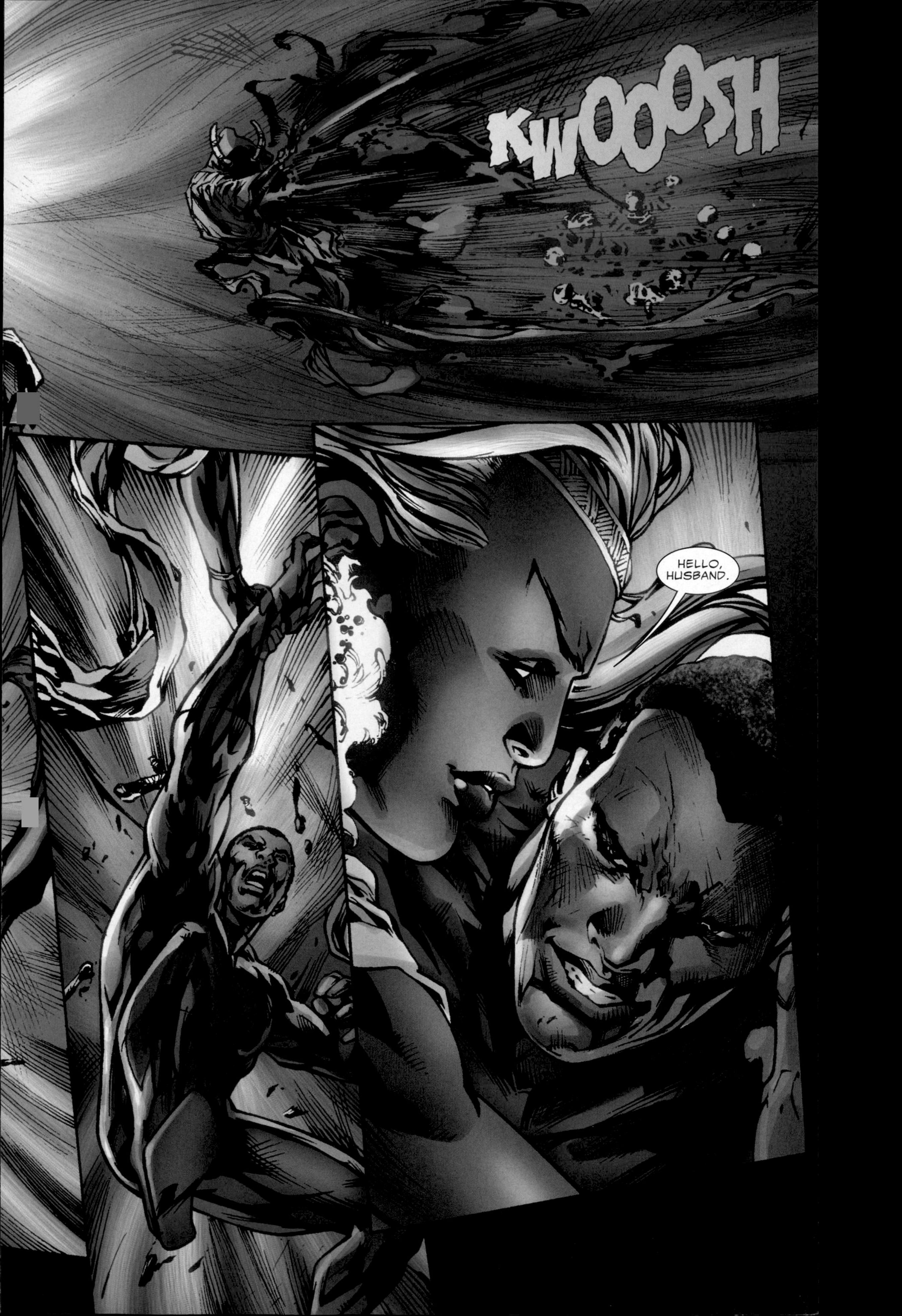
KWOOOSH
HELLO, HUSBAND.

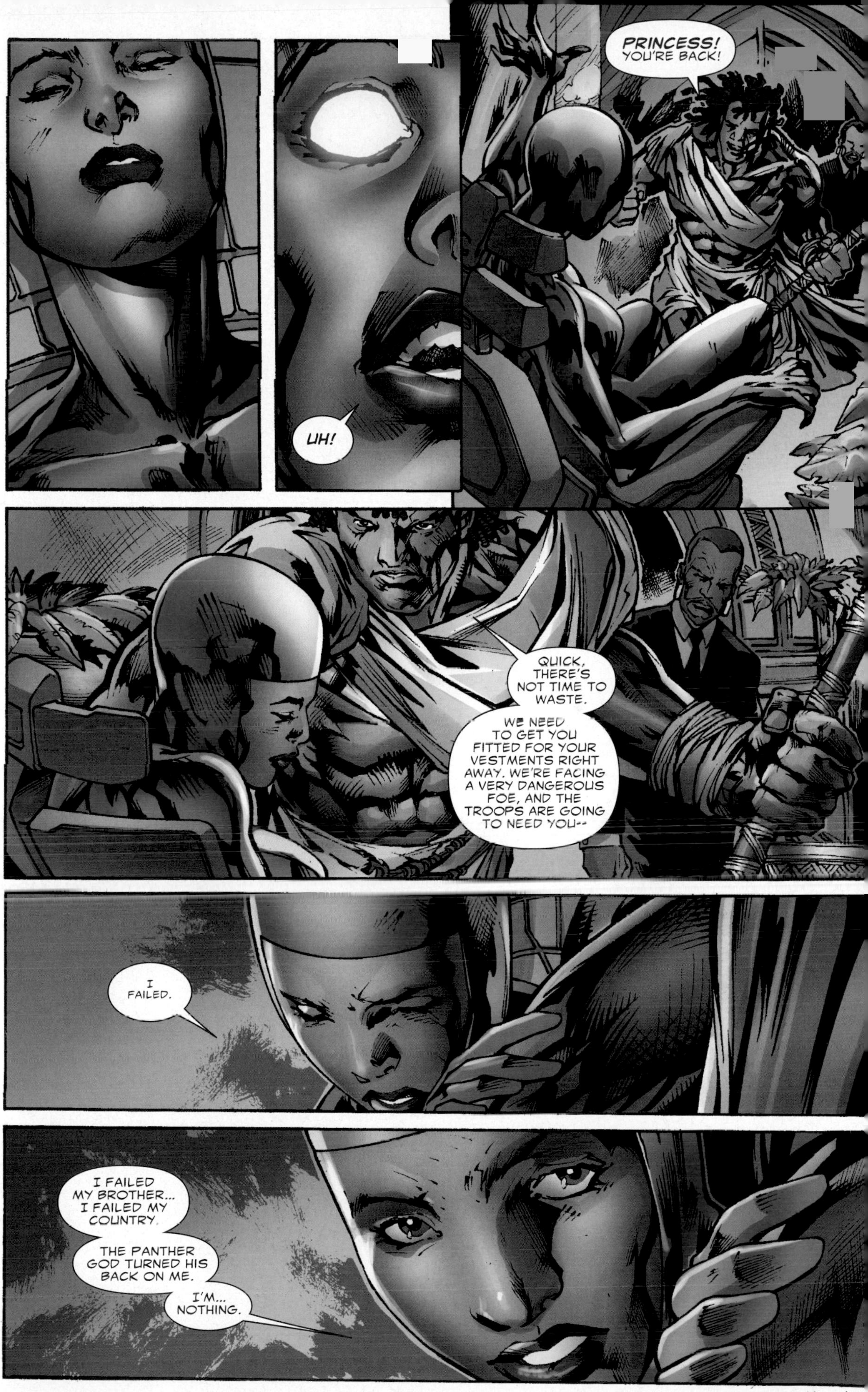
UH!
PRINCESS! YOU'RE BACK!
QUICK, THERE'S NOT TIME TO WASTE.
WE NEED TO GET YOU FITTED FOR YOUR VESTMENTS RIGHT AWAY. WE'RE FACING A VERY DANGEROUS FOE, AND THE TROOPS ARE GOING TO NEED YOU--
I FAILED.
I FAILED MY BROTHER... I FAILED MY COUNTRY.
THE PANTHER GOD TURNED HIS BACK ON ME.
I'M... NOTHING.

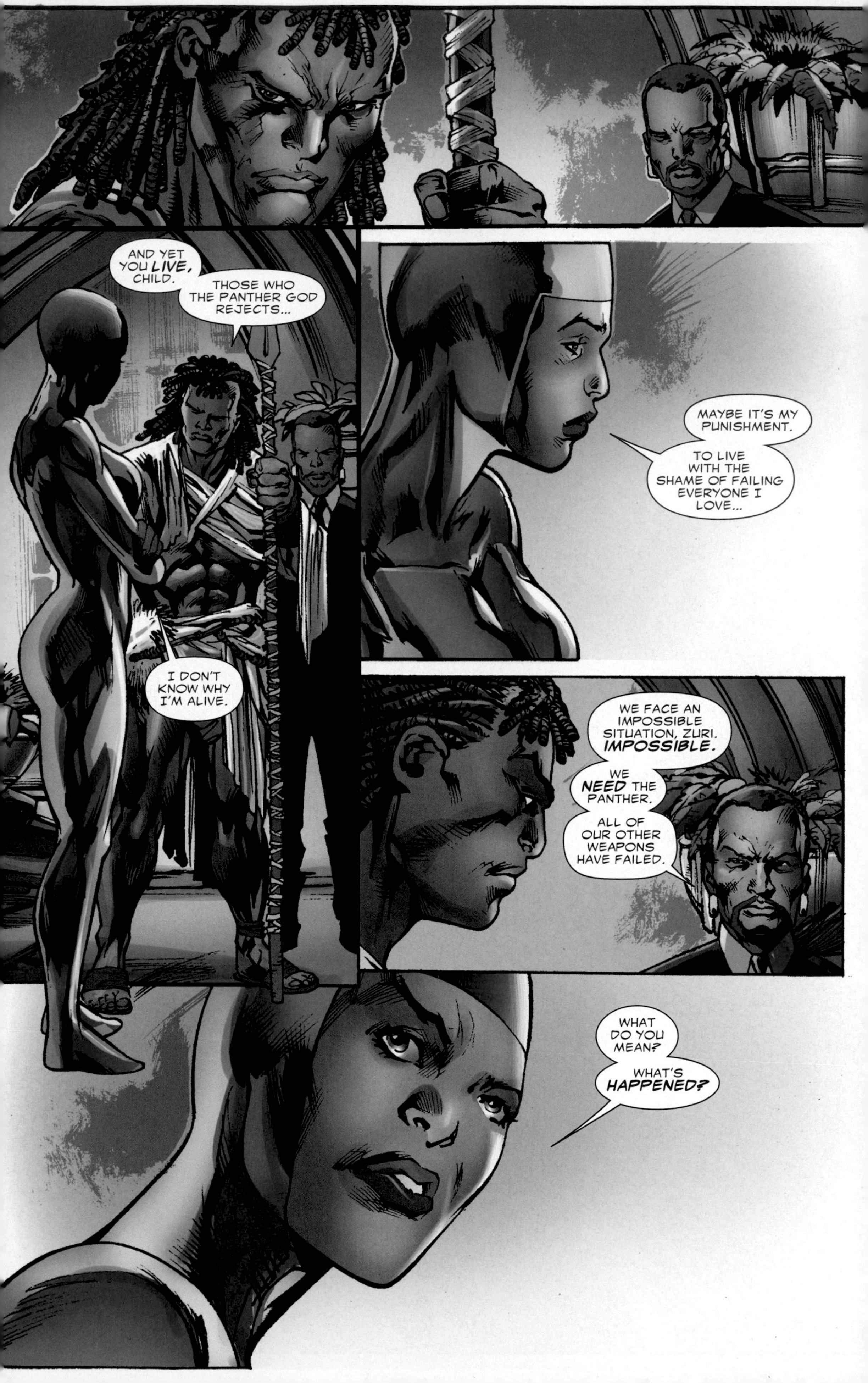

AND YET YOU LIVE, CHILD.
THOSE WHO THE PANTHER GOD REJECTS...
I DON'T KNOW WHY I'M ALIVE.
MAYBE IT'S MY PUNISHMENT.
TO LIVE WITH THE SHAME OF FAILING EVERYONE I LOVE...
WE FACE AN IMPOSSIBLE SITUATION, ZURI. IMPOSSIBLE.
WE NEED THE PANTHER.
ALL OF OUR OTHER WEAPONS HAVE FAILED.
WHAT DO YOU MEAN?
WHAT'S HAPPENED?

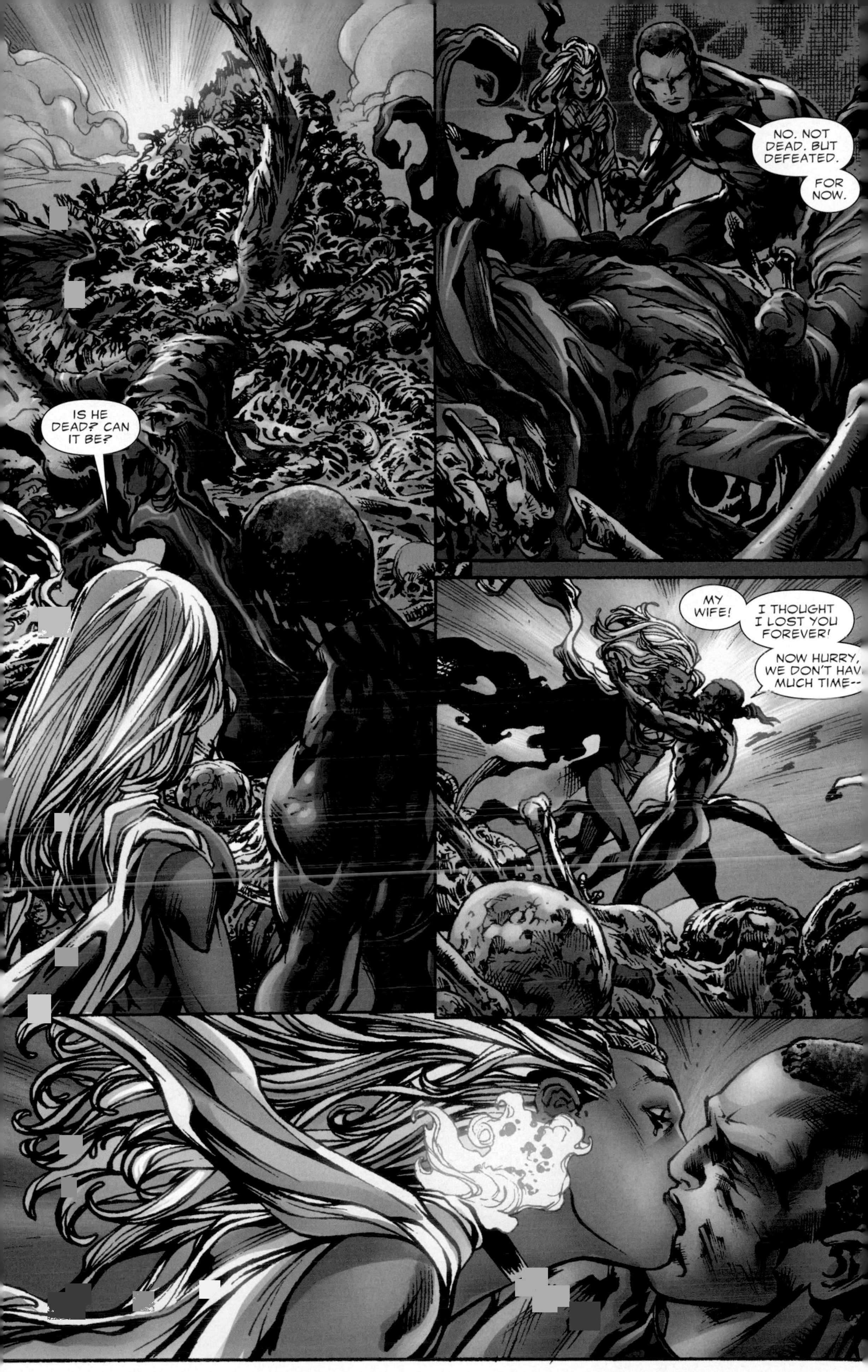
IS HE DEAD? CAN IT BE?
NO. NOT DEAD. BUT DEFEATED.
FOR NOW.
MY WIFE!
I THOUGHT I LOST YOU FOREVER!
NOW HURRY, WE DON'T HAV MUCH TIME--

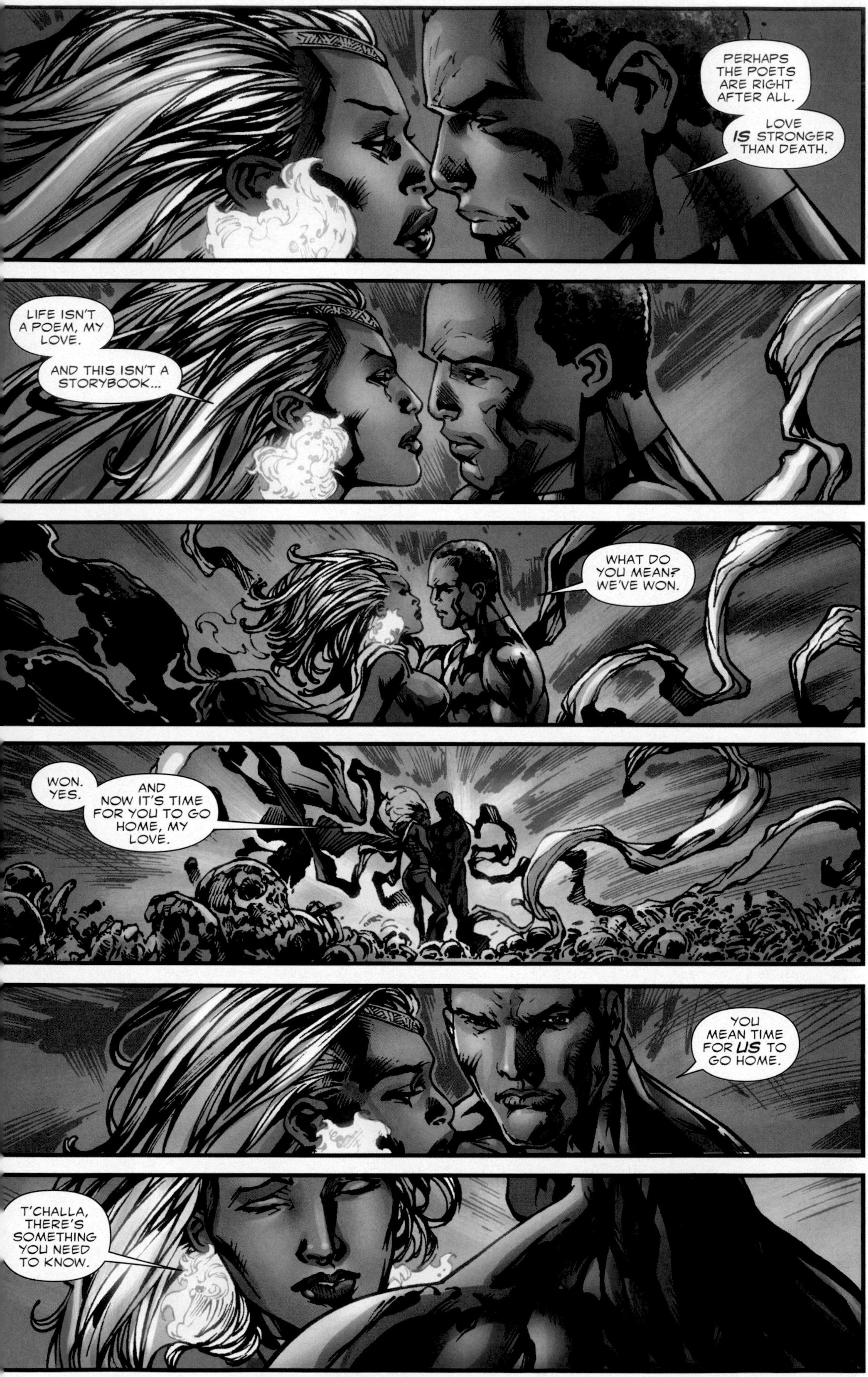
PERHAPS THE POETS ARE RIGHT AFTER ALL.
LOVE IS STRONGER THAN DEATH.
LIFE ISN'T A POEM, MY LOVE.
AND THIS ISN'T A STORYBOOK...
WHAT DO YOU MEAN? WE'VE WON.
WON. YES.
AND NOW IT'S TIME FOR YOU TO GO HOME, MY LOVE.
YOU MEAN TIME FOR US TO GO HOME.
T'CHALLA, THERE'S SOMETHING YOU NEED TO KNOW.

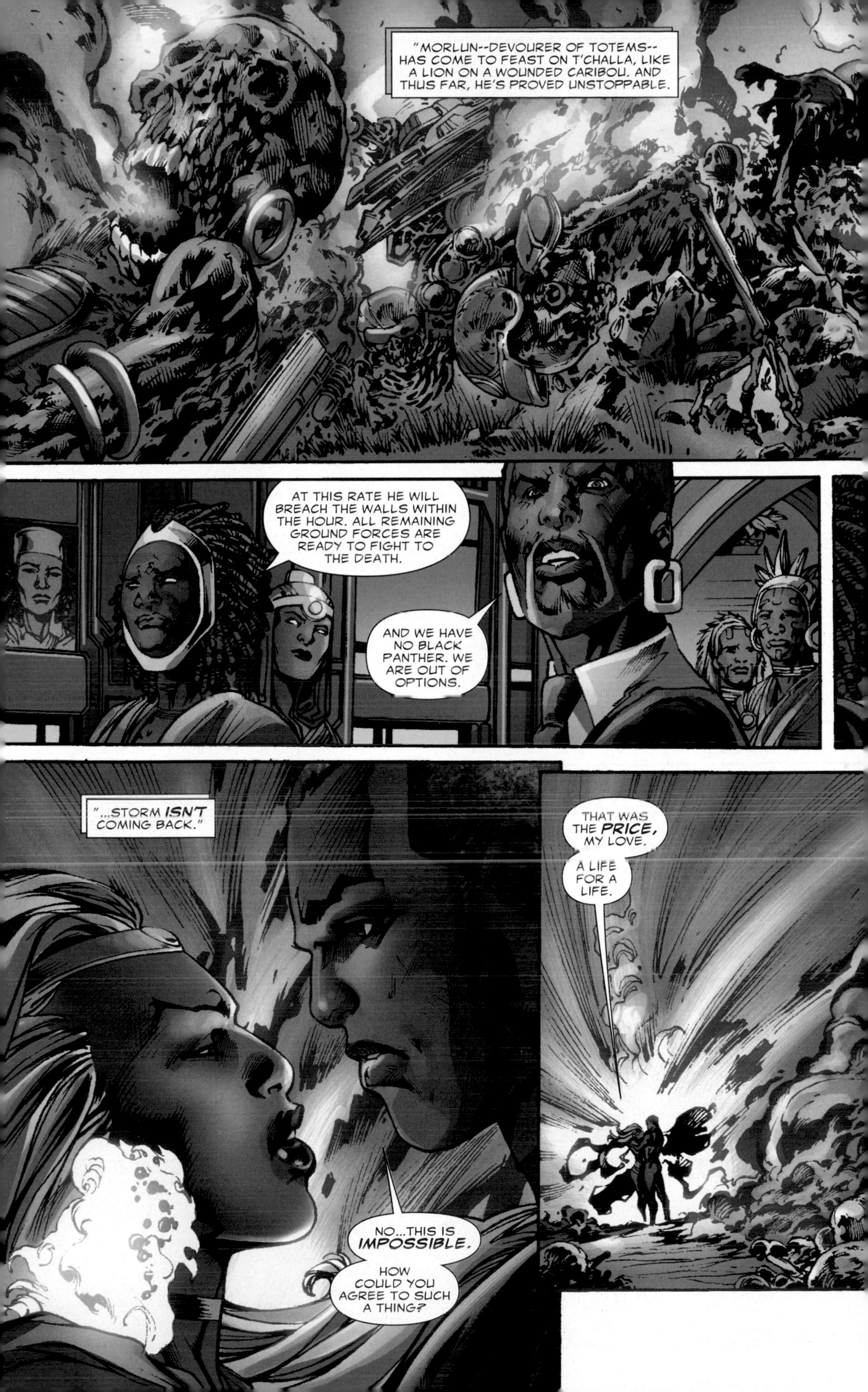
"MORLUN--DEVOURER OF TOTEMS-- HAS COME TO FEAST ON T'CHALLA, LIKE A LION ON A WOUNDED CARIBOU. AND THUS FAR, HE'S PROVED UNSTOPPABLE.
AT THIS RATE HE WILL BREACH THE WALLS WITHIN THE HOUR. ALL REMAINING GROUND FORCES ARE READY TO FIGHT TO THE DEATH.
AND WE HAVE NO BLACK PANTHER. WE ARE OUT OF OPTIONS.
"...STORM ISN'T COMING BACK."
NO...THIS IS IMPOSSIBLE.
HOW COULD YOU AGREE TO SUCH A THING?
THAT WAS THE PRICE, MY LOVE.
A LIFE FOR A LIFE.

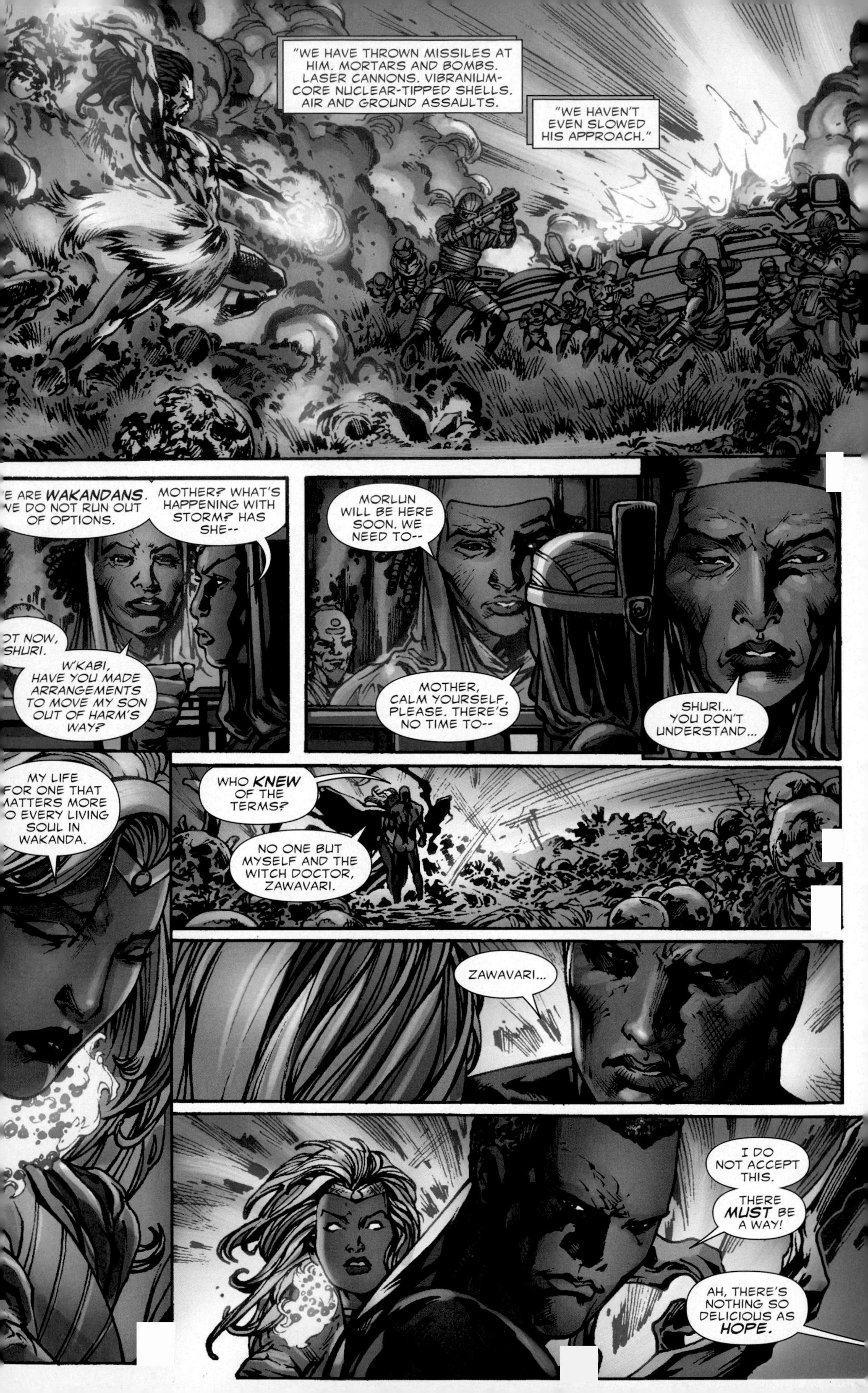
"WE HAVE THROWN MISSILES AT HIM. MORTARS AND BOMBS. LASER CANNONS. VIBRANIUM-CORE NUCLEAR-TIPPED SHELLS. AIR AND GROUND ASSAULTS.
"WE HAVEN'T EVEN SLOWED HIS APPROACH."
E ARE WAKANDANS. VE DO NOT RUN OUT OF OPTIONS.
MOTHER? WHAT'S HAPPENING WITH STORM? HAS SHE--
OT NOW, SHURI.
W'KABI, HAVE YOU MADE ARRANGEMENTS TO MOVE MY SON OUT OF HARM'S WAY?
MORLUN WILL BE HERE SOON. WE NEED TO--
MOTHER, CALM YOURSELF, PLEASE. THERE'S NO TIME TO--
SHURI... YOU DON'T UNDERSTAND...
MY LIFE FOR ONE THAT MATTERS MORE O EVERY LIVING SOUL IN WAKANDA.
WHO KNEW OF THE TERMS?
NO ONE BUT MYSELF AND THE WITCH DOCTOR, ZAWAVARI.
ZAWAVARI...
I DO NOT ACCEPT THIS.
THERE MUST BE A WAY!
AH, THERE'S NOTHING SO DELICIOUS AS HOPE.

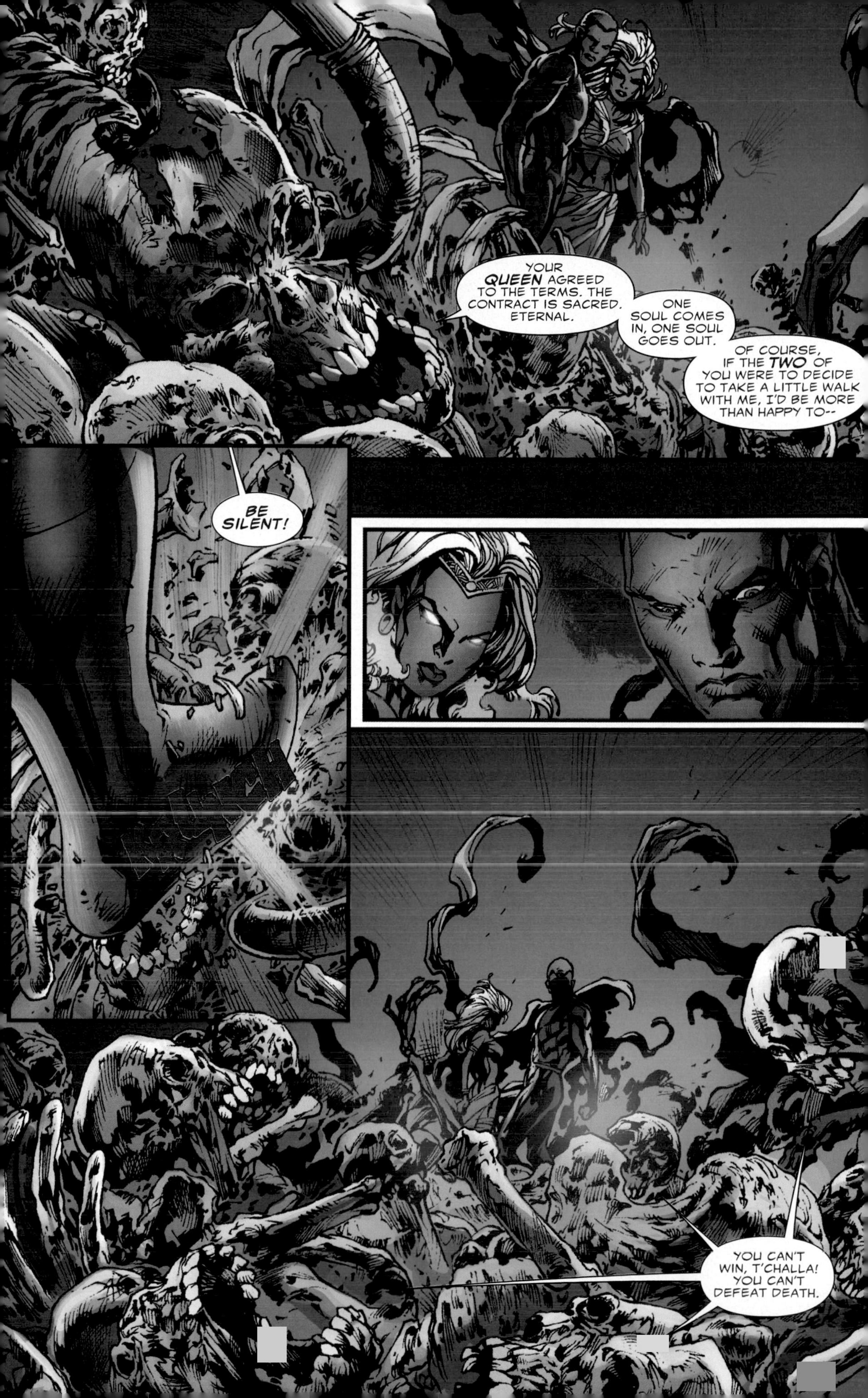
YOUR QUEEN AGREED TO THE TERMS. THE CONTRACT IS SACRED. ETERNAL.
ONE SOUL COMES IN, ONE SOUL GOES OUT.
OF COURSE, IF THE TWO OF YOU WERE TO DECIDE TO TAKE A LITTLE WALK WITH ME, I'D BE MORE THAN HAPPY TO--
BE SILENT!
YOU CAN'T WIN, T'CHALLA! YOU CAN'T DEFEAT DEATH.

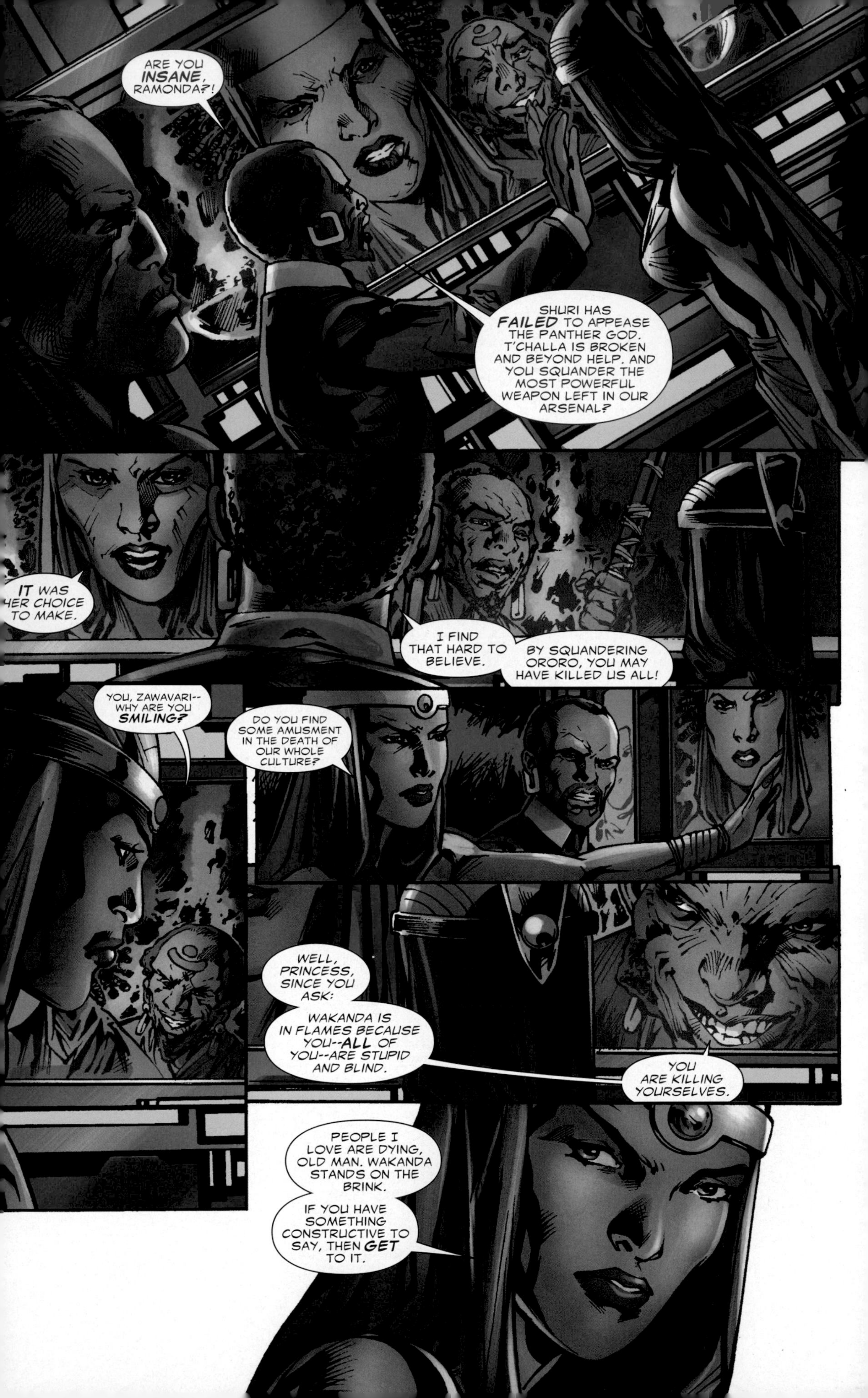
ARE YOU INSANE, RAMONDA?!
SHURI HAS FAILED TO APPEASE THE PANTHER GOD. T'CHALLA IS BROKEN AND BEYOND HELP. AND YOU SQUANDER THE MOST POWERFUL WEAPON LEFT IN OUR ARSENAL?
IT WAS HER CHOICE TO MAKE.
I FIND THAT HARD TO BELIEVE.
BY SQUANDERING ORORO, YOU MAY HAVE KILLED US ALL!
YOU, ZAWAVARI-- WHY ARE YOU SMILING?
DO YOU FIND SOME AMUSMENT IN THE DEATH OF OUR WHOLE CULTURE?
WELL, PRINCESS, SINCE YOU ASK:
WAKANDA IS IN FLAMES BECAUSE YOU--ALL OF YOU--ARE STUPID AND BLIND.
YOU ARE KILLING YOURSELVES.
PEOPLE I LOVE ARE DYING, OLD MAN. WAKANDA STANDS ON THE BRINK.
IF YOU HAVE SOMETHING CONSTRUCTIVE TO SAY, THEN GET TO IT.

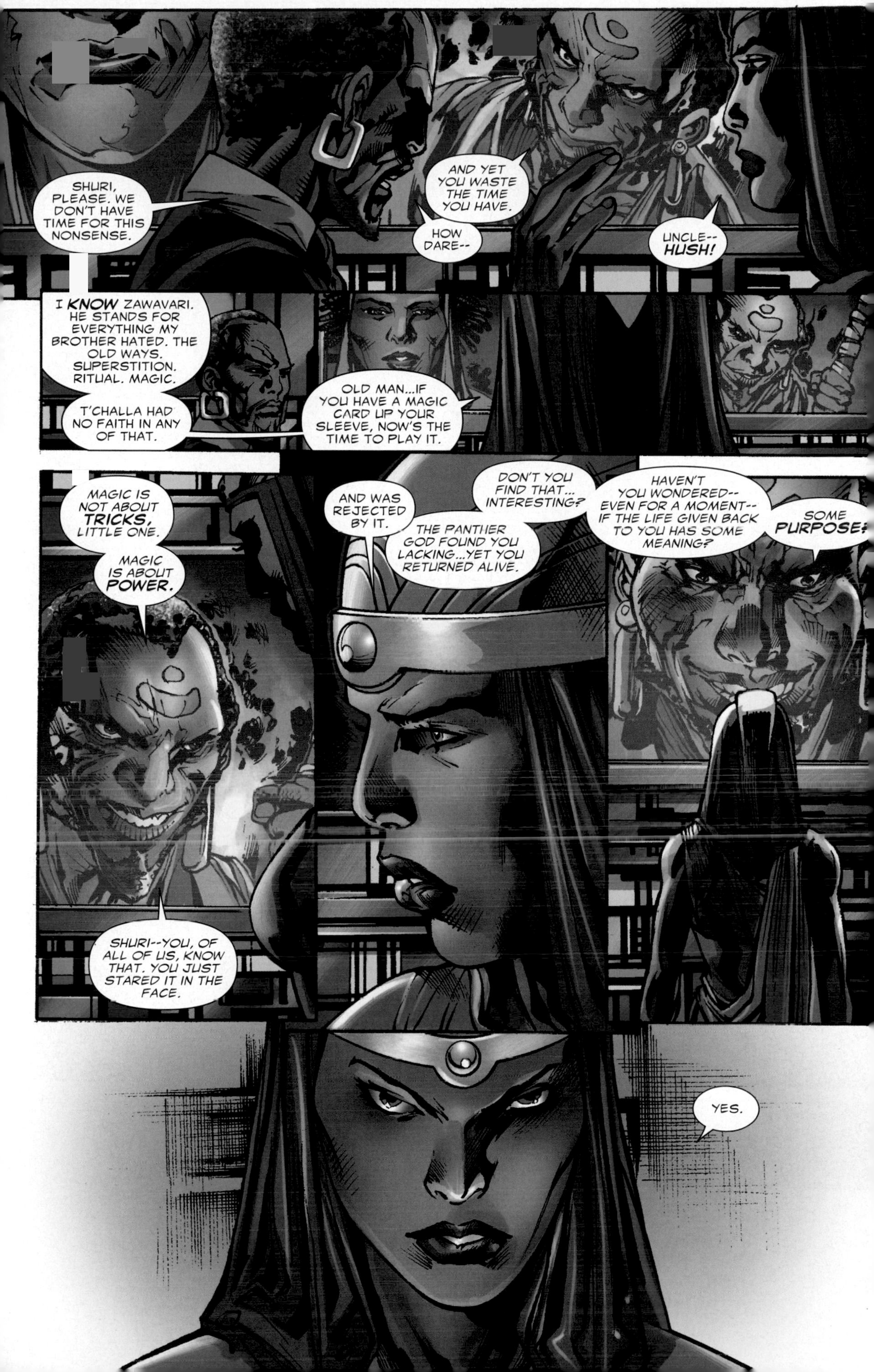
SHURI, PLEASE. WE DON'T HAVE TIME FOR THIS NONSENSE.
HOW DARE--
AND YET YOU WASTE THE TIME YOU HAVE.
UNCLE-- **HUSH!**
I **KNOW** ZAWAVARI. HE STANDS FOR EVERYTHING MY BROTHER HATED. THE OLD WAYS. SUPERSTITION. RITUAL. MAGIC.
T'CHALLA HAD NO FAITH IN ANY OF THAT.
OLD MAN...IF YOU HAVE A MAGIC CARD UP YOUR SLEEVE, NOW'S THE TIME TO PLAY IT.
MAGIC IS NOT ABOUT **TRICKS**, LITTLE ONE.
MAGIC IS ABOUT **POWER.**
SHURI--YOU, OF ALL OF US, KNOW THAT. YOU JUST STARED IT IN THE FACE.
AND WAS REJECTED BY IT.
THE PANTHER GOD FOUND YOU LACKING...YET YOU RETURNED ALIVE.
DON'T YOU FIND THAT... INTERESTING?
HAVEN'T YOU WONDERED-- EVEN FOR A MOMENT-- IF THE LIFE GIVEN BACK TO YOU HAS SOME MEANING?
SOME **PURPOSE?**
YES.

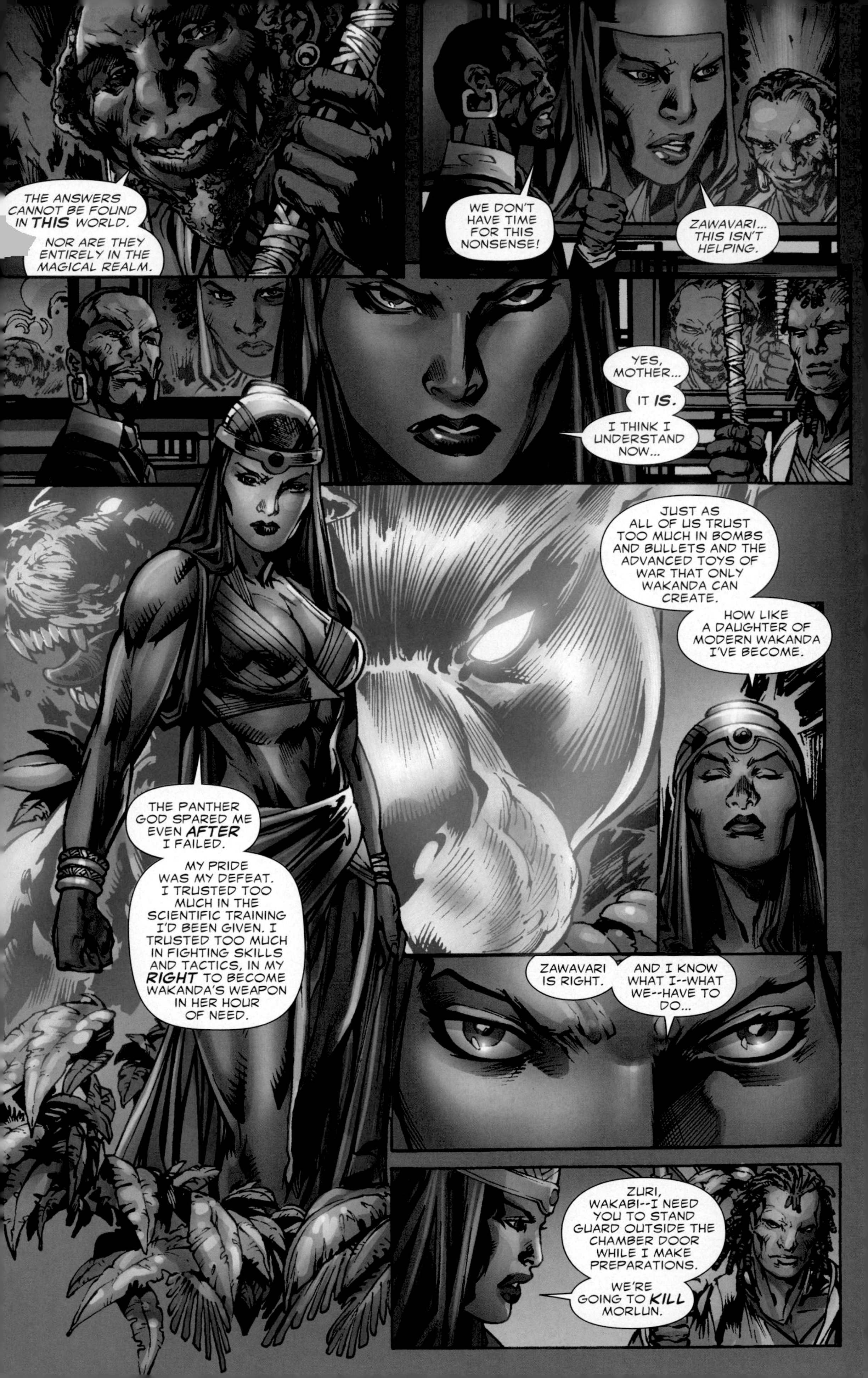
THE ANSWERS CANNOT BE FOUND IN THIS WORLD.
NOR ARE THEY ENTIRELY IN THE MAGICAL REALM.
WE DON'T HAVE TIME FOR THIS NONSENSE!
ZAWAVARI... THIS ISN'T HELPING.
YES, MOTHER...
IT IS.
I THINK I UNDERSTAND NOW...
THE PANTHER GOD SPARED ME EVEN AFTER I FAILED.
MY PRIDE WAS MY DEFEAT. I TRUSTED TOO MUCH IN THE SCIENTIFIC TRAINING I'D BEEN GIVEN. I TRUSTED TOO MUCH IN FIGHTING SKILLS AND TACTICS, IN MY RIGHT TO BECOME WAKANDA'S WEAPON IN HER HOUR OF NEED.
JUST AS ALL OF US TRUST TOO MUCH IN BOMBS AND BULLETS AND THE ADVANCED TOYS OF WAR THAT ONLY WAKANDA CAN CREATE.
HOW LIKE A DAUGHTER OF MODERN WAKANDA I'VE BECOME.
ZAWAVARI IS RIGHT.
AND I KNOW WHAT I--WHAT WE--HAVE TO DO...
ZURI, WAKABI--I NEED YOU TO STAND GUARD OUTSIDE THE CHAMBER DOOR WHILE I MAKE PREPARATIONS.
WE'RE GOING TO KILL MORLUN.

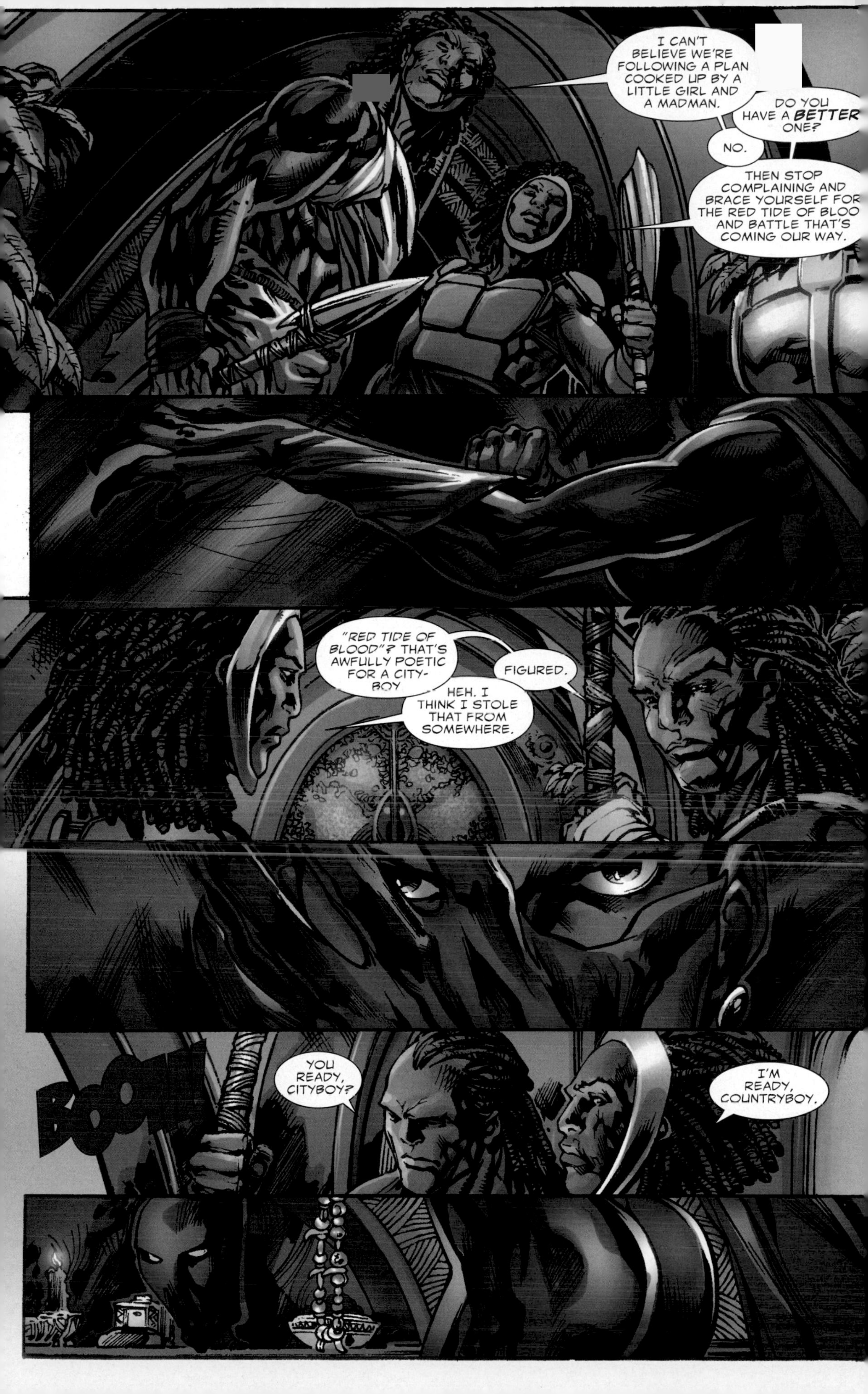
I CAN'T BELIEVE WE'RE FOLLOWING A PLAN COOKED UP BY A LITTLE GIRL AND A MADMAN.
DO YOU HAVE A **BETTER** ONE?
NO.
THEN STOP COMPLAINING AND BRACE YOURSELF FOR THE RED TIDE OF BLOO AND BATTLE THAT'S COMING OUR WAY.
"RED TIDE OF BLOOD"? THAT'S AWFULLY POETIC FOR A CITY-BOY
HEH. I THINK I STOLE THAT FROM SOMEWHERE.
FIGURED.
YOU READY, CITYBOY?
I'M READY, COUNTRYBOY.

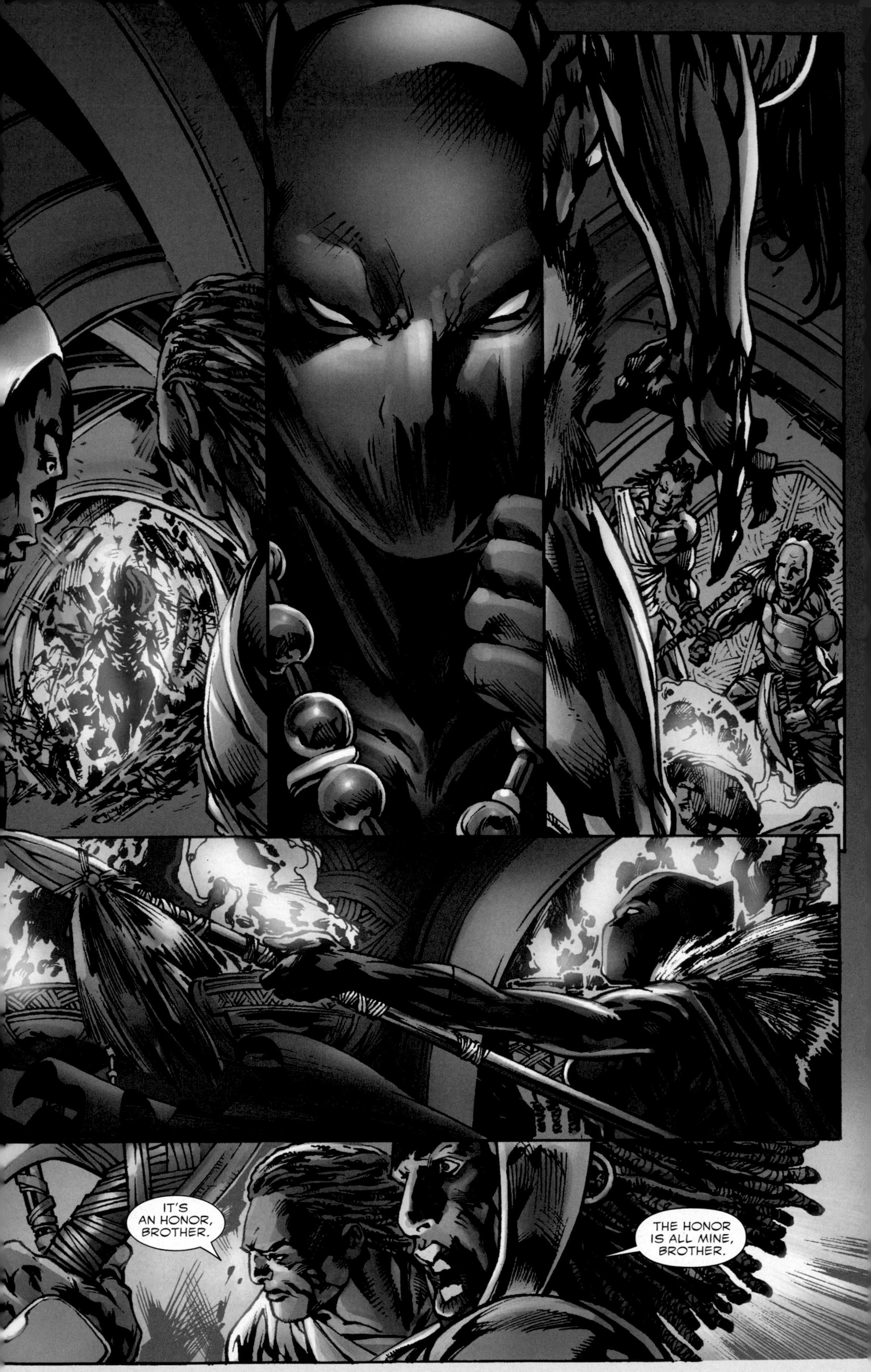
IT'S AN HONOR, BROTHER.
THE HONOR IS ALL MINE, BROTHER.

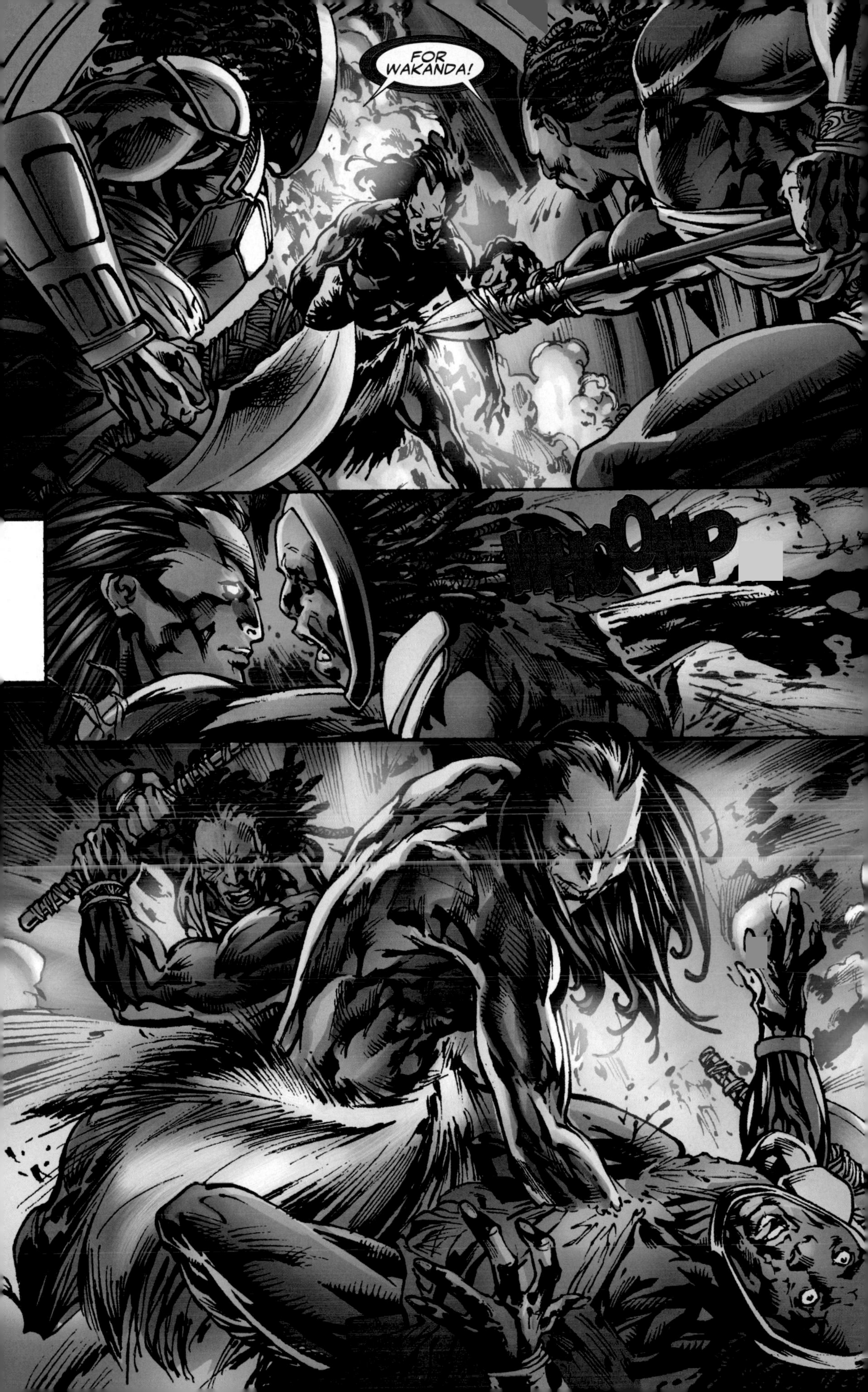
FOR WAKANDA!

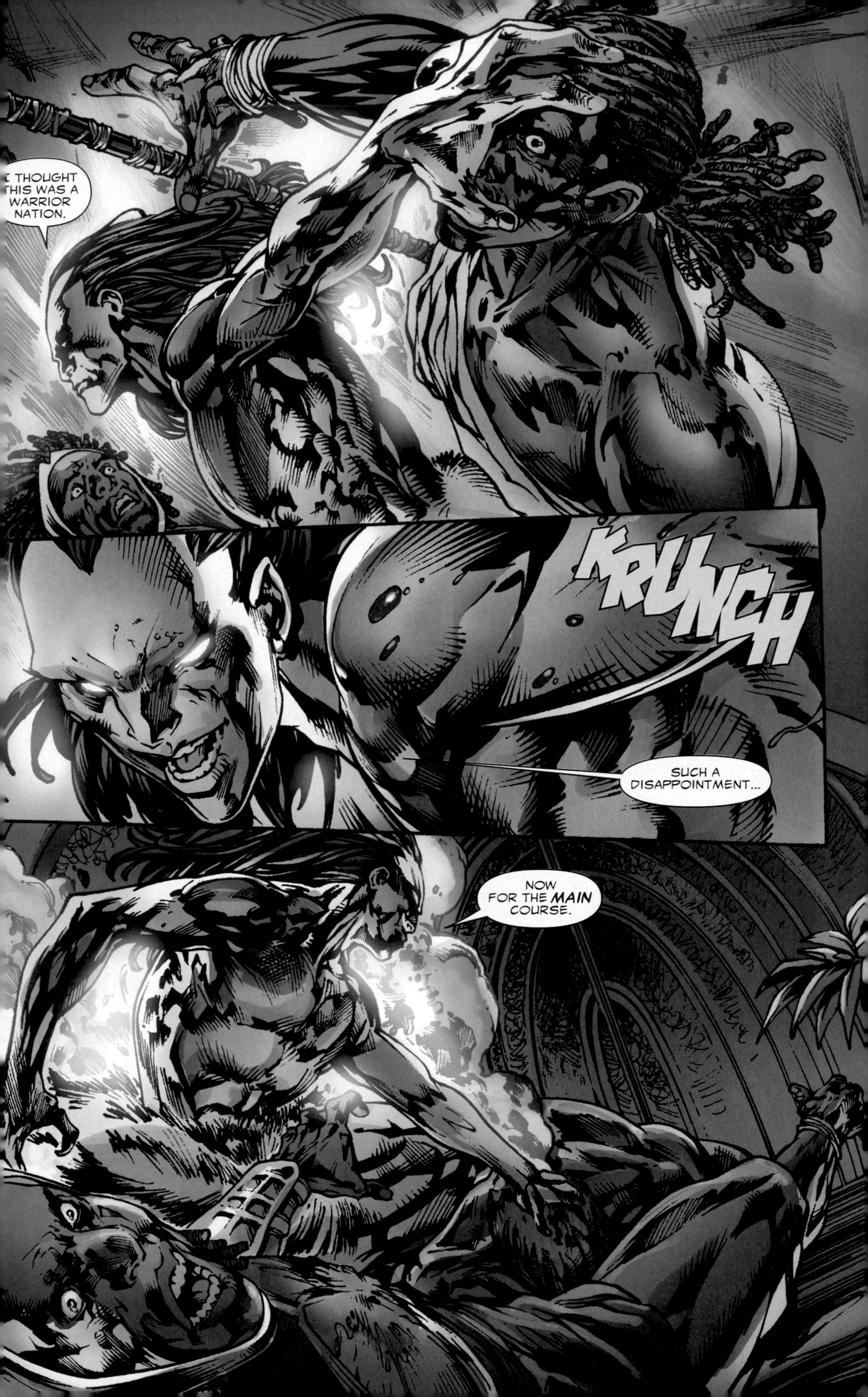
I THOUGHT THIS WAS A WARRIOR NATION.
KRUNCH
SUCH A DISAPPOINTMENT...
NOW FOR THE *MAIN* COURSE.

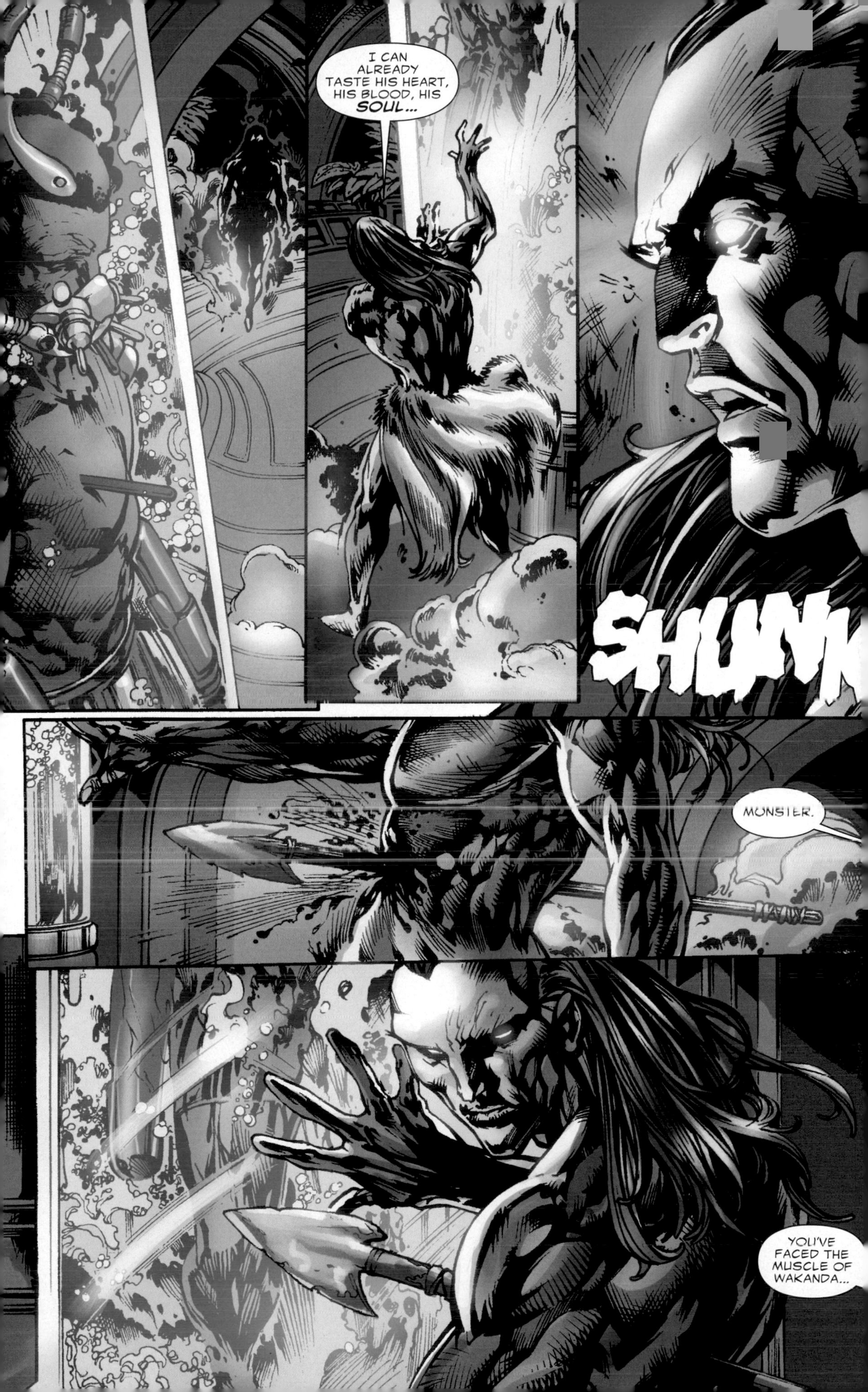
I CAN ALREADY TASTE HIS HEART, HIS BLOOD, HIS SOUL...
SHUNK
MONSTER.
YOU'VE FACED THE MUSCLE OF WAKANDA...

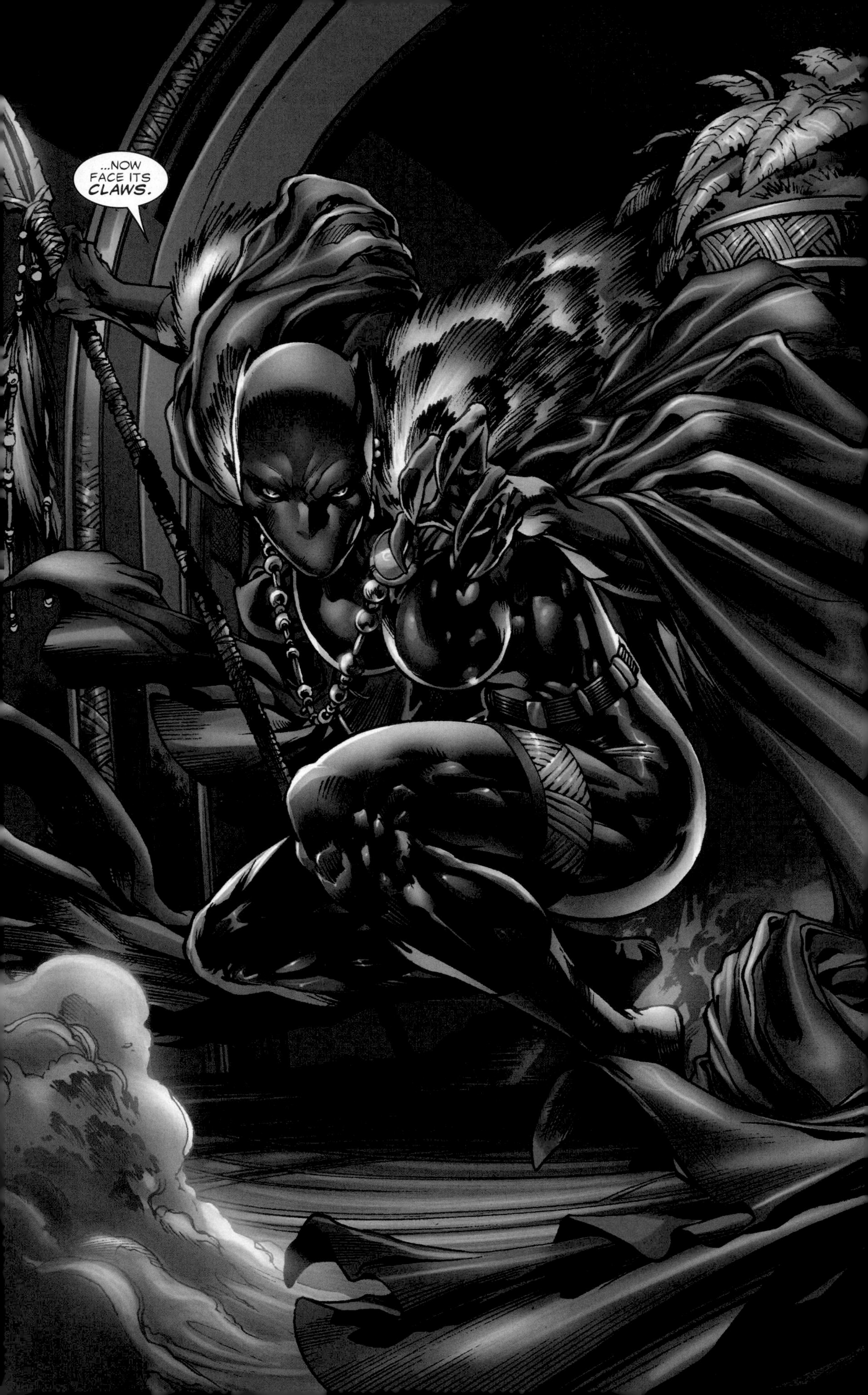
...NOW FACE ITS CLAWS.

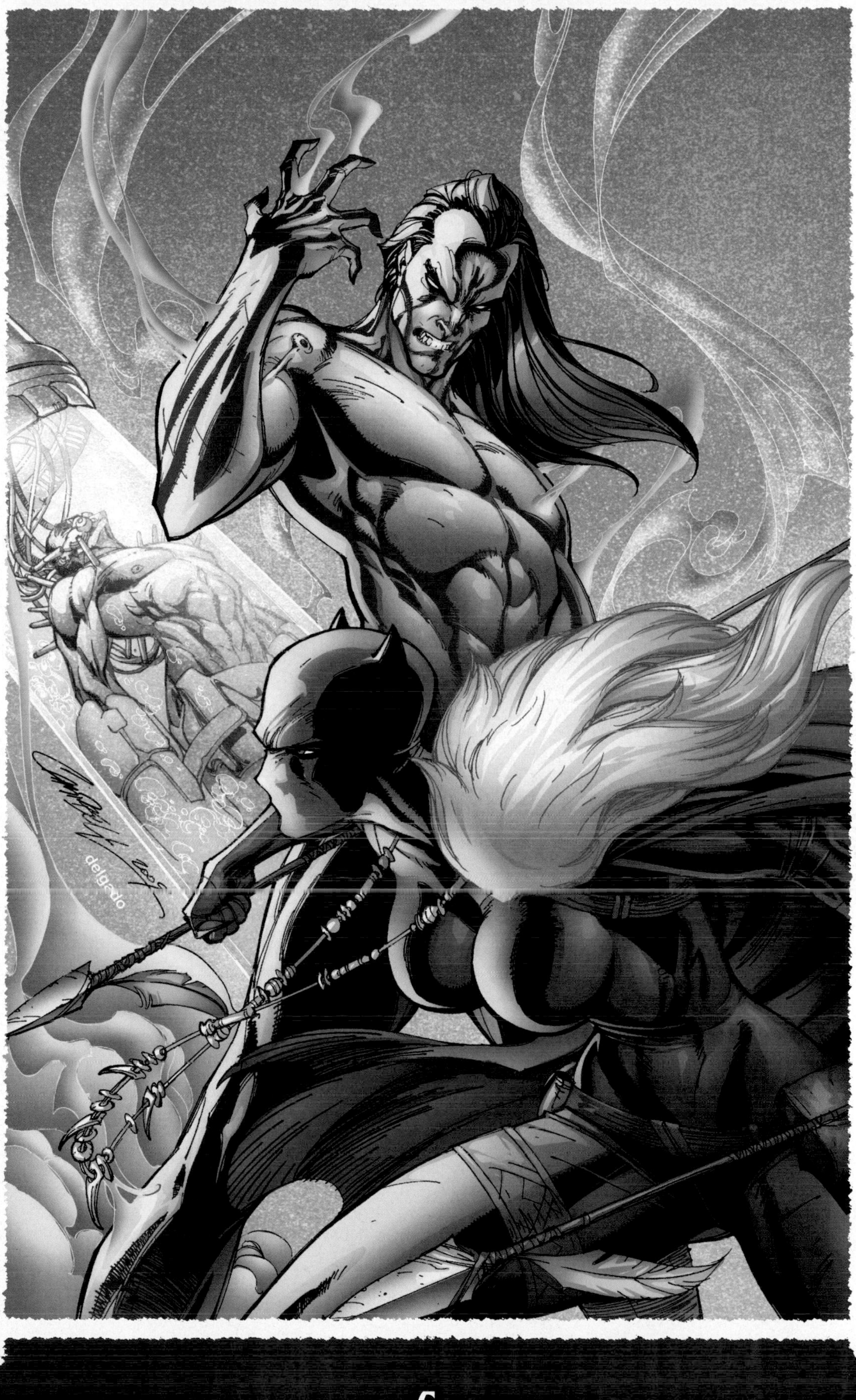
delgado

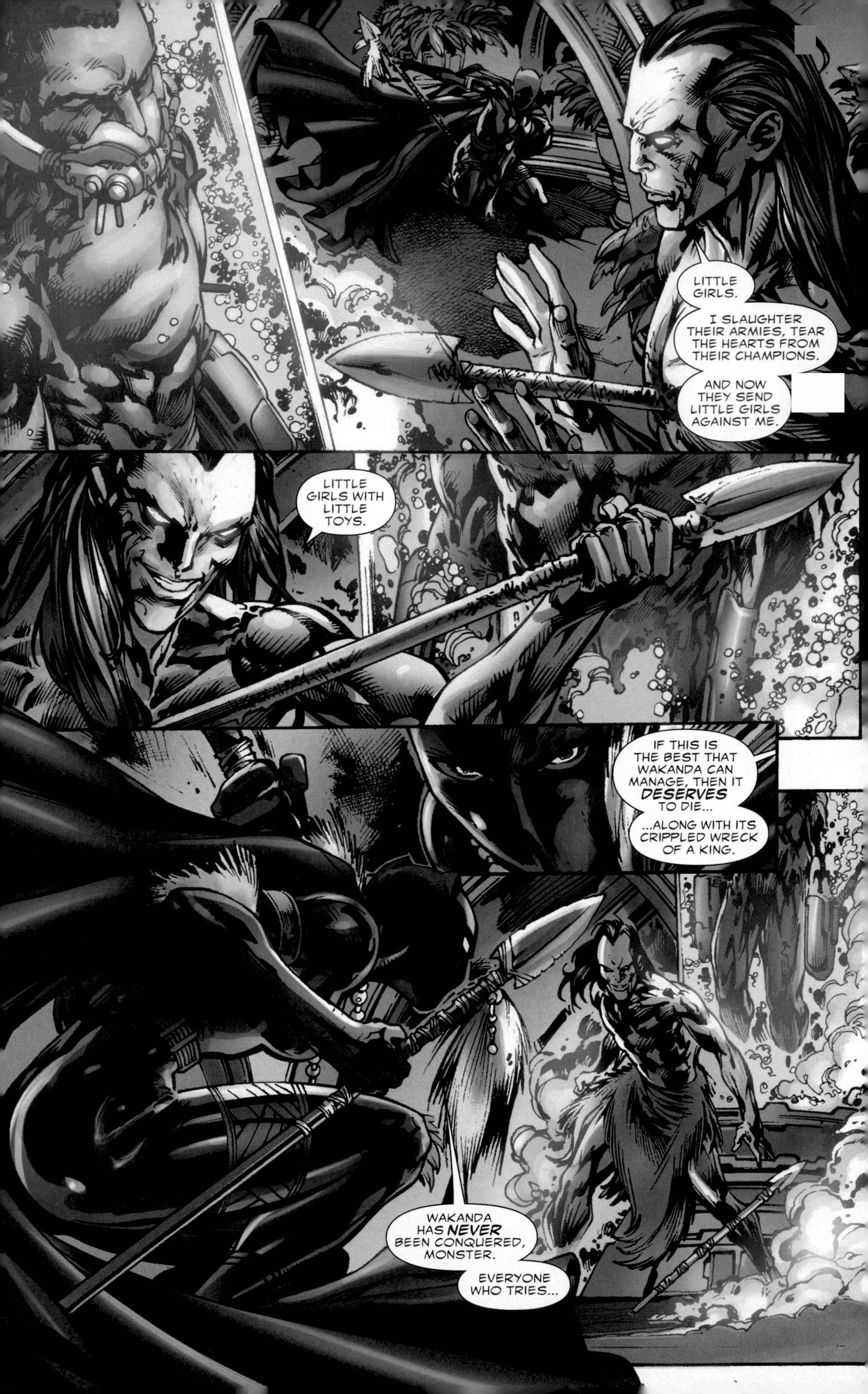
LITTLE GIRLS.
I SLAUGHTER THEIR ARMIES, TEAR THE HEARTS FROM THEIR CHAMPIONS.
AND NOW THEY SEND LITTLE GIRLS AGAINST ME.
LITTLE GIRLS WITH LITTLE TOYS.
IF THIS IS THE BEST THAT WAKANDA CAN MANAGE, THEN IT DESERVES TO DIE...
...ALONG WITH ITS CRIPPLED WRECK OF A KING.
WAKANDA HAS NEVER BEEN CONQUERED, MONSTER.
EVERYONE WHO TRIES...

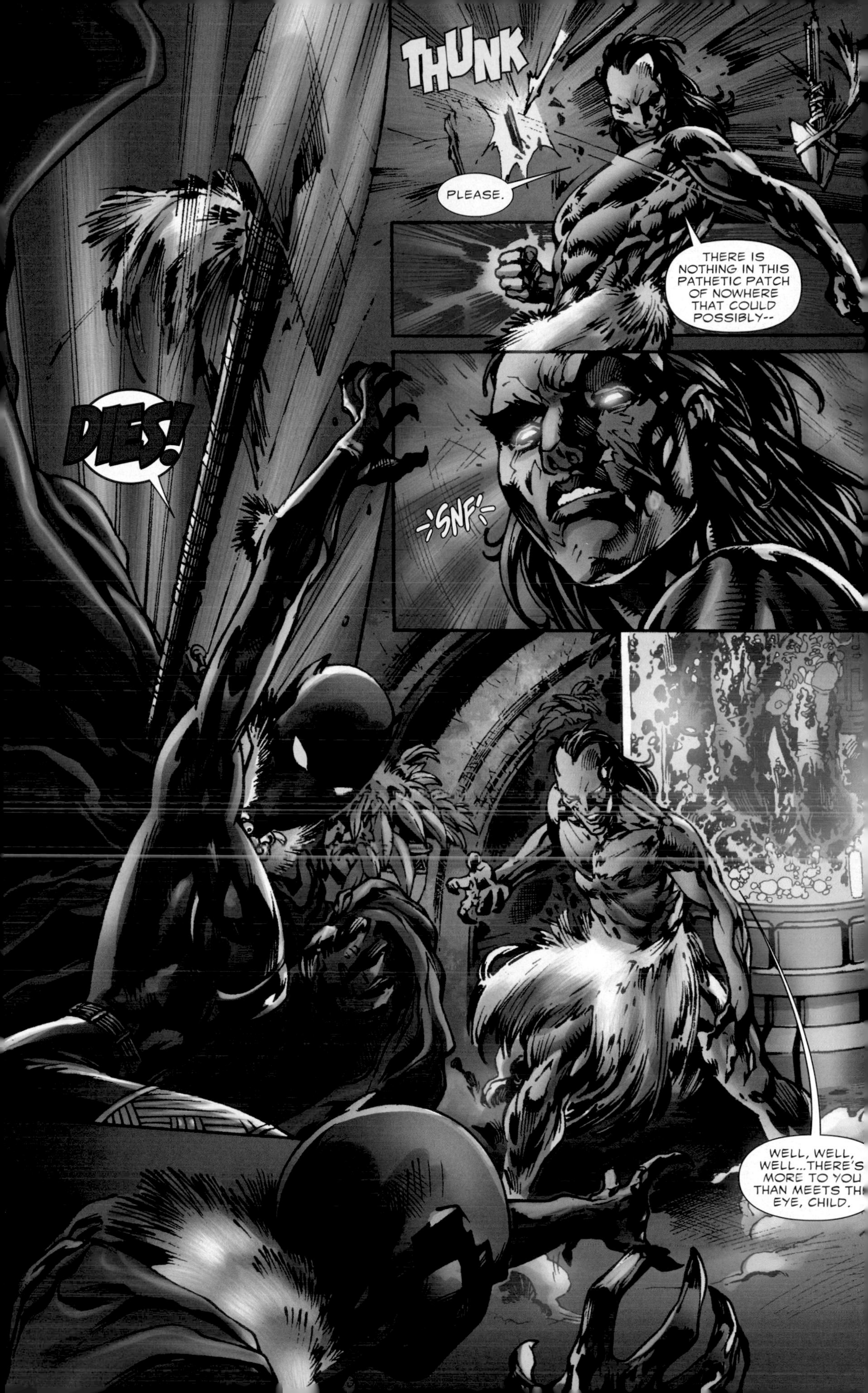
THUNK
PLEASE.
THERE IS NOTHING IN THIS PATHETIC PATCH OF NOWHERE THAT COULD POSSIBLY--
DIES!
SNF
WELL, WELL, WELL...THERE'S MORE TO YOU THAN MEETS TH EYE, CHILD.

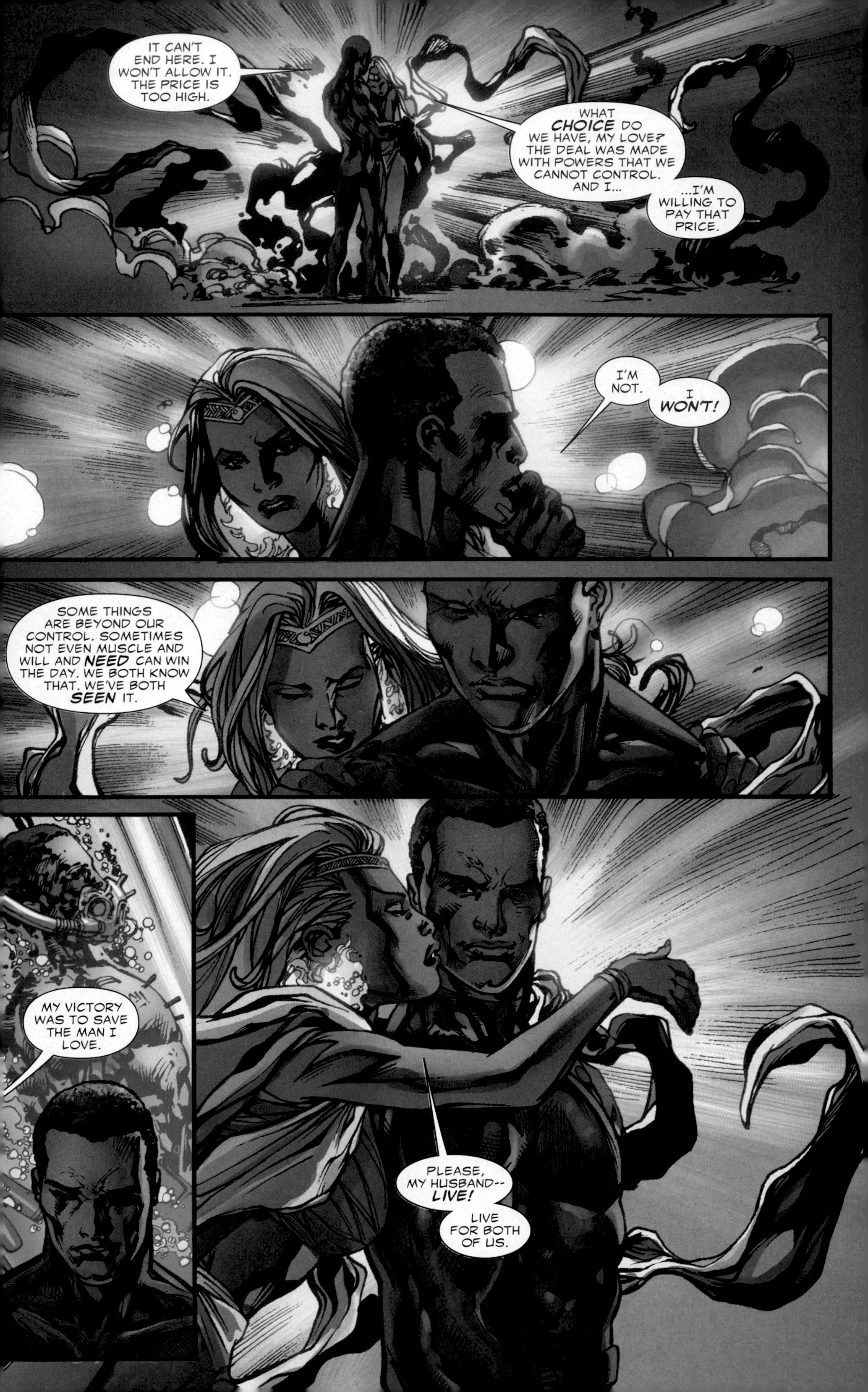

IT CAN'T END HERE. I WON'T ALLOW IT. THE PRICE IS TOO HIGH.
WHAT CHOICE DO WE HAVE, MY LOVE? THE DEAL WAS MADE WITH POWERS THAT WE CANNOT CONTROL. AND I...
...I'M WILLING TO PAY THAT PRICE.
I'M NOT.
I WON'T!
SOME THINGS ARE BEYOND OUR CONTROL. SOMETIMES NOT EVEN MUSCLE AND WILL AND NEED CAN WIN THE DAY. WE BOTH KNOW THAT. WE'VE BOTH SEEN IT.
MY VICTORY WAS TO SAVE THE MAN I LOVE.
PLEASE, MY HUSBAND-- LIVE!
LIVE FOR BOTH OF US.

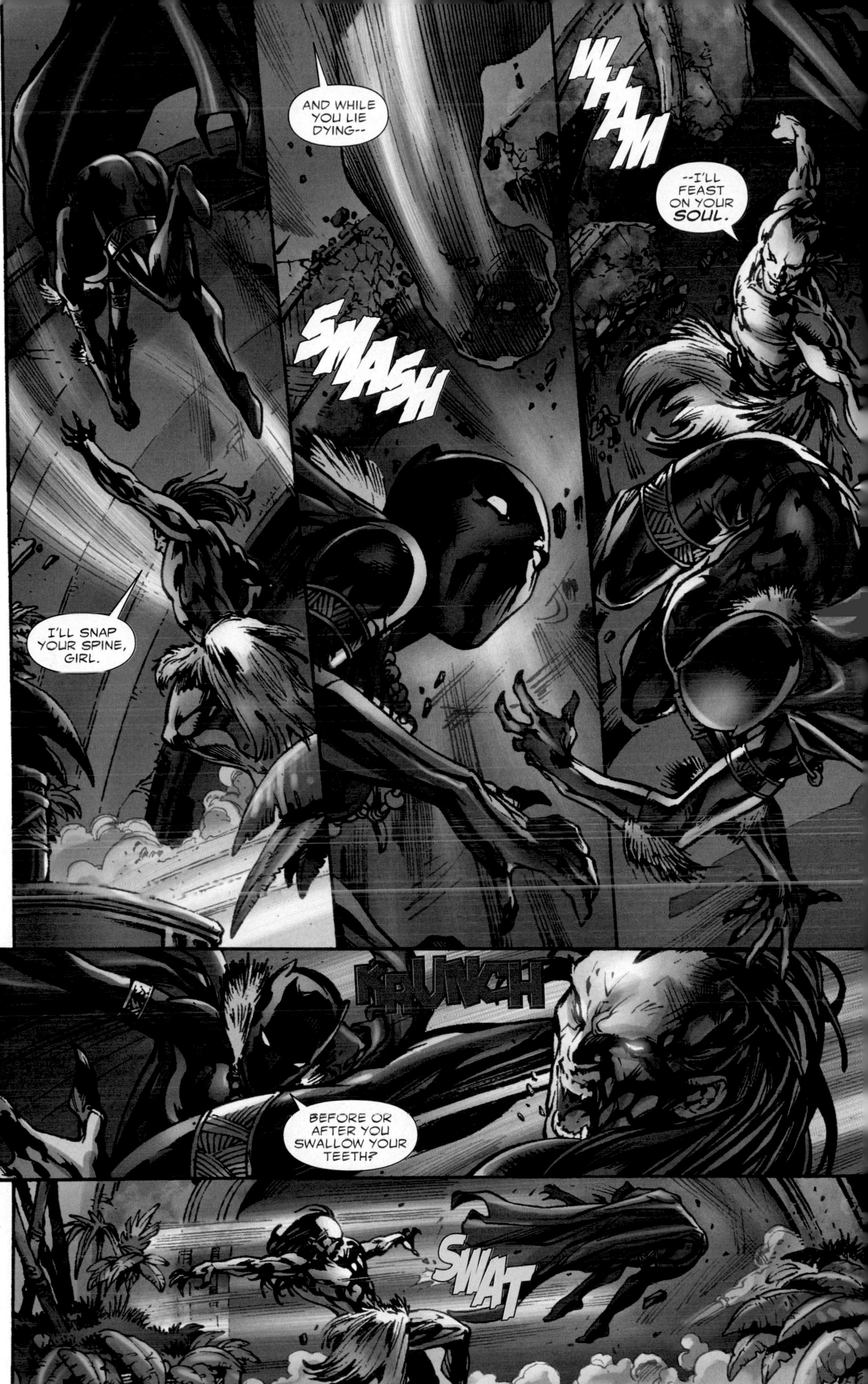
I'LL SNAP YOUR SPINE, GIRL.
AND WHILE YOU LIE DYING--
SMASH
WHAM
--I'LL FEAST ON YOUR SOUL.
KRUNCH
BEFORE OR AFTER YOU SWALLOW YOUR TEETH?
SWAT

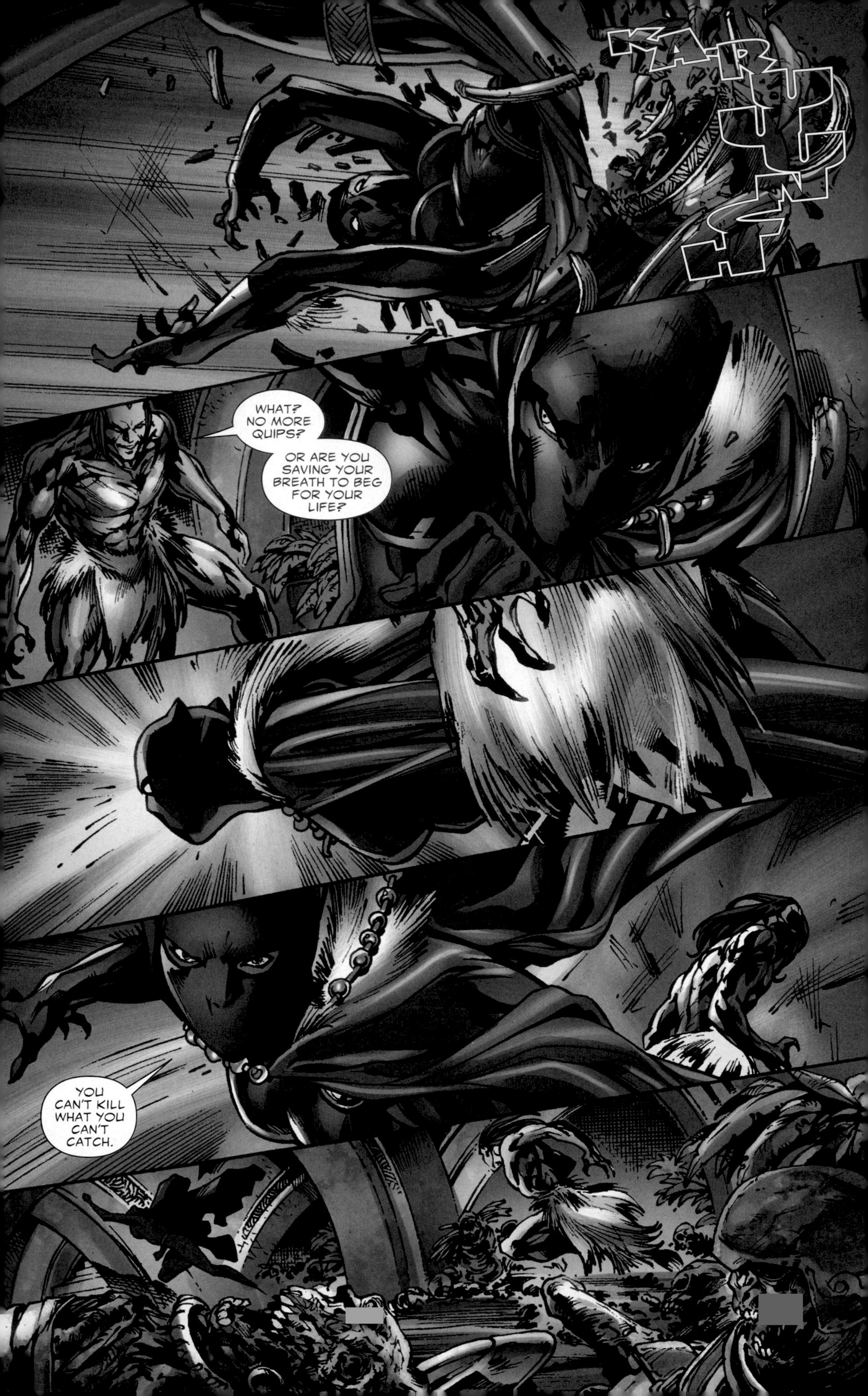
KA-RUUUNCH
WHAT? NO MORE QUIPS?
OR ARE YOU SAVING YOUR BREATH TO BEG FOR YOUR LIFE?
YOU CAN'T KILL WHAT YOU CAN'T CATCH.

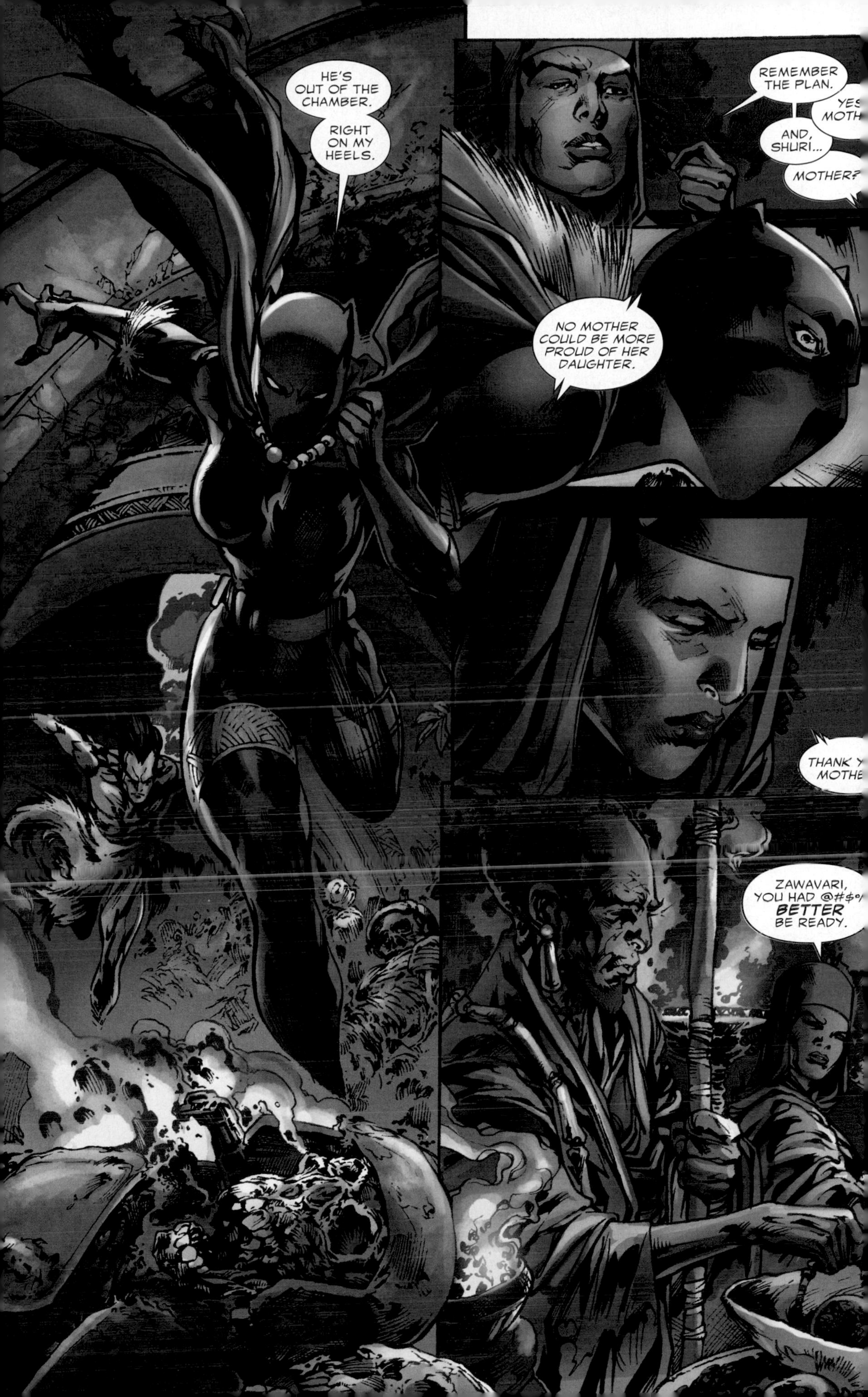
HE'S OUT OF THE CHAMBER.
RIGHT ON MY HEELS.
REMEMBER THE PLAN.
YES MOTH
AND, SHURI...
MOTHER?
NO MOTHER COULD BE MORE PROUD OF HER DAUGHTER.
THANK MOTHE
ZAWAVARI, YOU HAD @#$ BETTER BE READY.

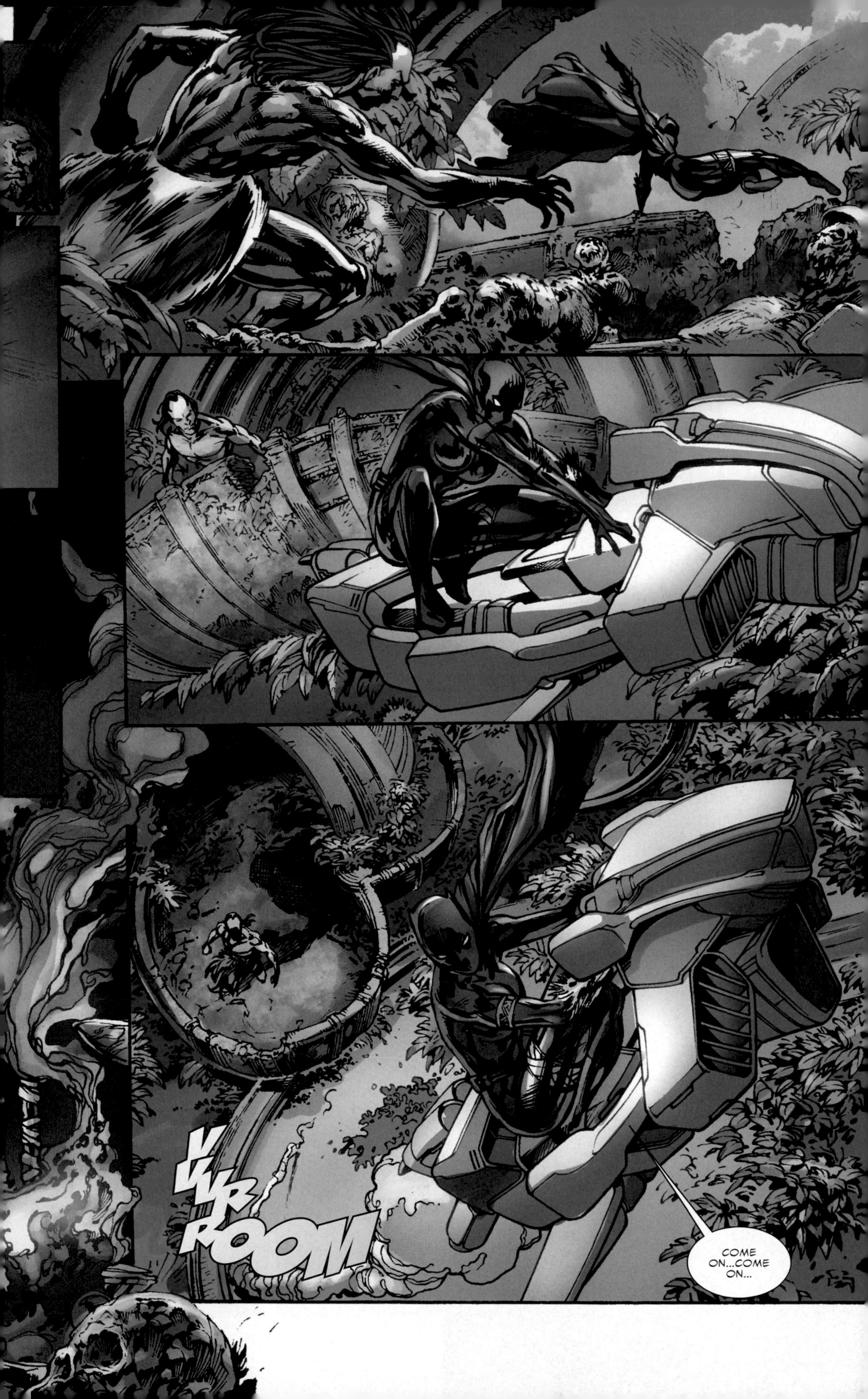
VVVRROOOM
COME ON...COME ON...

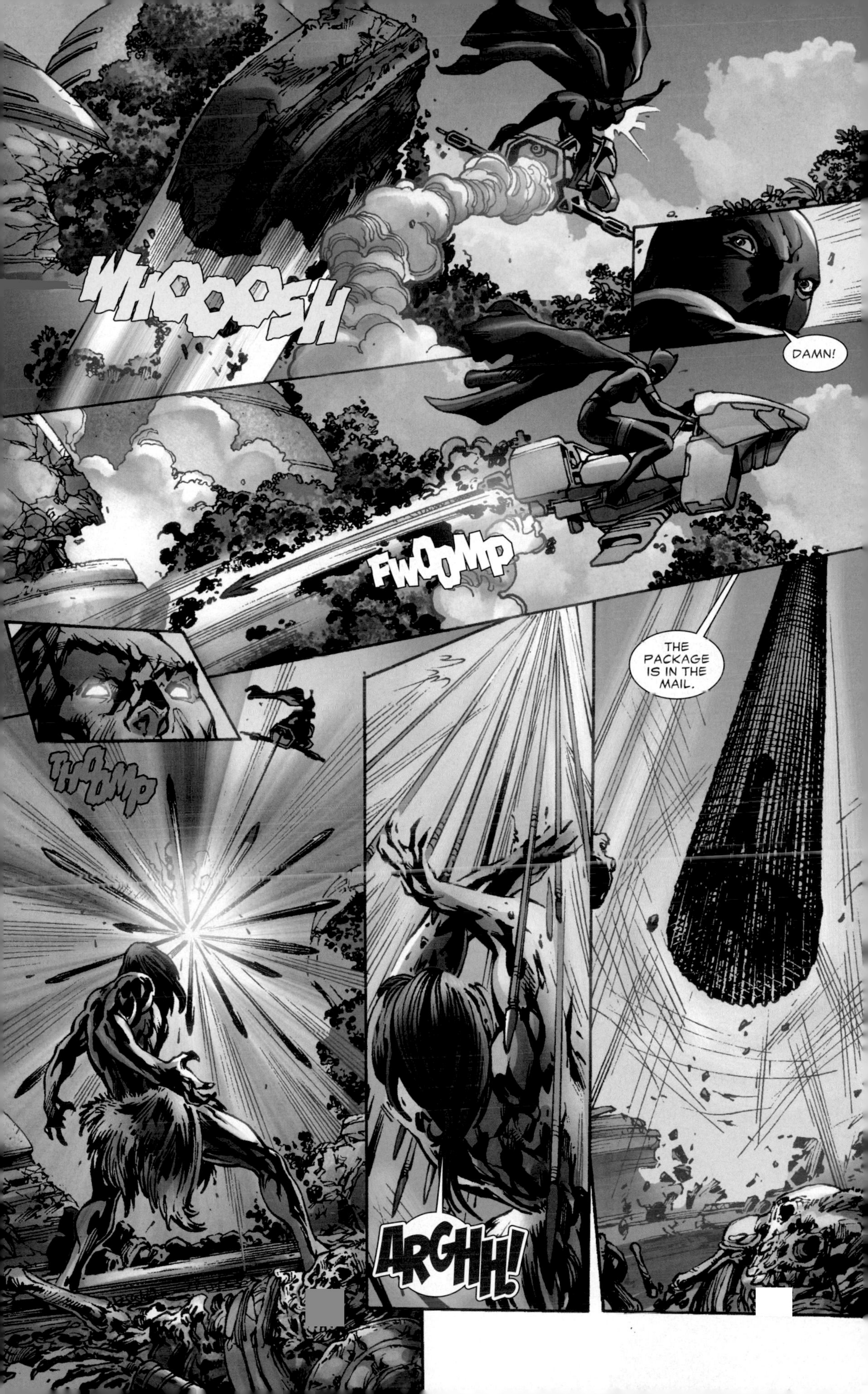
WHOOOSH
DAMN!
FWOOMP
THOOMP
THE PACKAGE IS IN THE MAIL.
ARGHH!

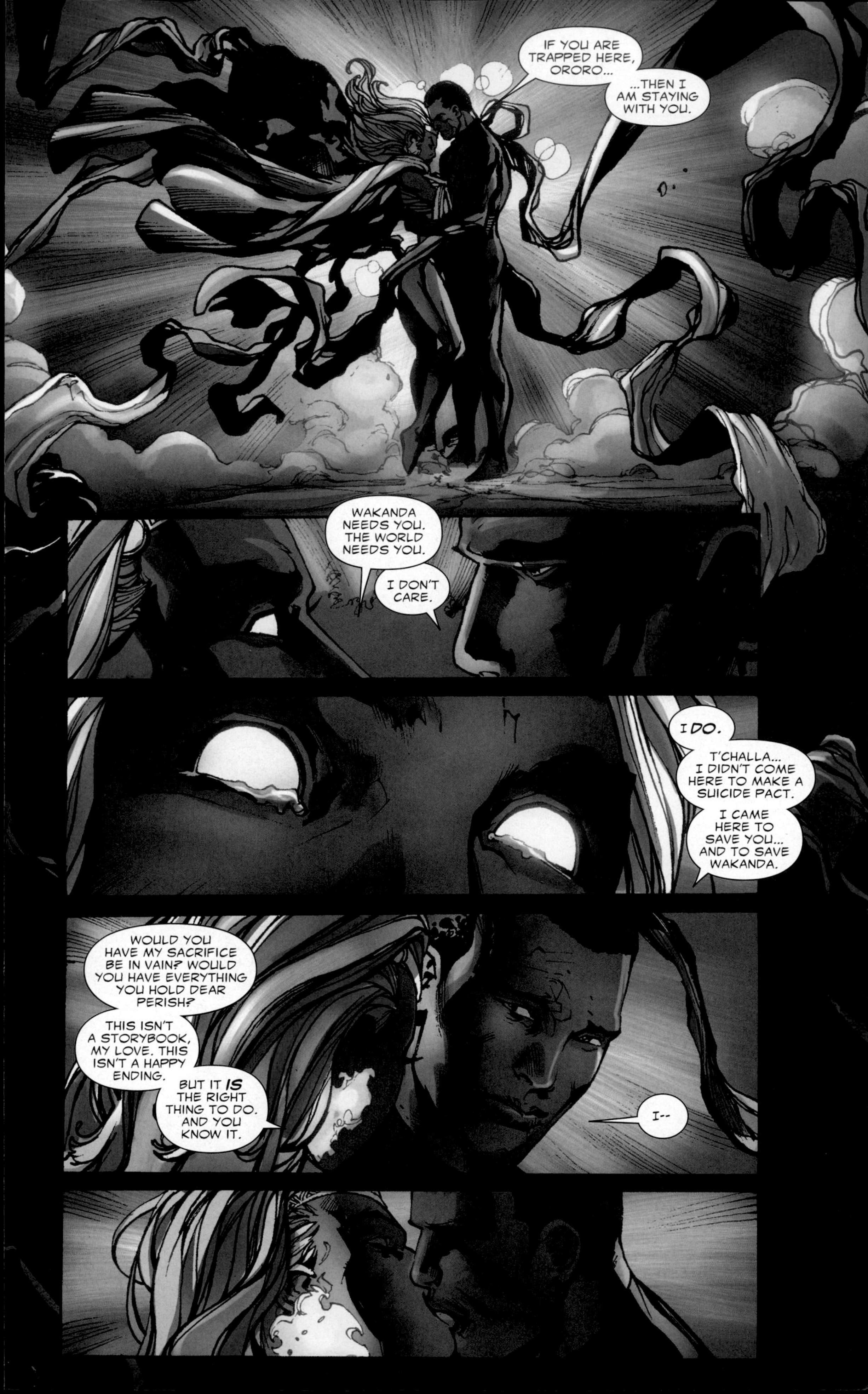
IF YOU ARE TRAPPED HERE, ORORO...
...THEN I AM STAYING WITH YOU.
WAKANDA NEEDS YOU. THE WORLD NEEDS YOU.
I DON'T CARE.
I DO.
T'CHALLA... I DIDN'T COME HERE TO MAKE A SUICIDE PACT.
I CAME HERE TO SAVE YOU... AND TO SAVE WAKANDA.
WOULD YOU HAVE MY SACRIFICE BE IN VAIN? WOULD YOU HAVE EVERYTHING YOU HOLD DEAR PERISH?
THIS ISN'T A STORYBOOK, MY LOVE. THIS ISN'T A HAPPY ENDING.
BUT IT IS THE RIGHT THING TO DO. AND YOU KNOW IT.
I--

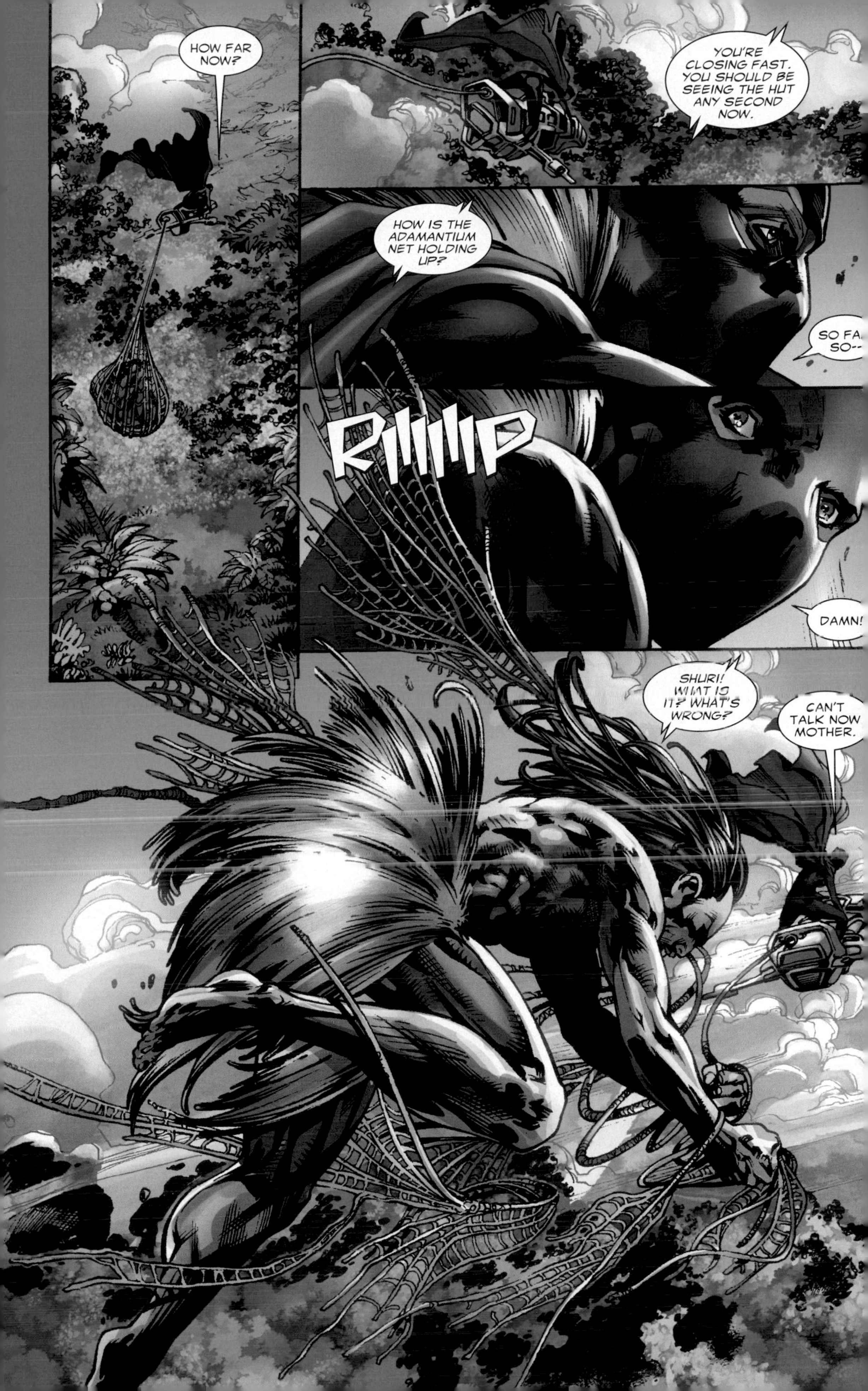
HOW FAR NOW?
YOU'RE CLOSING FAST. YOU SHOULD BE SEEING THE HUT ANY SECOND NOW.
HOW IS THE ADAMANTIUM NET HOLDING UP?
SO FA SO--
RIIIIIP
DAMN!
SHURI! WHAT IS IT? WHAT'S WRONG?
CAN'T TALK NOW MOTHER.

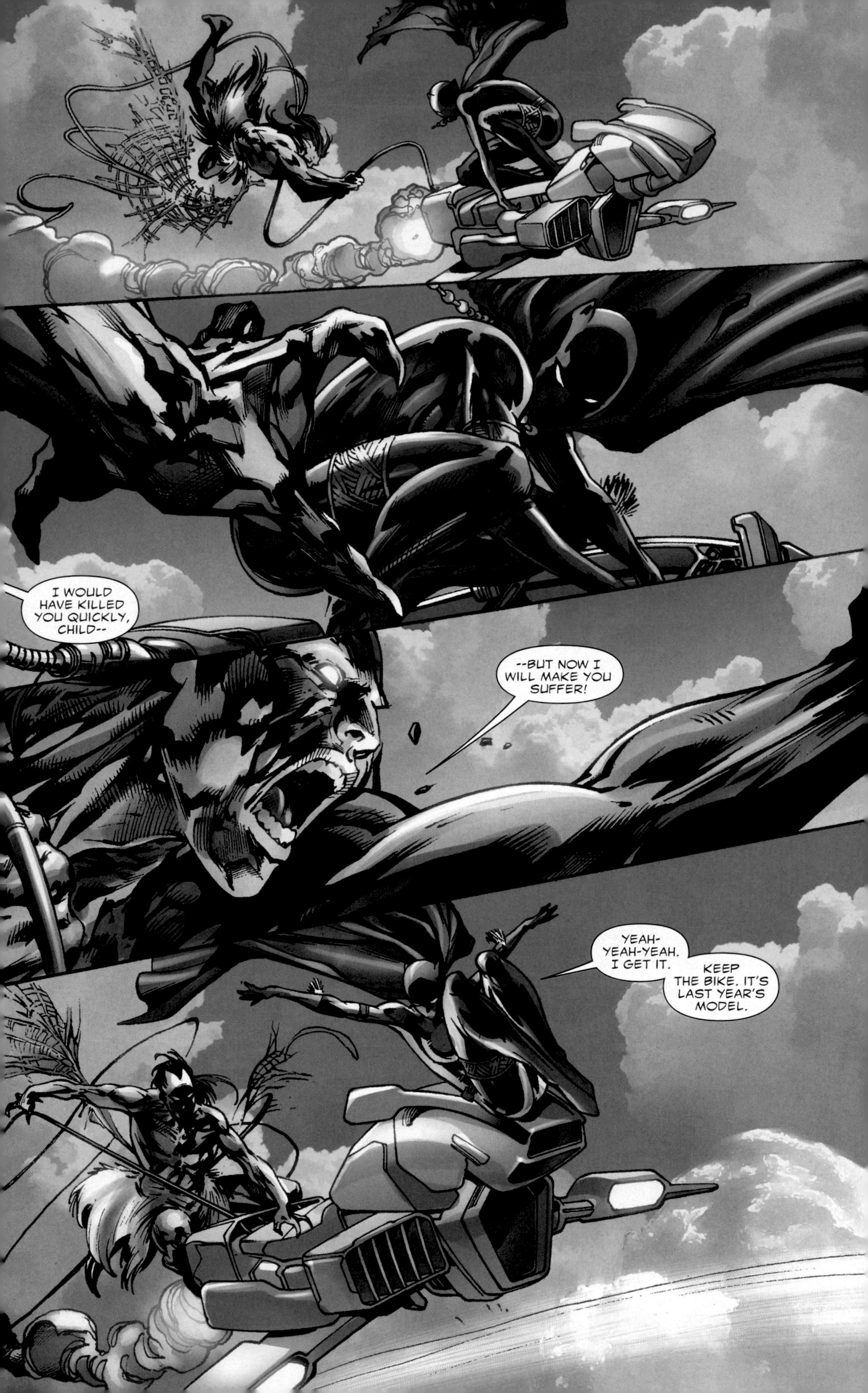

I WOULD HAVE KILLED YOU QUICKLY, CHILD--
--BUT NOW I WILL MAKE YOU SUFFER!
YEAH-YEAH-YEAH. I GET IT.
KEEP THE BIKE. IT'S LAST YEAR'S MODEL.

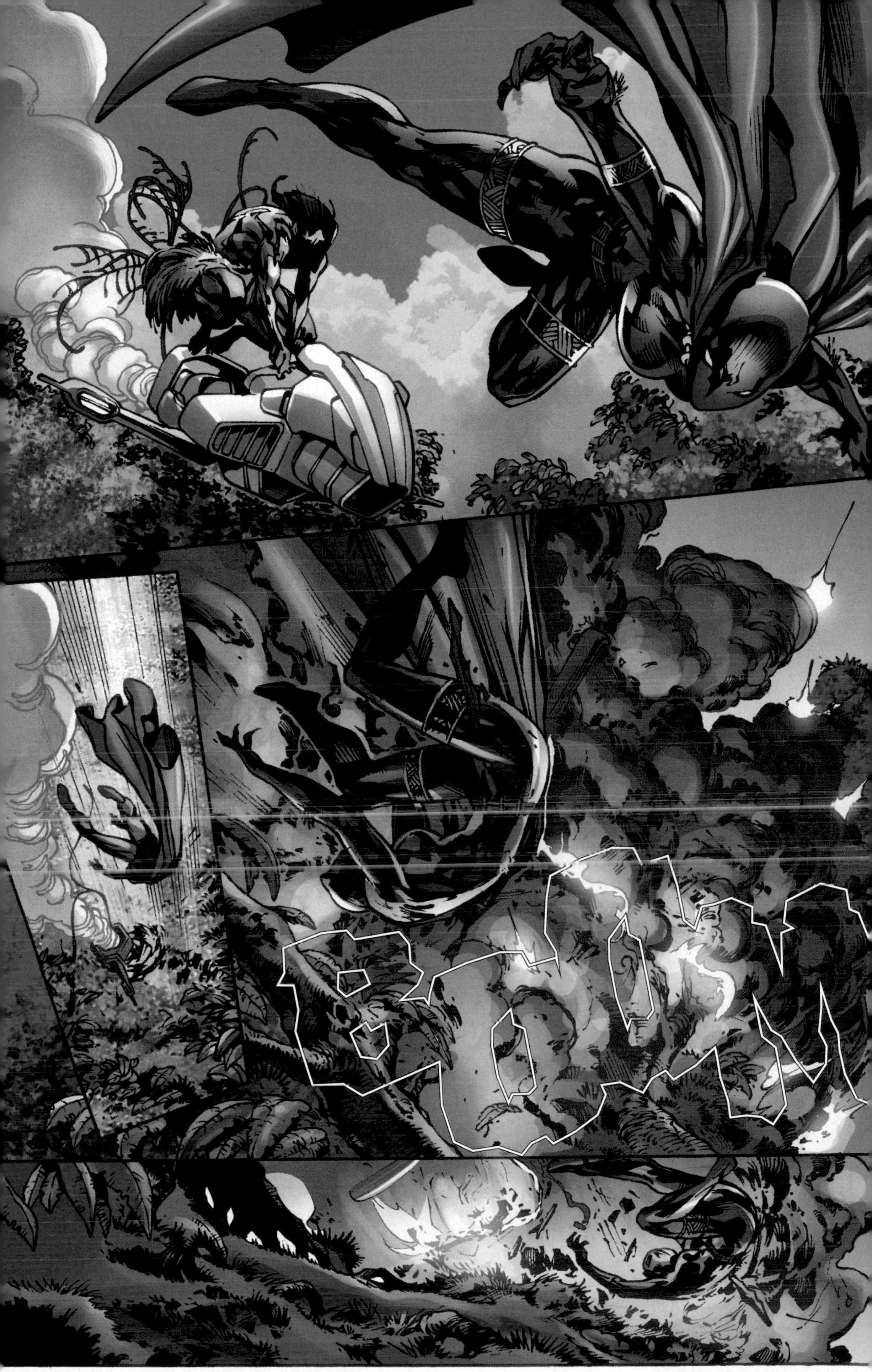
BOOM

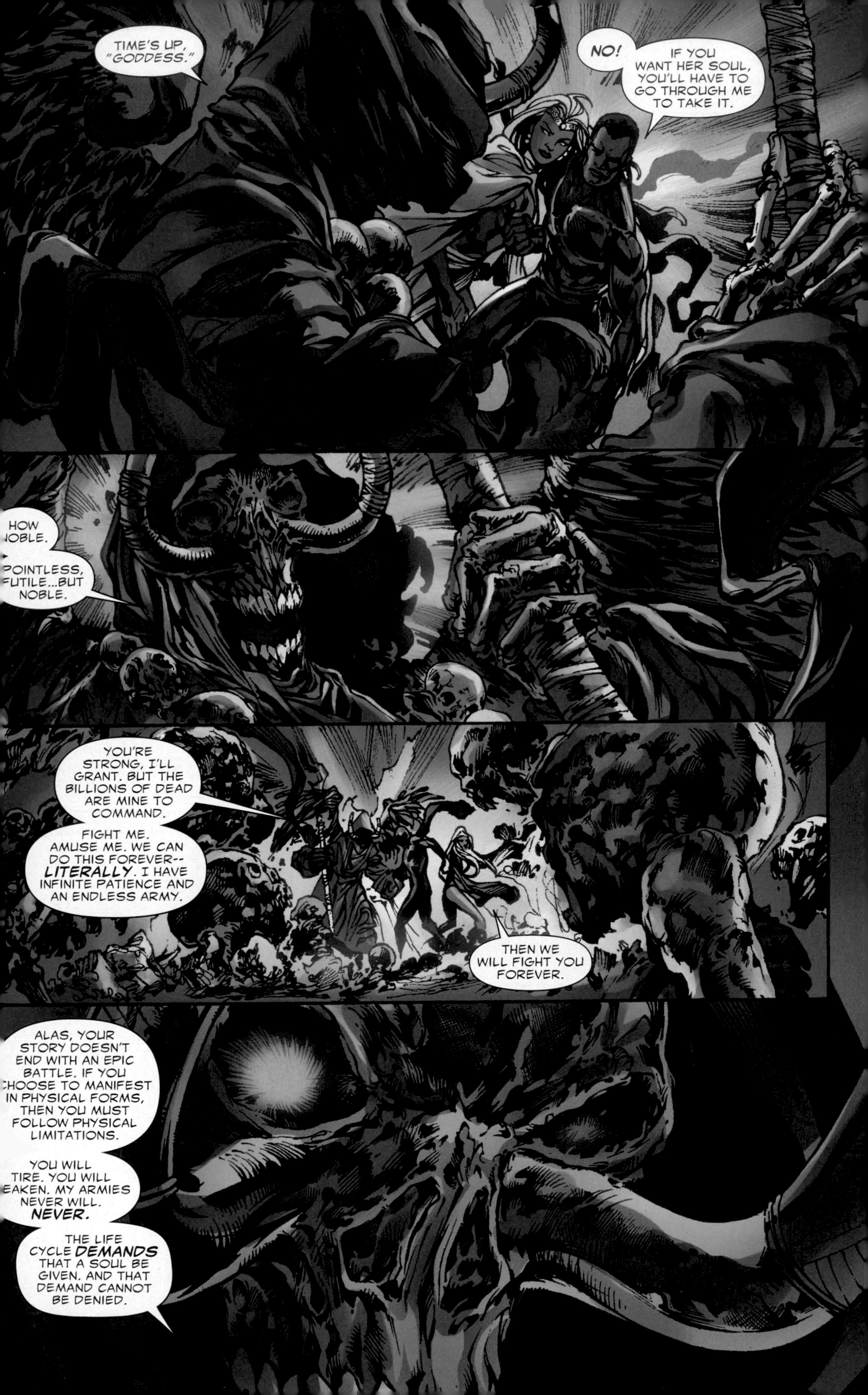

TIME'S UP, "GODDESS."
NO!
IF YOU WANT HER SOUL, YOU'LL HAVE TO GO THROUGH ME TO TAKE IT.
HOW NOBLE.
POINTLESS, FUTILE...BUT NOBLE.
YOU'RE STRONG, I'LL GRANT. BUT THE BILLIONS OF DEAD ARE MINE TO COMMAND.
FIGHT ME. AMUSE ME. WE CAN DO THIS FOREVER-- **LITERALLY**. I HAVE INFINITE PATIENCE AND AN ENDLESS ARMY.
THEN WE WILL FIGHT YOU FOREVER.
ALAS, YOUR STORY DOESN'T END WITH AN EPIC BATTLE. IF YOU CHOOSE TO MANIFEST IN PHYSICAL FORMS, THEN YOU MUST FOLLOW PHYSICAL LIMITATIONS.
YOU WILL TIRE. YOU WILL WEAKEN. MY ARMIES NEVER WILL. **NEVER.**
THE LIFE CYCLE **DEMANDS** THAT A SOUL BE GIVEN. AND THAT DEMAND CANNOT BE DENIED.

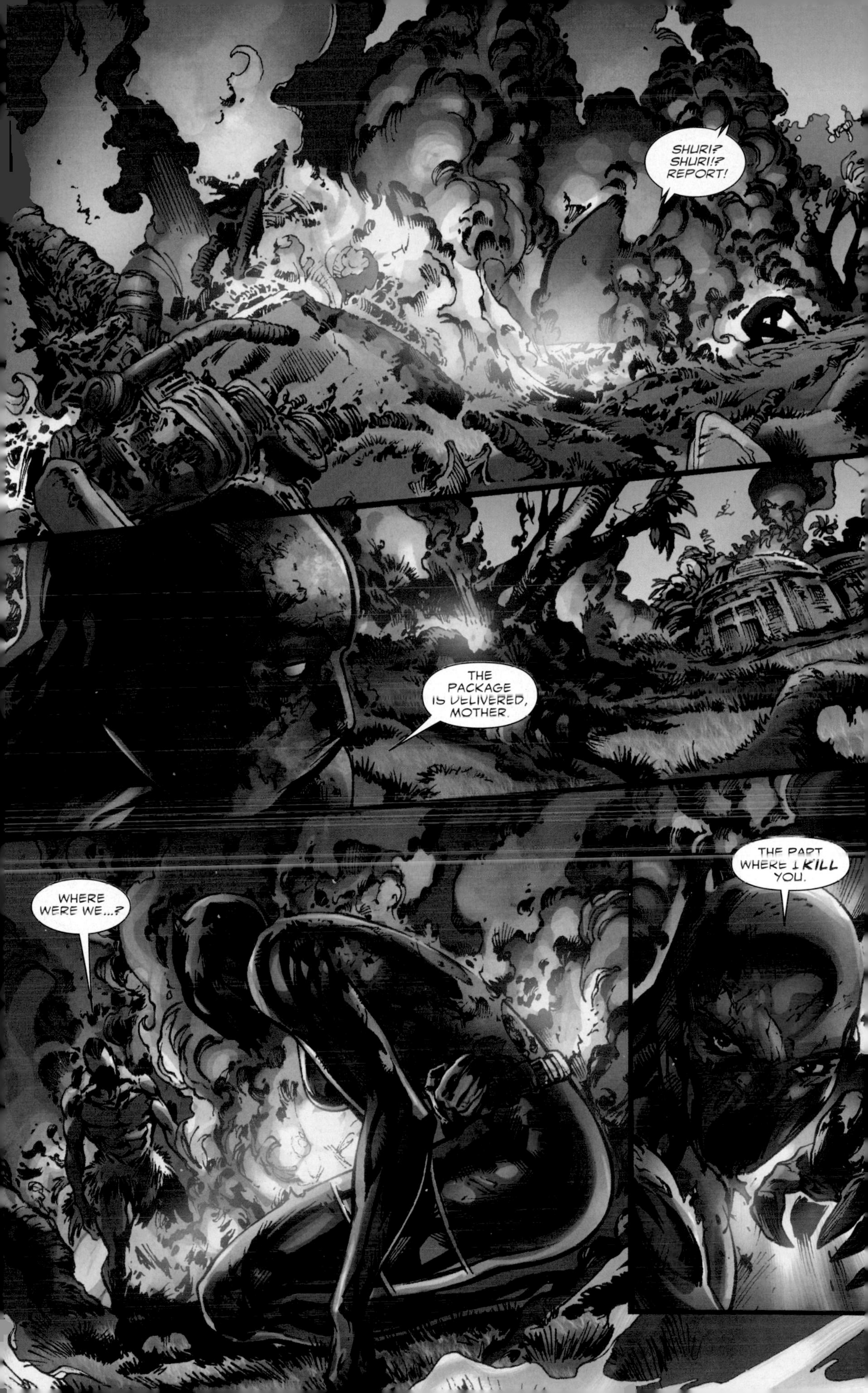
SHURI!? SHURI!? REPORT!
THE PACKAGE IS DELIVERED, MOTHER.
WHERE WERE WE...?
THE PART WHERE I KILL YOU.

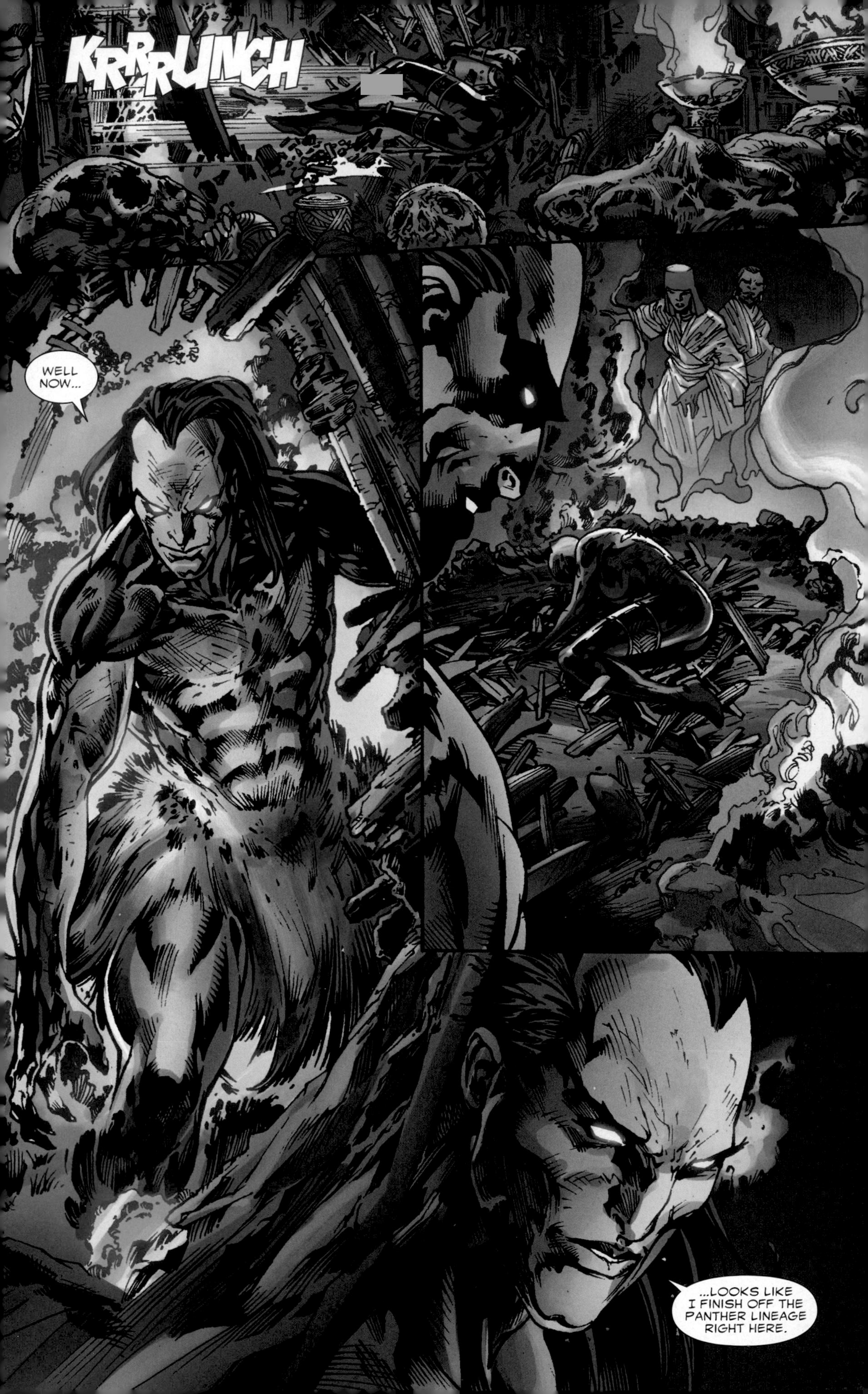
KRRRUNCH
WELL NOW...
...LOOKS LIKE I FINISH OFF THE PANTHER LINEAGE RIGHT HERE.

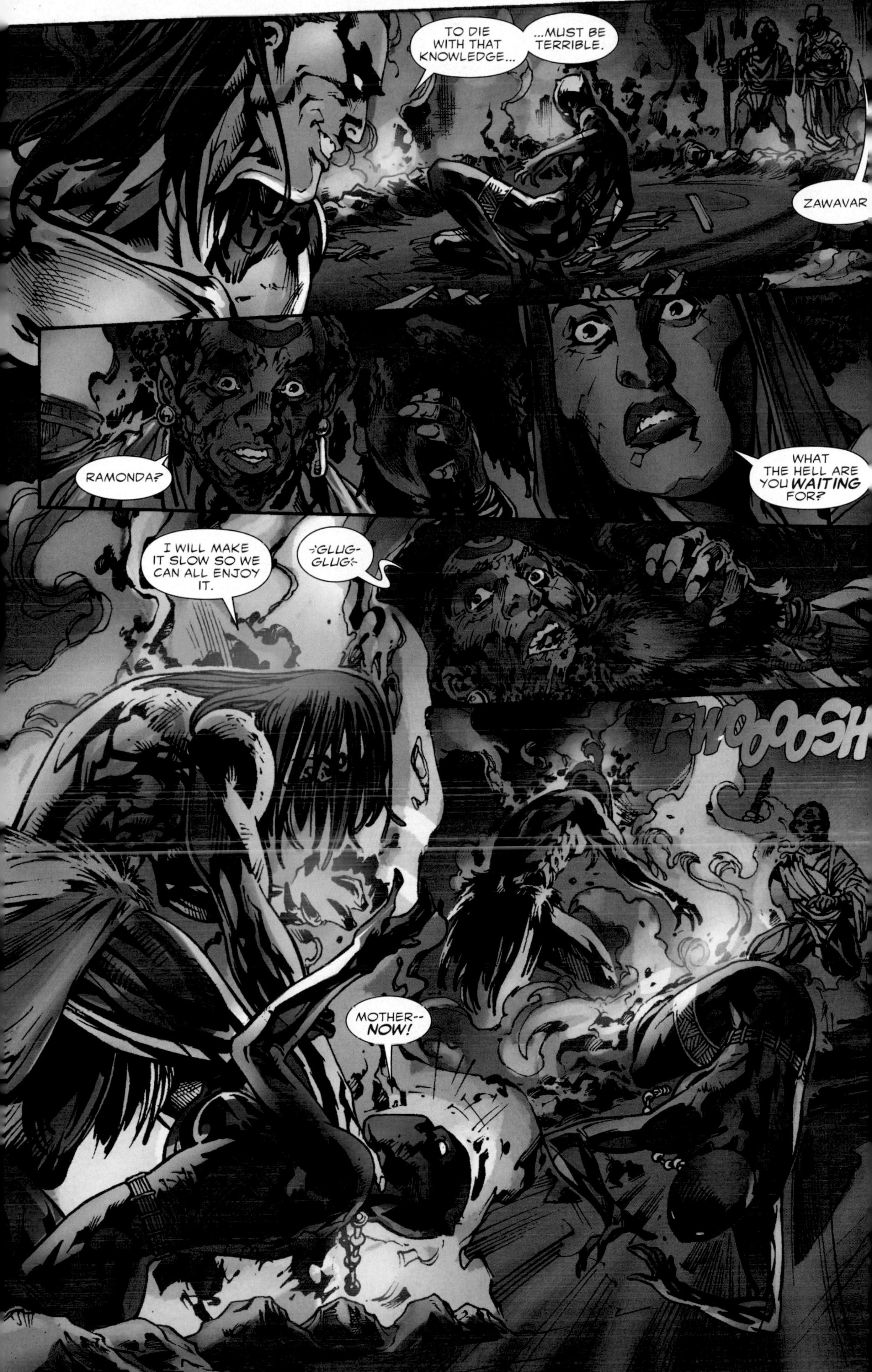
TO DIE WITH THAT KNOWLEDGE...
...MUST BE TERRIBLE.
ZAWAVAR
RAMONDA?
WHAT THE HELL ARE YOU WAITING FOR?
I WILL MAKE IT SLOW SO WE CAN ALL ENJOY IT.
-GLUG-GLUG-
FWOOOOSH
MOTHER-- NOW!

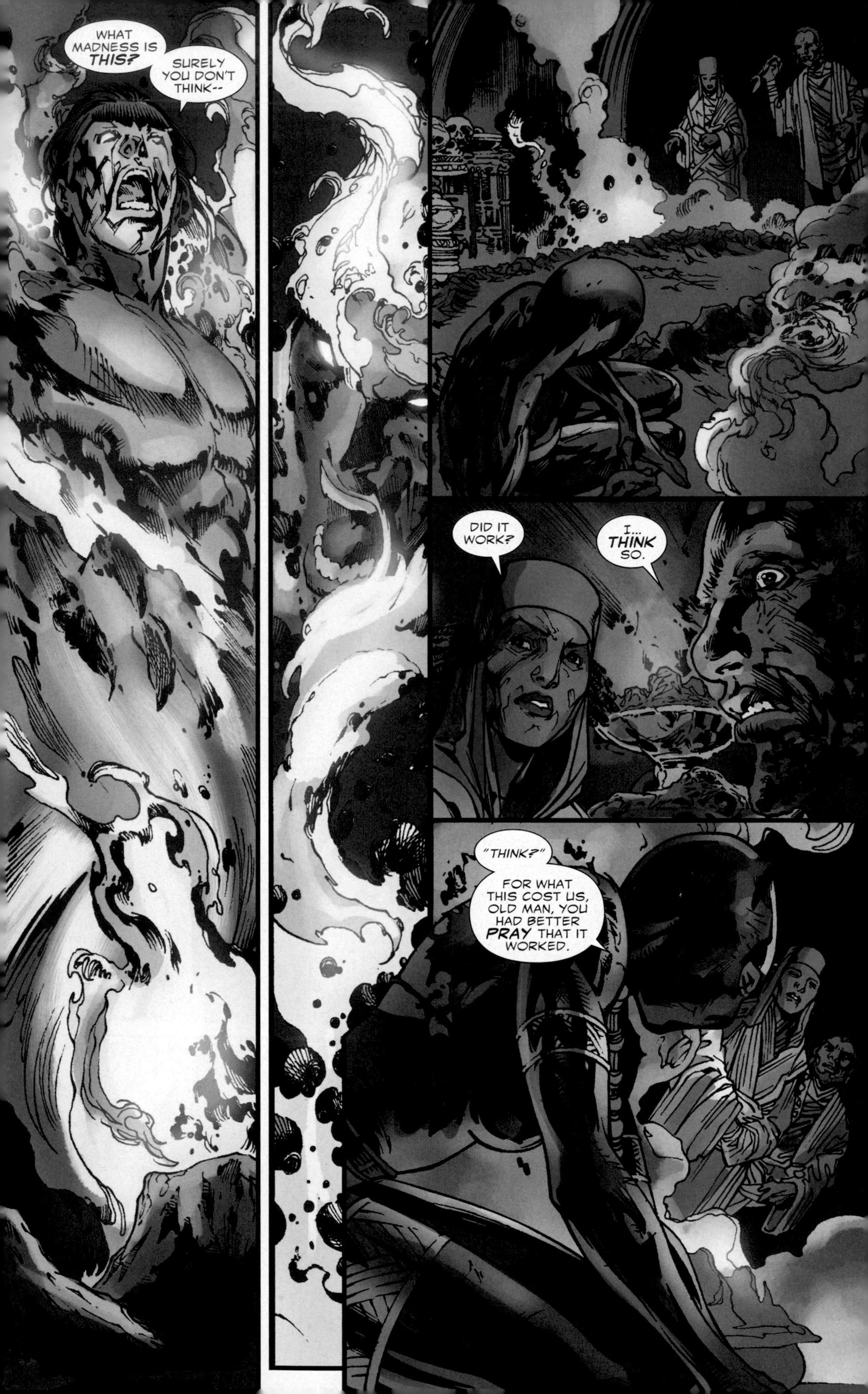
WHAT MADNESS IS THIS?
SURELY YOU DON'T THINK--
DID IT WORK?
I... THINK SO.
"THINK?"
FOR WHAT THIS COST US, OLD MAN, YOU HAD BETTER PRAY THAT IT WORKED.

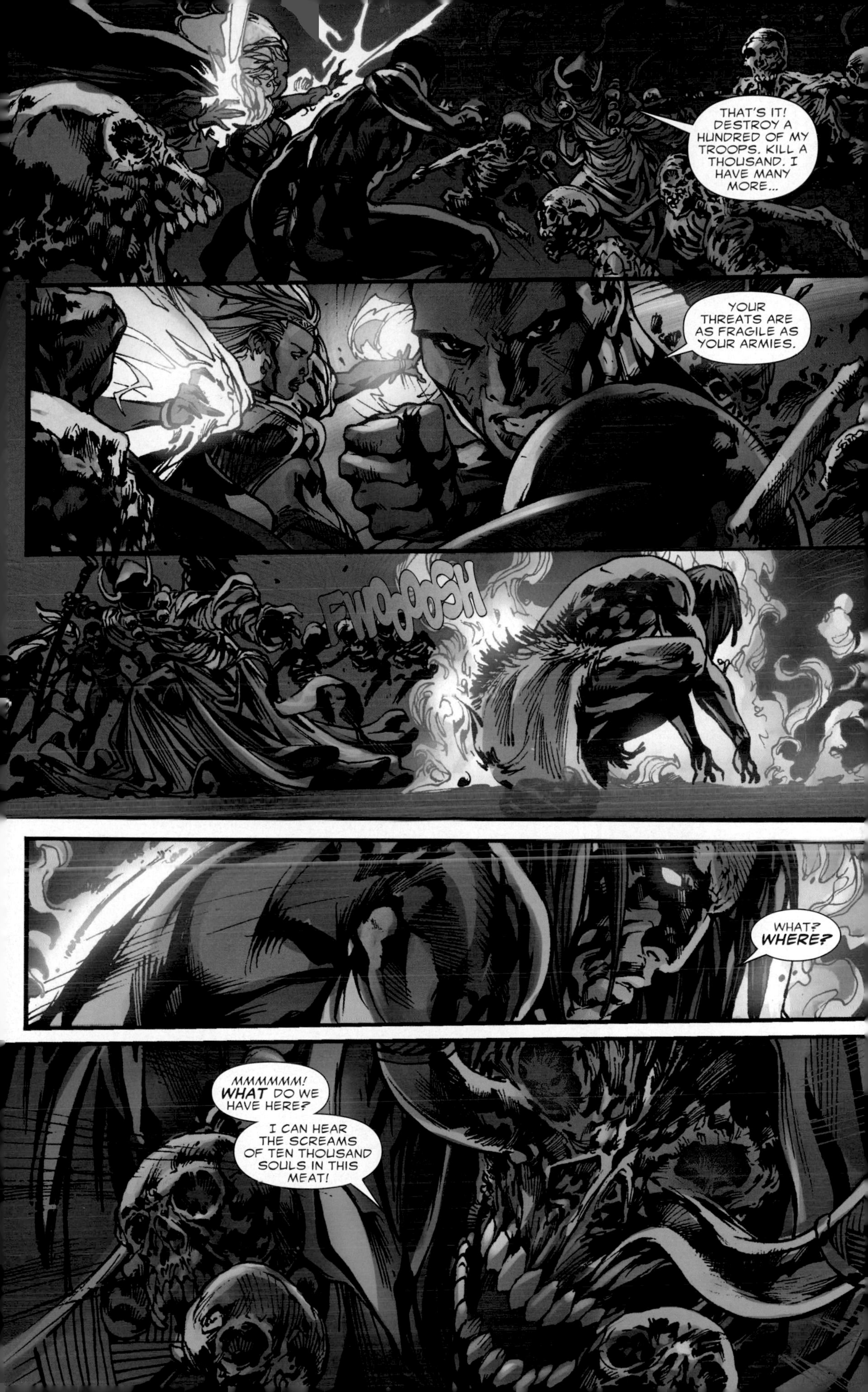
THAT'S IT! DESTROY A HUNDRED OF MY TROOPS. KILL A THOUSAND. I HAVE MANY MORE...
YOUR THREATS ARE AS FRAGILE AS YOUR ARMIES.
FWOOOOSH
WHAT? WHERE?
MMMMMM! WHAT DO WE HAVE HERE?
I CAN HEAR THE SCREAMS OF TEN THOUSAND SOULS IN THIS MEAT!

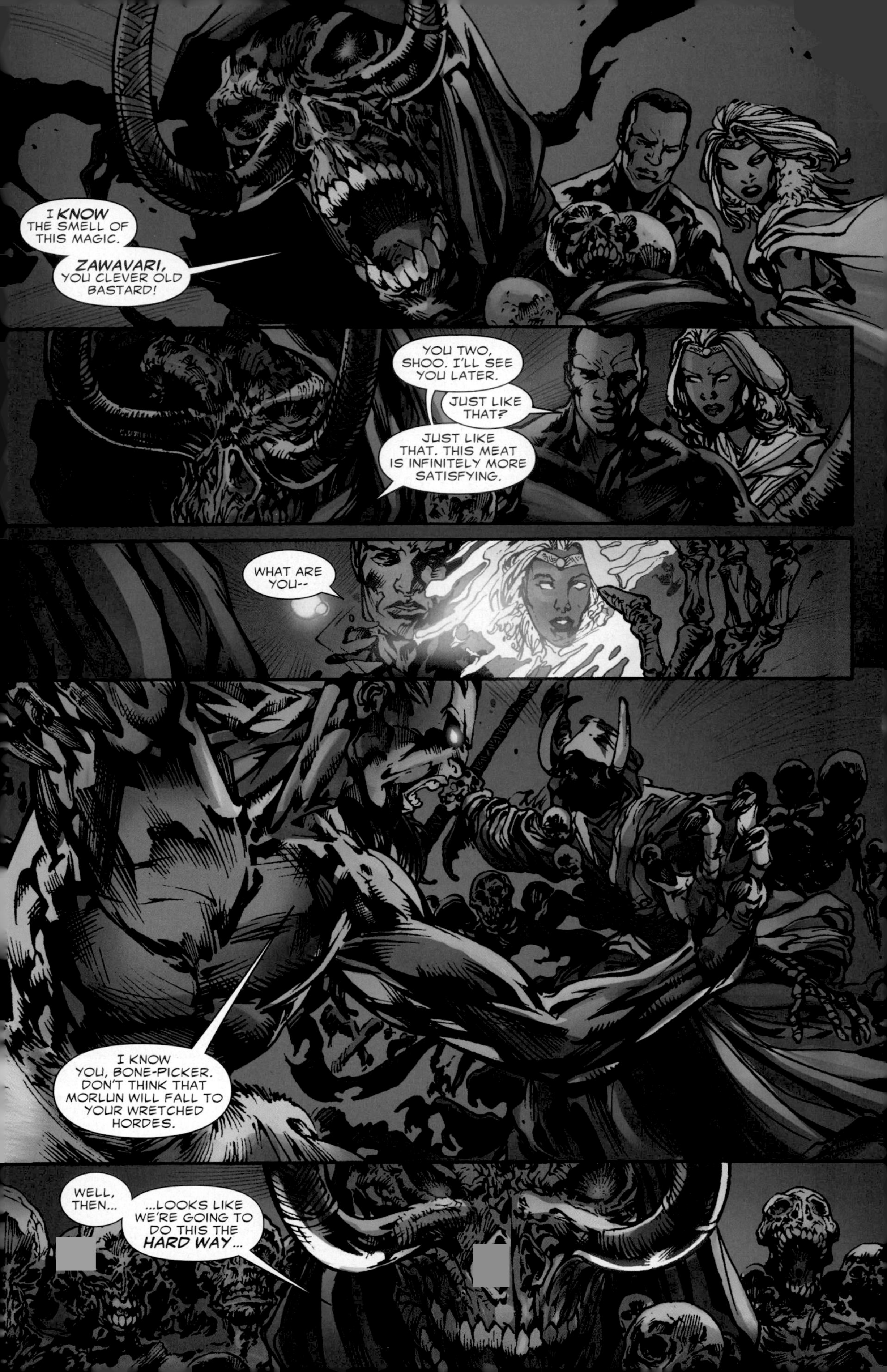
I KNOW THE SMELL OF THIS MAGIC.
ZAWAVARI, YOU CLEVER OLD BASTARD!
YOU TWO, SHOO. I'LL SEE YOU LATER.
JUST LIKE THAT?
JUST LIKE THAT. THIS MEAT IS INFINITELY MORE SATISFYING.
WHAT ARE YOU--
I KNOW YOU, BONE-PICKER. DON'T THINK THAT MORLUN WILL FALL TO YOUR WRETCHED HORDES.
WELL, THEN...
...LOOKS LIKE WE'RE GOING TO DO THIS THE HARD WAY...

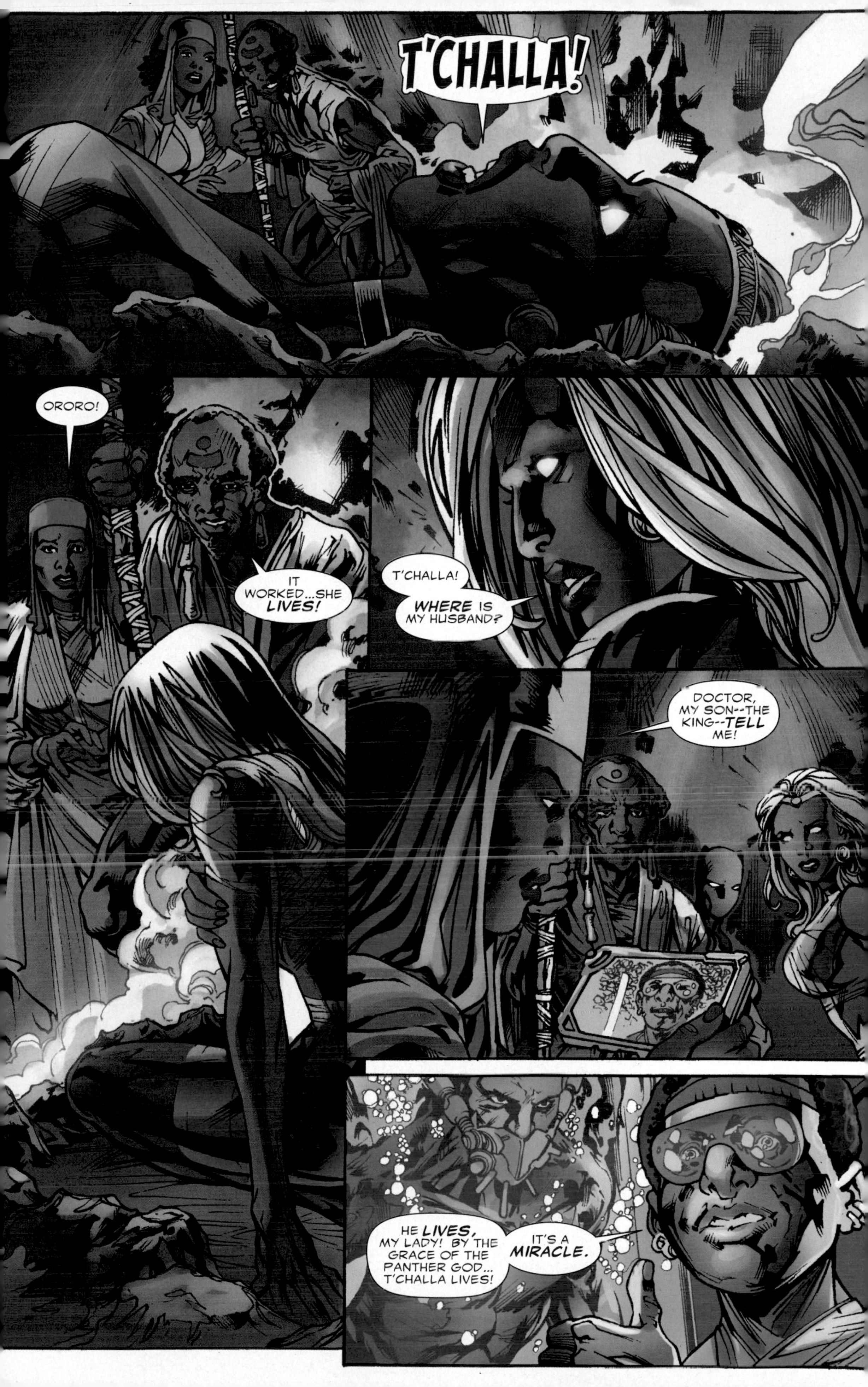
T'CHALLA!
ORORO!
IT WORKED...SHE LIVES!
T'CHALLA! WHERE IS MY HUSBAND?
DOCTOR, MY SON--THE KING--TELL ME!
IT'S A MIRACLE.
HE LIVES, MY LADY! BY THE GRACE OF THE PANTHER GOD... T'CHALLA LIVES!

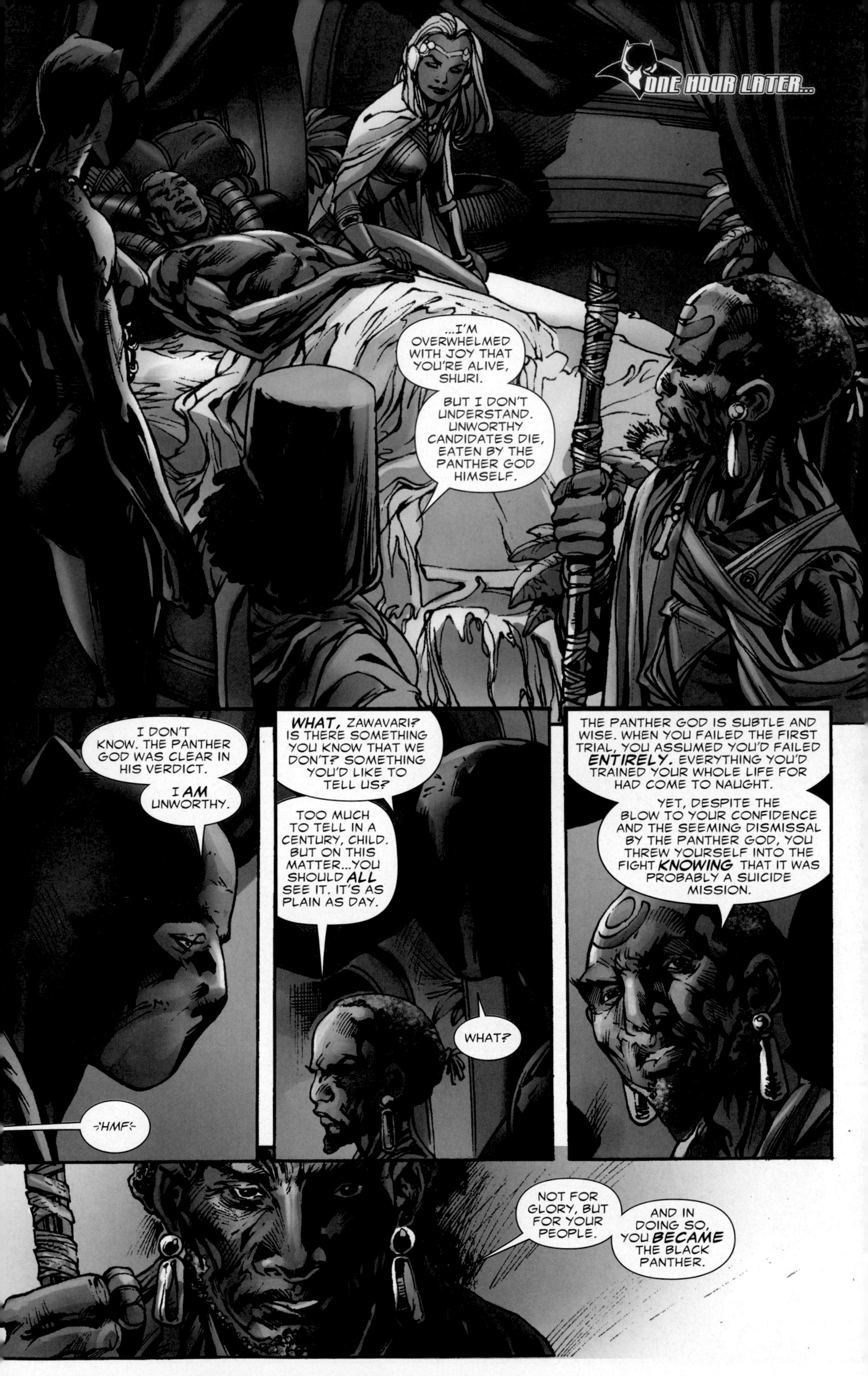
ONE HOUR LATER...
...I'M OVERWHELMED WITH JOY THAT YOU'RE ALIVE, SHURI.
BUT I DON'T UNDERSTAND. UNWORTHY CANDIDATES DIE, EATEN BY THE PANTHER GOD HIMSELF.
I DON'T KNOW. THE PANTHER GOD WAS CLEAR IN HIS VERDICT.
I *AM* UNWORTHY.
-HMF-
WHAT, ZAWAVARI? IS THERE SOMETHING YOU KNOW THAT WE DON'T? SOMETHING YOU'D LIKE TO TELL US?
TOO MUCH TO TELL IN A CENTURY, CHILD. BUT ON THIS MATTER...YOU SHOULD *ALL* SEE IT. IT'S AS PLAIN AS DAY.
WHAT?
THE PANTHER GOD IS SUBTLE AND WISE. WHEN YOU FAILED THE FIRST TRIAL, YOU ASSUMED YOU'D FAILED *ENTIRELY.* EVERYTHING YOU'D TRAINED YOUR WHOLE LIFE FOR HAD COME TO NAUGHT.
YET, DESPITE THE BLOW TO YOUR CONFIDENCE AND THE SEEMING DISMISSAL BY THE PANTHER GOD, YOU THREW YOURSELF INTO THE FIGHT *KNOWING* THAT IT WAS PROBABLY A SUICIDE MISSION.
NOT FOR GLORY, BUT FOR YOUR PEOPLE.
AND IN DOING SO, YOU *BECAME* THE BLACK PANTHER.

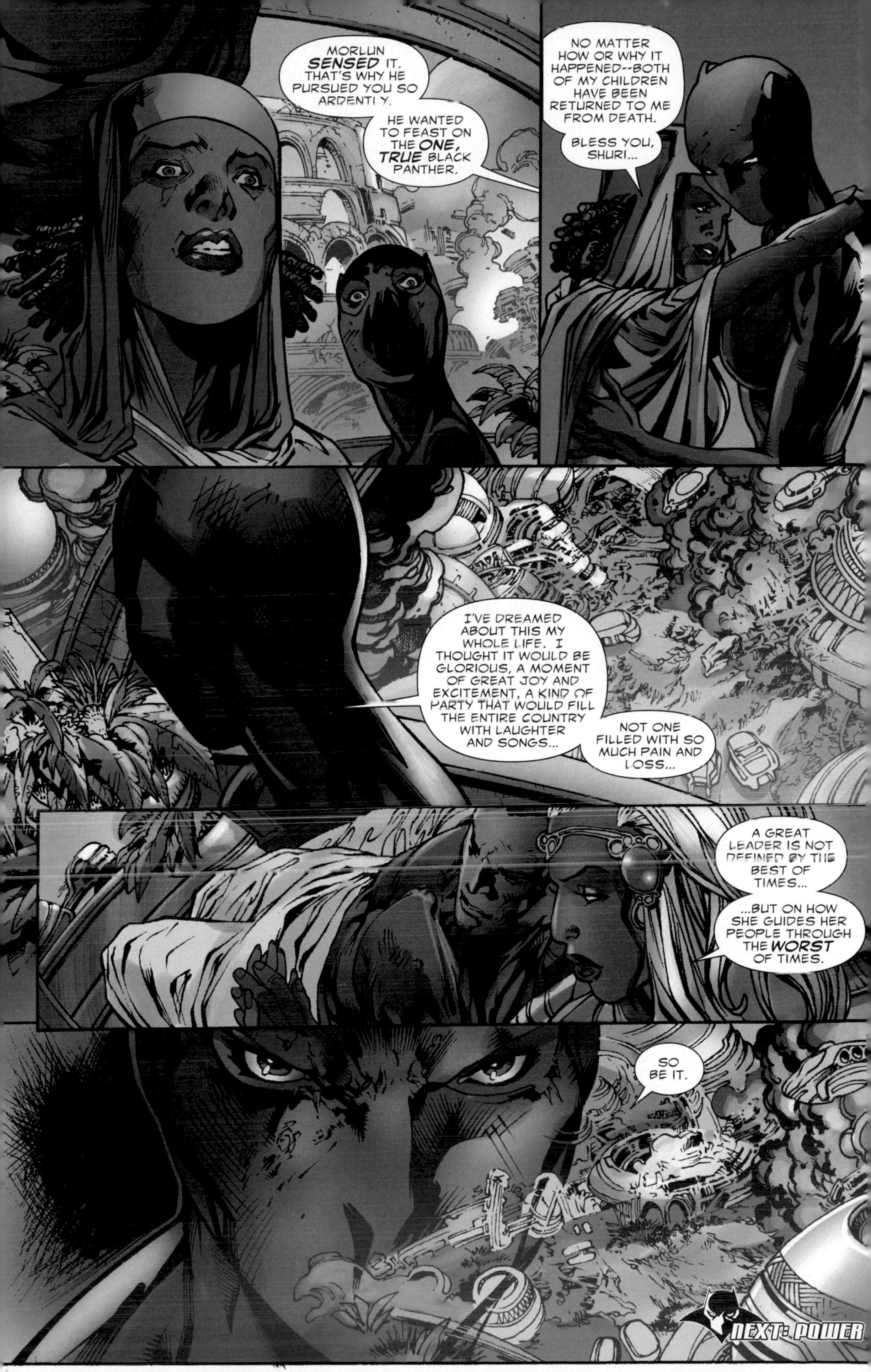
MORLUN SENSED IT. THAT'S WHY HE PURSUED YOU SO ARDENTLY.
HE WANTED TO FEAST ON THE ONE, TRUE BLACK PANTHER.
NO MATTER HOW OR WHY IT HAPPENED--BOTH OF MY CHILDREN HAVE BEEN RETURNED TO ME FROM DEATH.
BLESS YOU, SHURI...
I'VE DREAMED ABOUT THIS MY WHOLE LIFE. I THOUGHT IT WOULD BE GLORIOUS, A MOMENT OF GREAT JOY AND EXCITEMENT, A KIND OF PARTY THAT WOULD FILL THE ENTIRE COUNTRY WITH LAUGHTER AND SONGS...
NOT ONE FILLED WITH SO MUCH PAIN AND LOSS...
A GREAT LEADER IS NOT DEFINED BY THE BEST OF TIMES...
...BUT ON HOW SHE GUIDES HER PEOPLE THROUGH THE WORST OF TIMES.
SO BE IT.
NEXT: POWER

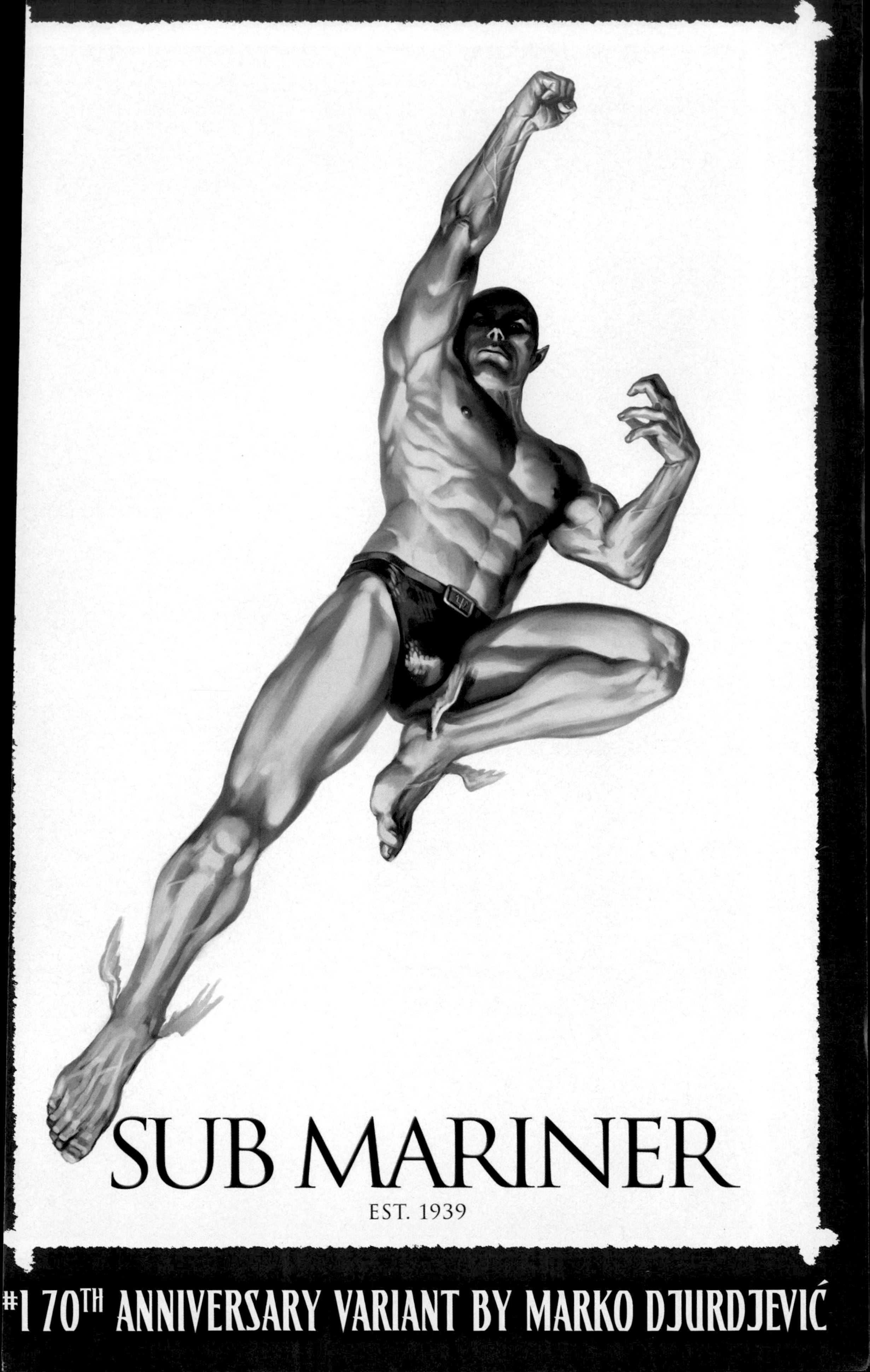
SUB MARINER
EST. 1939

#1 70TH ANNIVERSARY VARIANT BY MARKO DJURDJEVIĆ

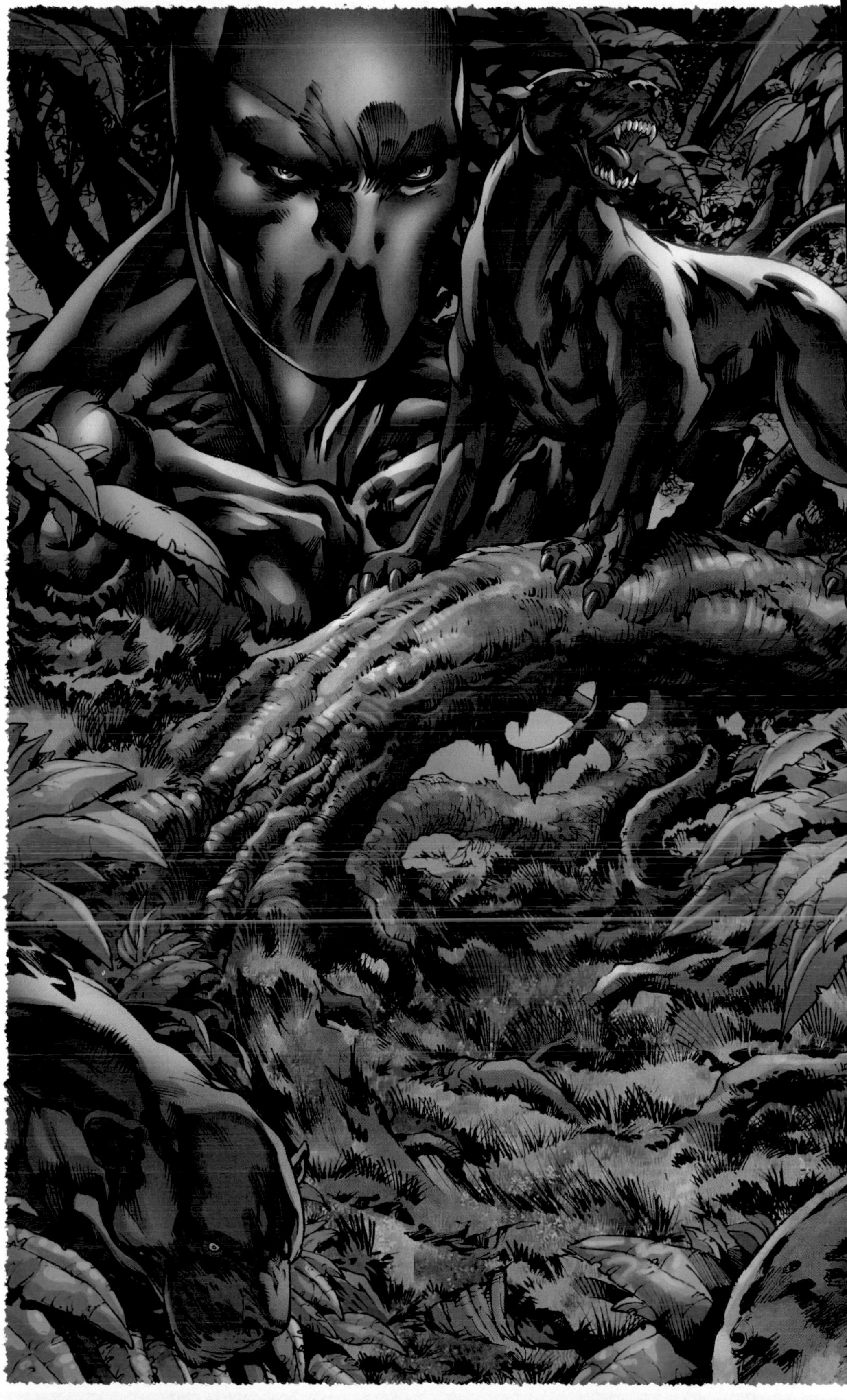

#1 WRAPAROUND VARIANT BY KEN LASHLEY,
PAUL NEARY & PAUL MOUNTS

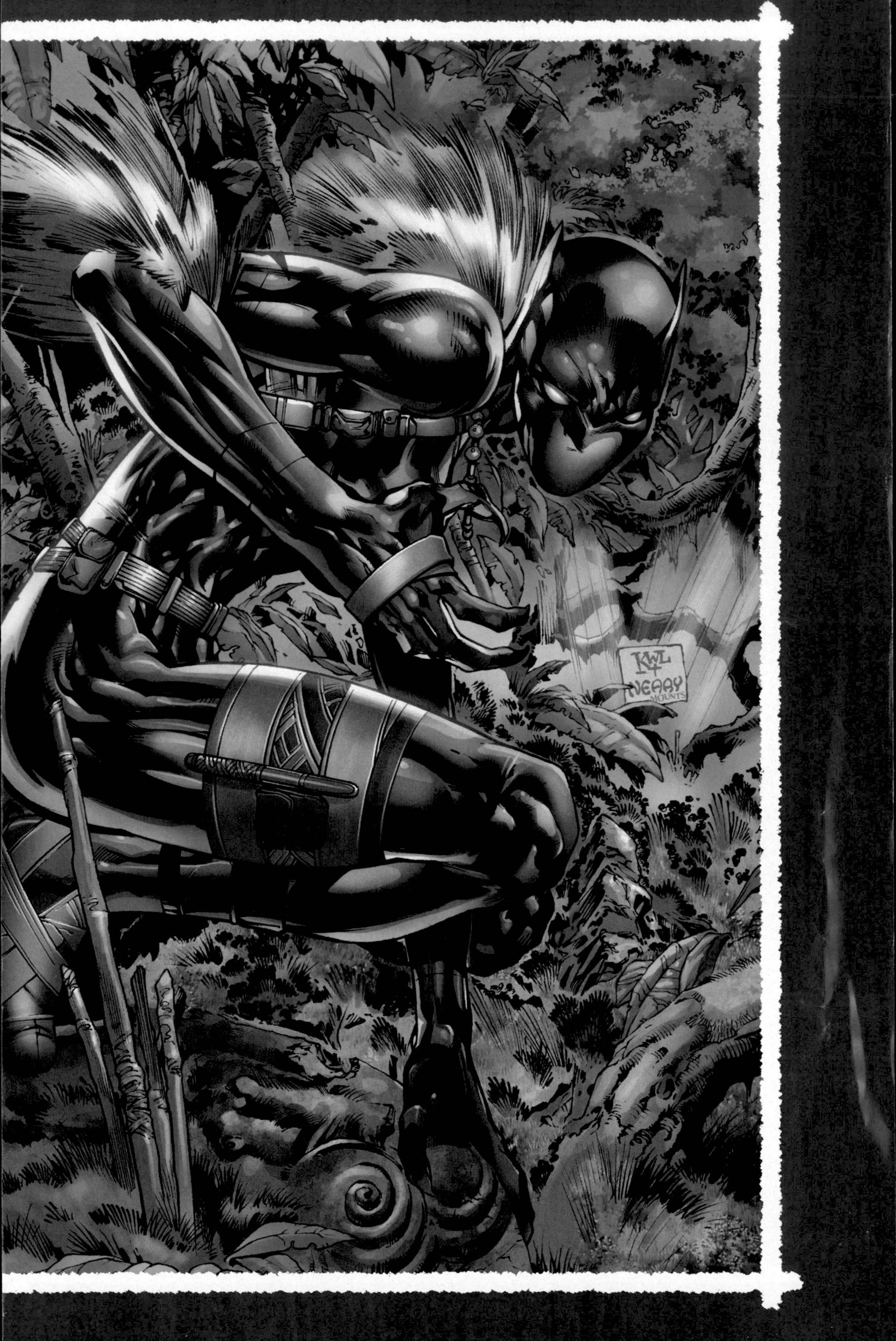

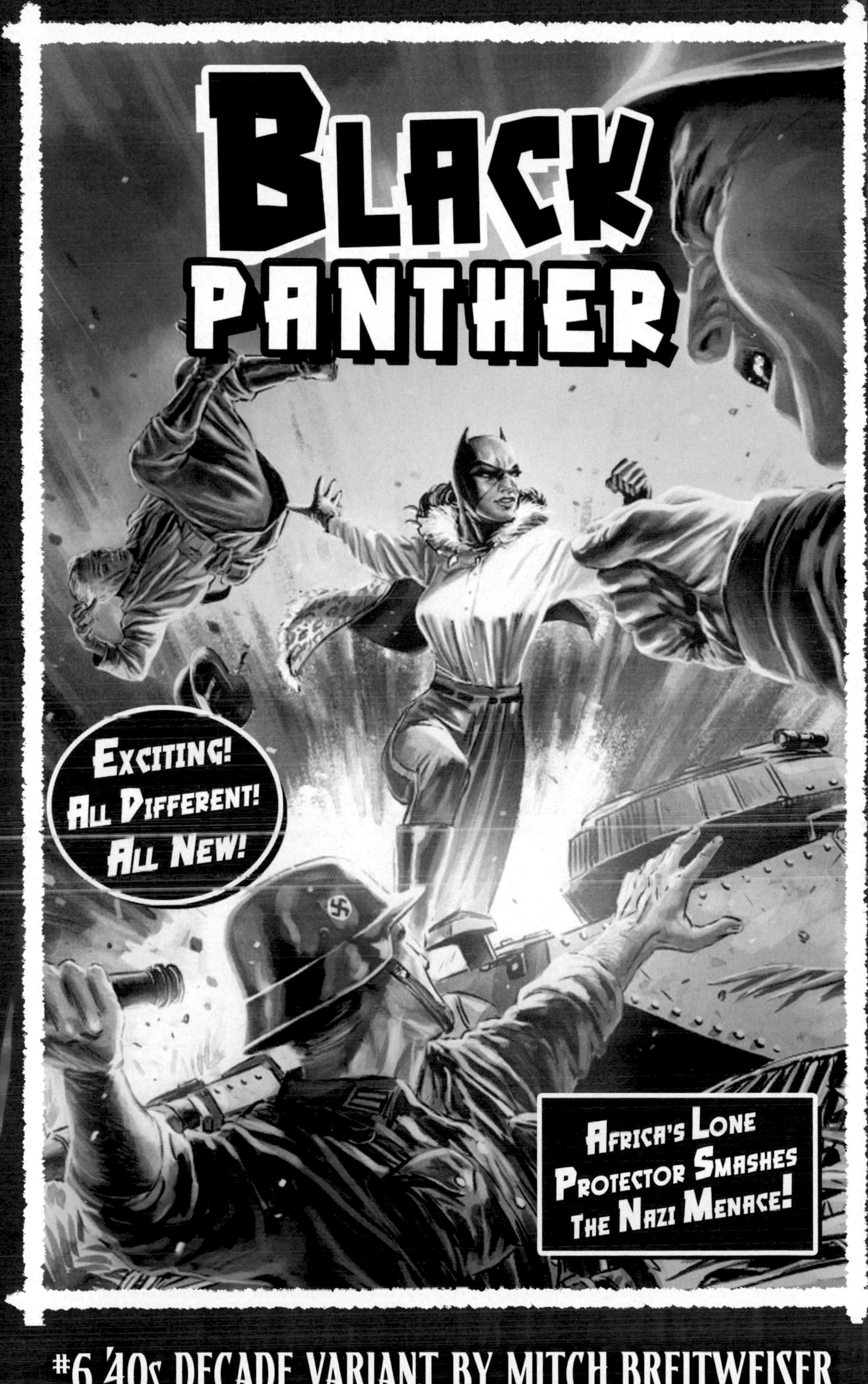
BLACK PANTHER
EXCITING! ALL DIFFERENT! ALL NEW!
AFRICA'S LONE PROTECTOR SMASHES THE NAZI MENACE!

#6 '40s DECADE VARIANT BY MITCH BREITWEISER

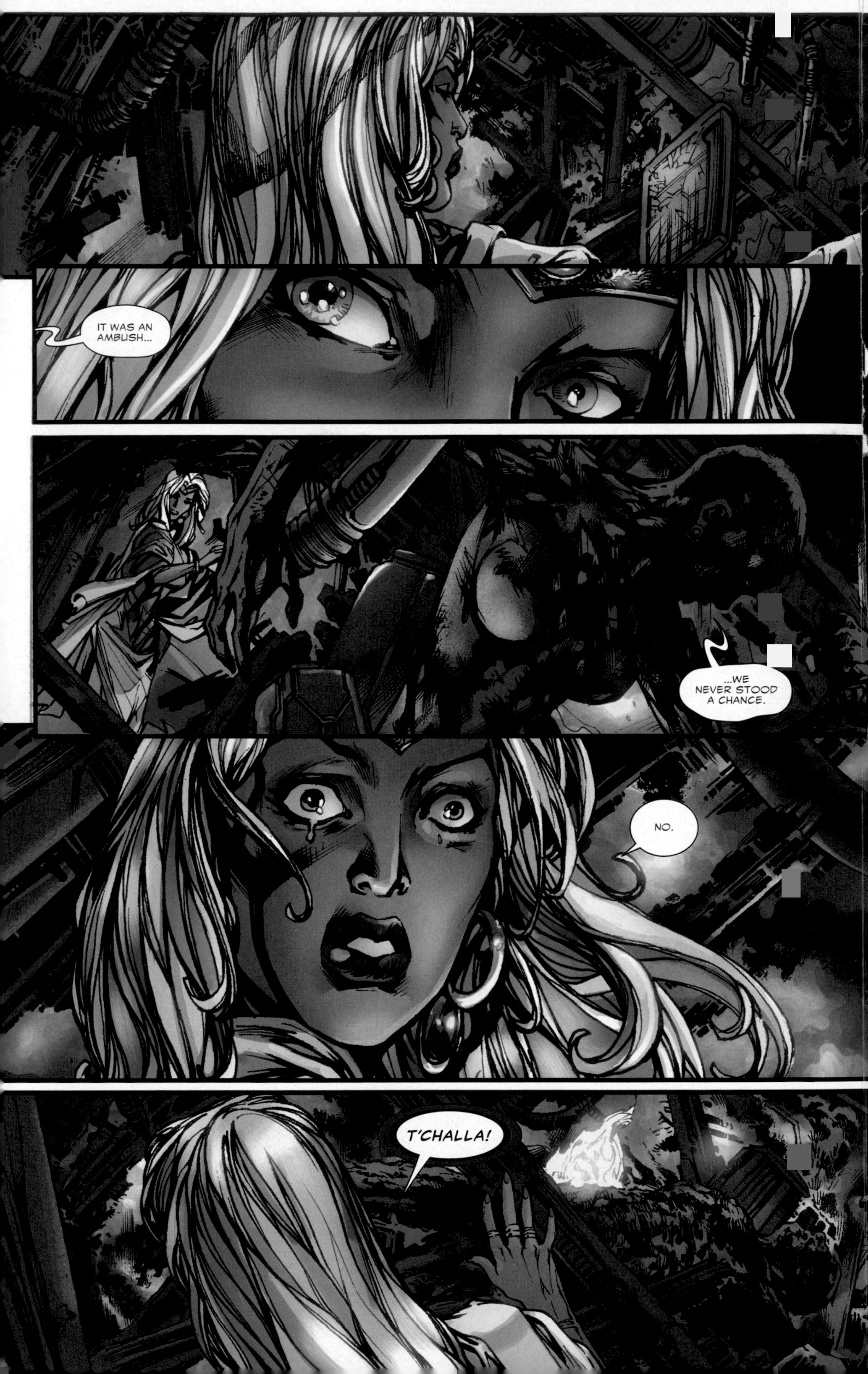
IT WAS AN AMBUSH...
...WE NEVER STOOD A CHANCE.
NO.
T'CHALLA!

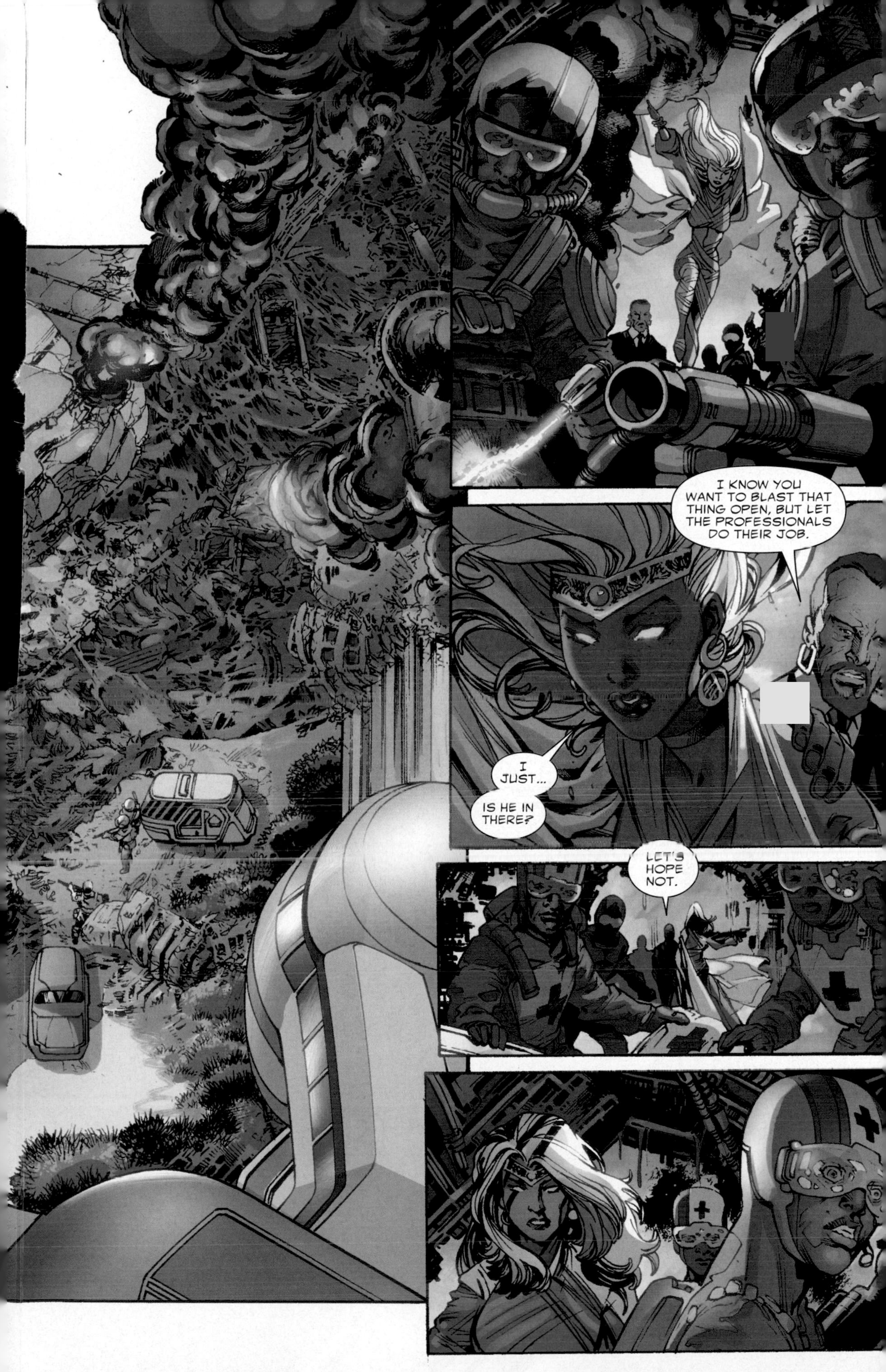
I KNOW YOU WANT TO BLAST THAT THING OPEN, BUT LET THE PROFESSIONALS DO THEIR JOB.
I JUST...
IS HE IN THERE?
LET'S HOPE NOT.

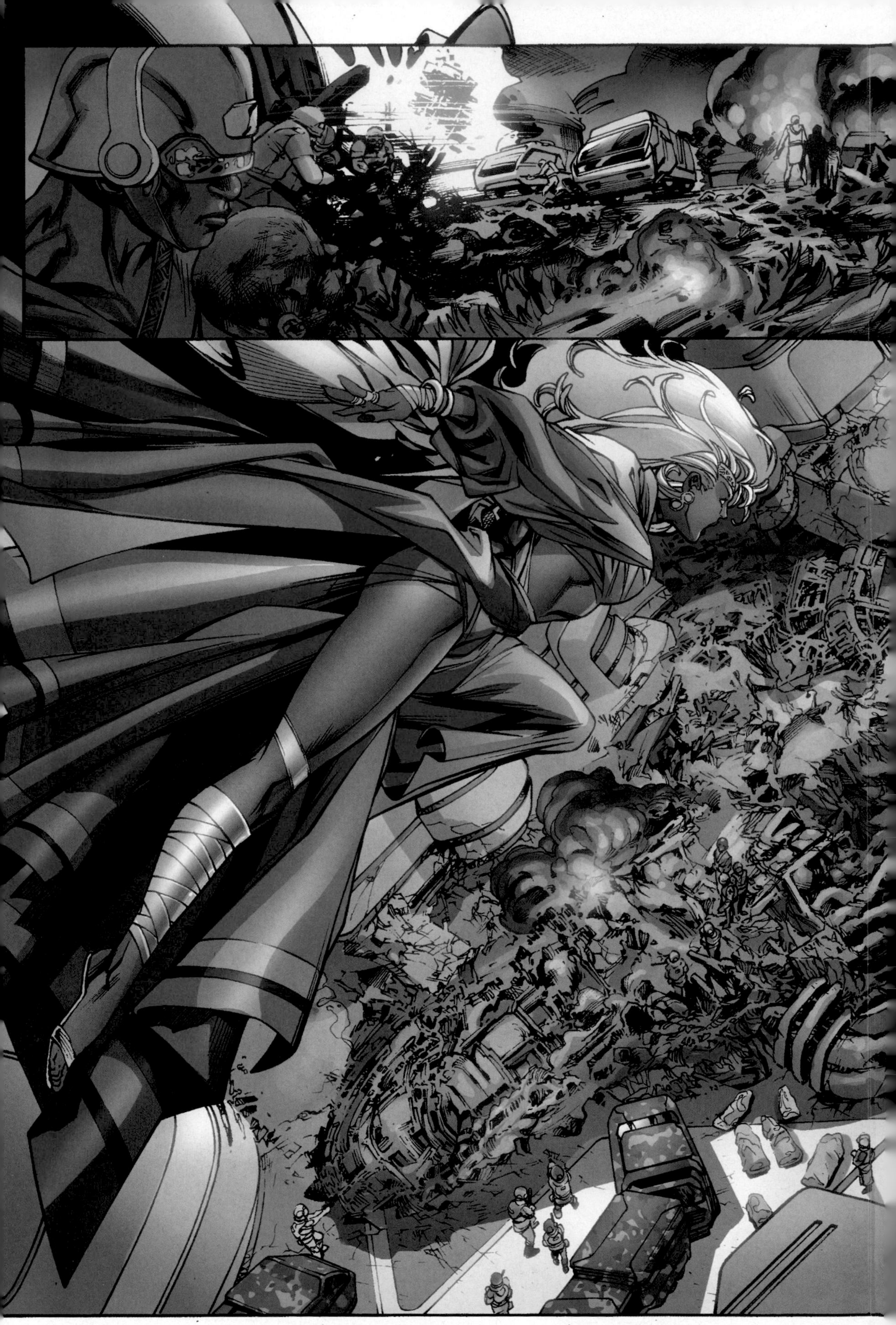

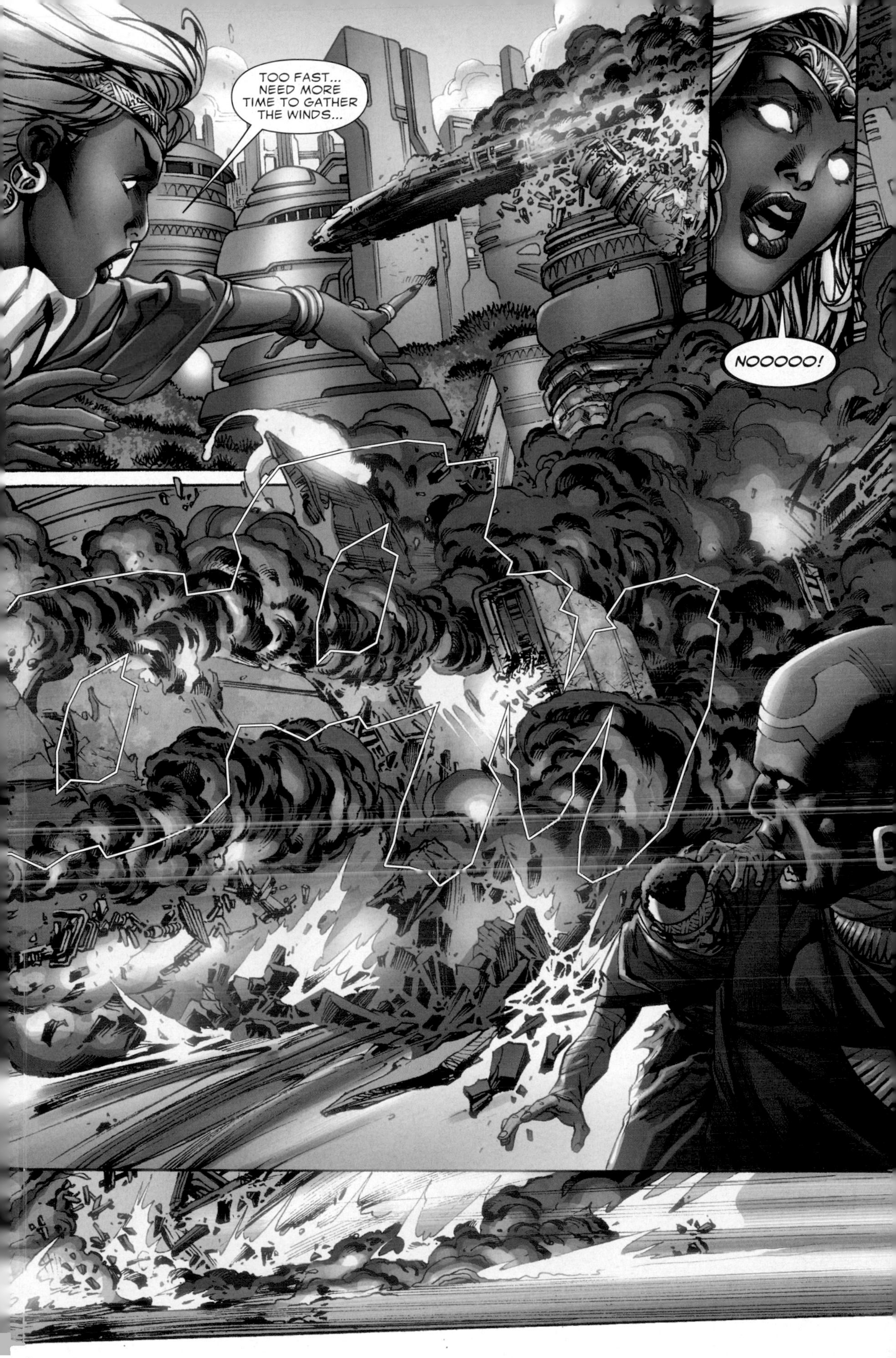

TOO FAST... NEED MORE TIME TO GATHER THE WINDS...
NOOOOO!

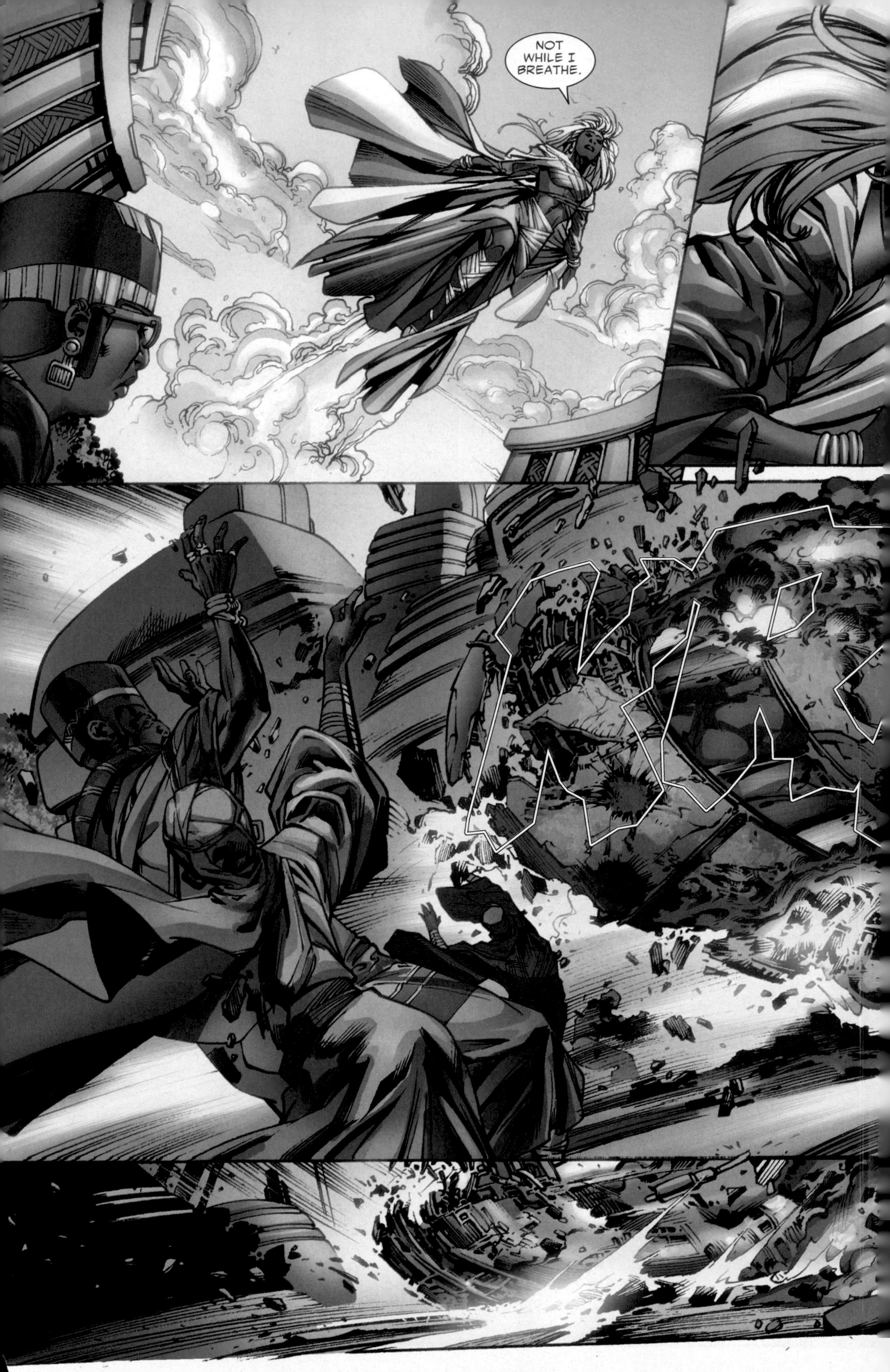
NOT WHILE I BREATHE.

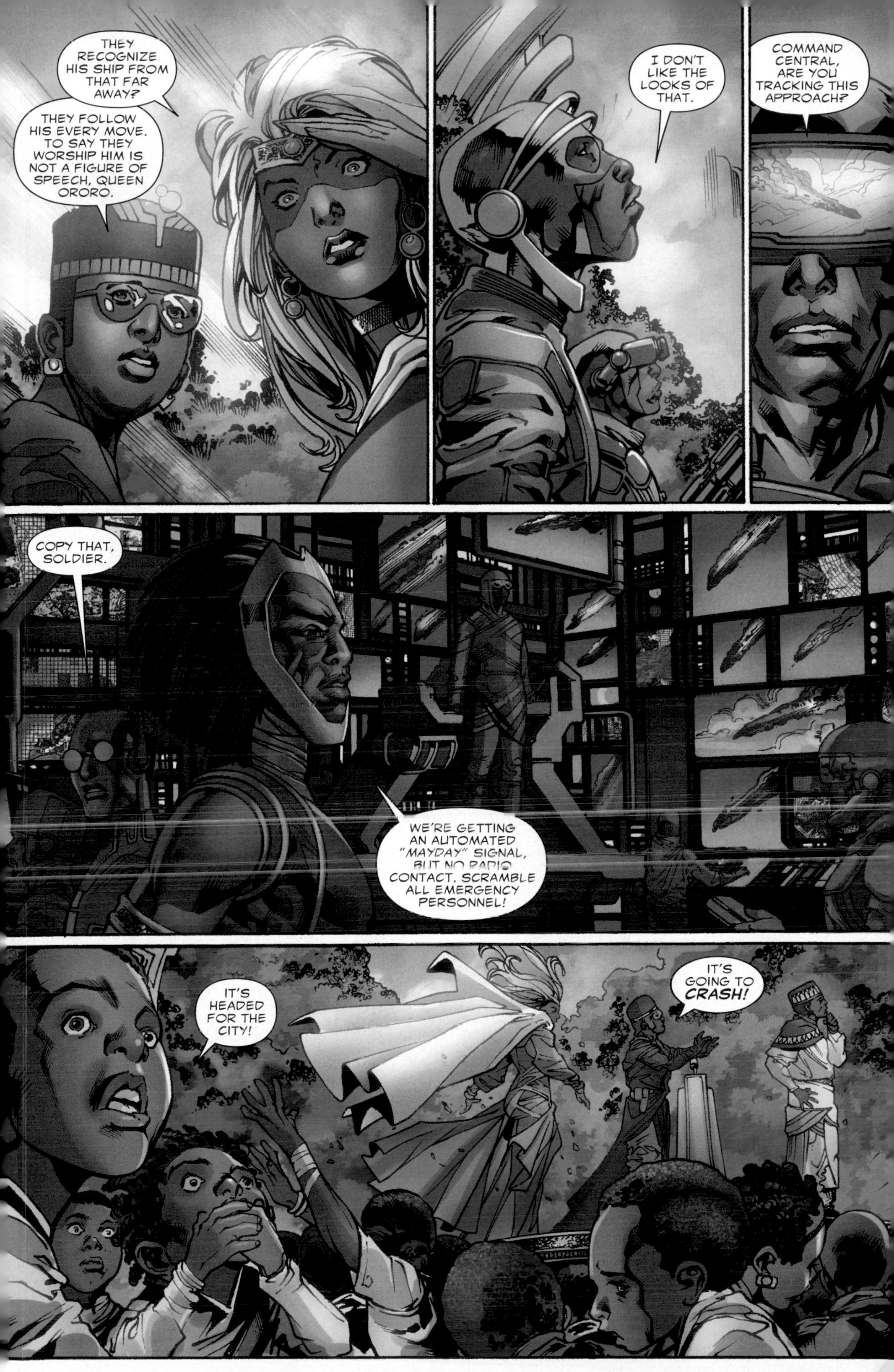
THEY RECOGNIZE HIS SHIP FROM THAT FAR AWAY?
THEY FOLLOW HIS EVERY MOVE. TO SAY THEY WORSHIP HIM IS NOT A FIGURE OF SPEECH, QUEEN ORORO.
I DON'T LIKE THE LOOKS OF THAT.
COMMAND CENTRAL, ARE YOU TRACKING THIS APPROACH?
COPY THAT, SOLDIER.
WE'RE GETTING AN AUTOMATED "MAYDAY" SIGNAL, BUT NO RADIO CONTACT. SCRAMBLE ALL EMERGENCY PERSONNEL!
IT'S HEADED FOR THE CITY!
IT'S GOING TO CRASH!

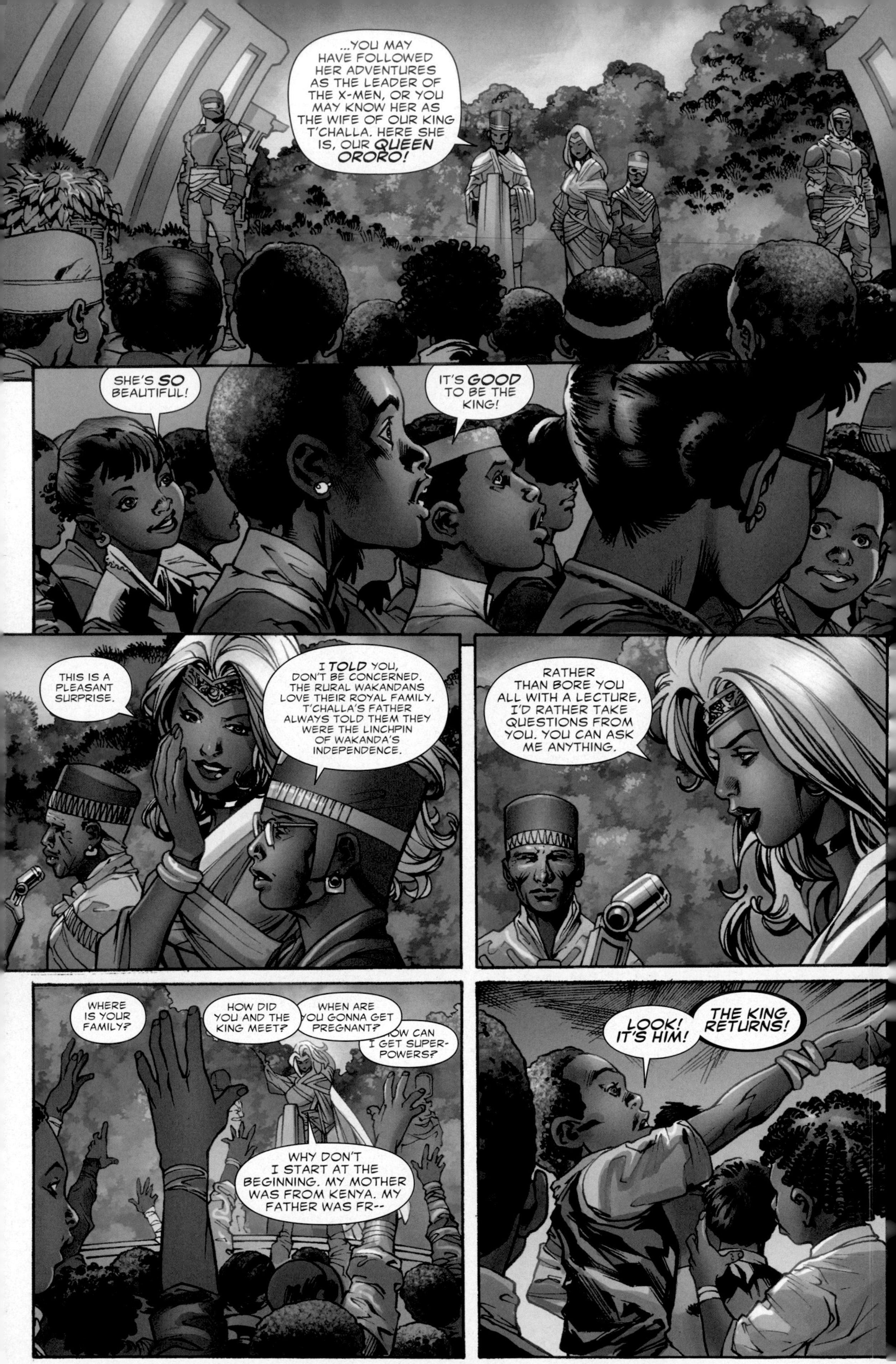

...YOU MAY HAVE FOLLOWED HER ADVENTURES AS THE LEADER OF THE X-MEN, OR YOU MAY KNOW HER AS THE WIFE OF OUR KING T'CHALLA. HERE SHE IS, OUR **QUEEN ORORO!**
SHE'S **SO** BEAUTIFUL!
IT'S **GOOD** TO BE THE KING!
THIS IS A PLEASANT SURPRISE.
I **TOLD** YOU, DON'T BE CONCERNED. THE RURAL WAKANDANS LOVE THEIR ROYAL FAMILY. T'CHALLA'S FATHER ALWAYS TOLD THEM THEY WERE THE LINCHPIN OF WAKANDA'S INDEPENDENCE.
RATHER THAN BORE YOU ALL WITH A LECTURE, I'D RATHER TAKE QUESTIONS FROM YOU. YOU CAN ASK ME ANYTHING.
WHERE IS YOUR FAMILY?
HOW DID YOU AND THE KING MEET?
WHEN ARE YOU GONNA GET PREGNANT?
HOW CAN I GET SUPER-POWERS?
WHY DON'T I START AT THE BEGINNING. MY MOTHER WAS FROM KENYA. MY FATHER WAS FR--
LOOK! IT'S HIM!
THE KING RETURNS!

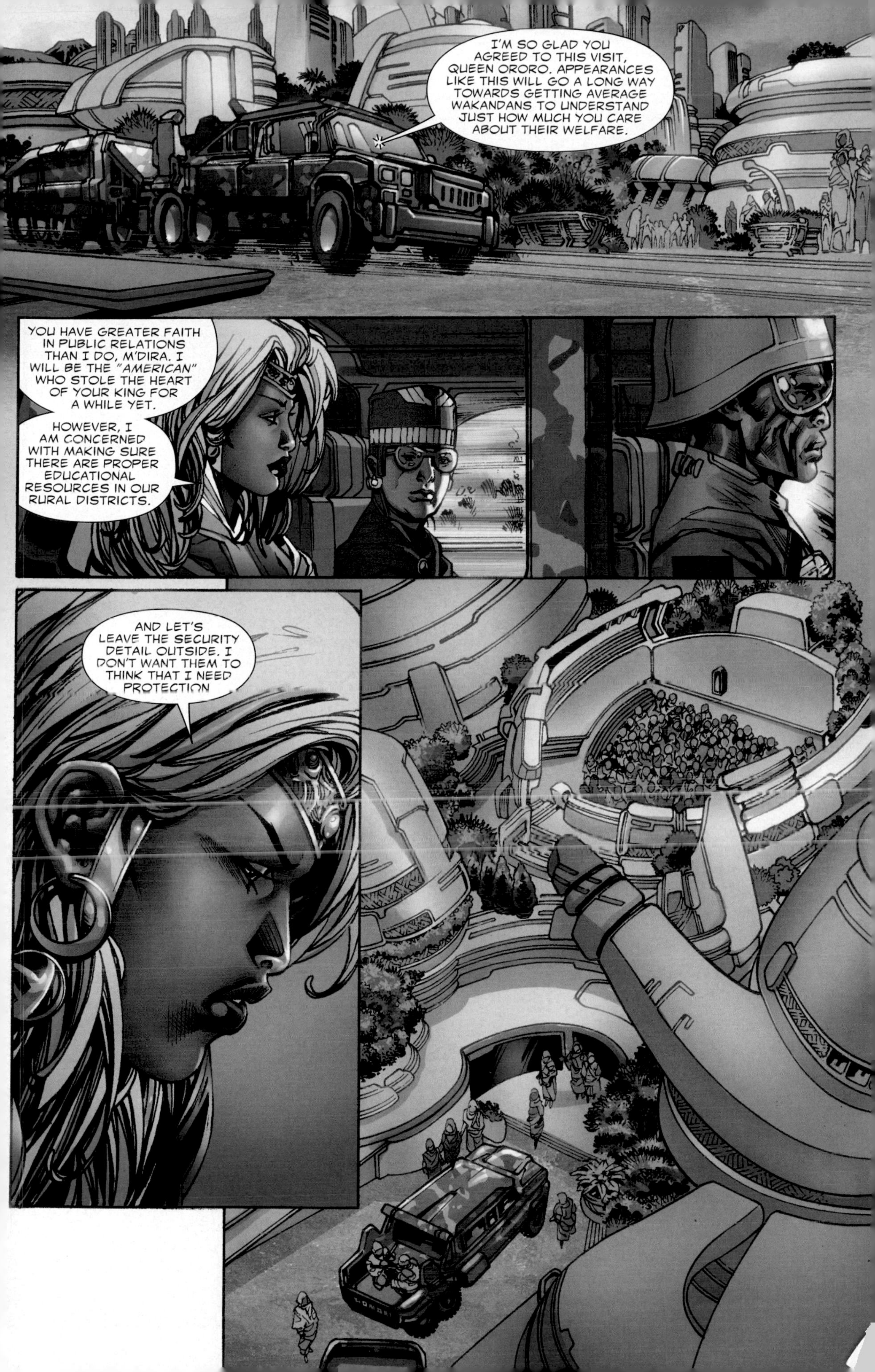
I'M SO GLAD YOU AGREED TO THIS VISIT, QUEEN ORORO. APPEARANCES LIKE THIS WILL GO A LONG WAY TOWARDS GETTING AVERAGE WAKANDANS TO UNDERSTAND JUST HOW MUCH YOU CARE ABOUT THEIR WELFARE.
YOU HAVE GREATER FAITH IN PUBLIC RELATIONS THAN I DO, M'DIRA. I WILL BE THE "AMERICAN" WHO STOLE THE HEART OF YOUR KING FOR A WHILE YET.
HOWEVER, I AM CONCERNED WITH MAKING SURE THERE ARE PROPER EDUCATIONAL RESOURCES IN OUR RURAL DISTRICTS.
AND LET'S LEAVE THE SECURITY DETAIL OUTSIDE. I DON'T WANT THEM TO THINK THAT I NEED PROTECTION

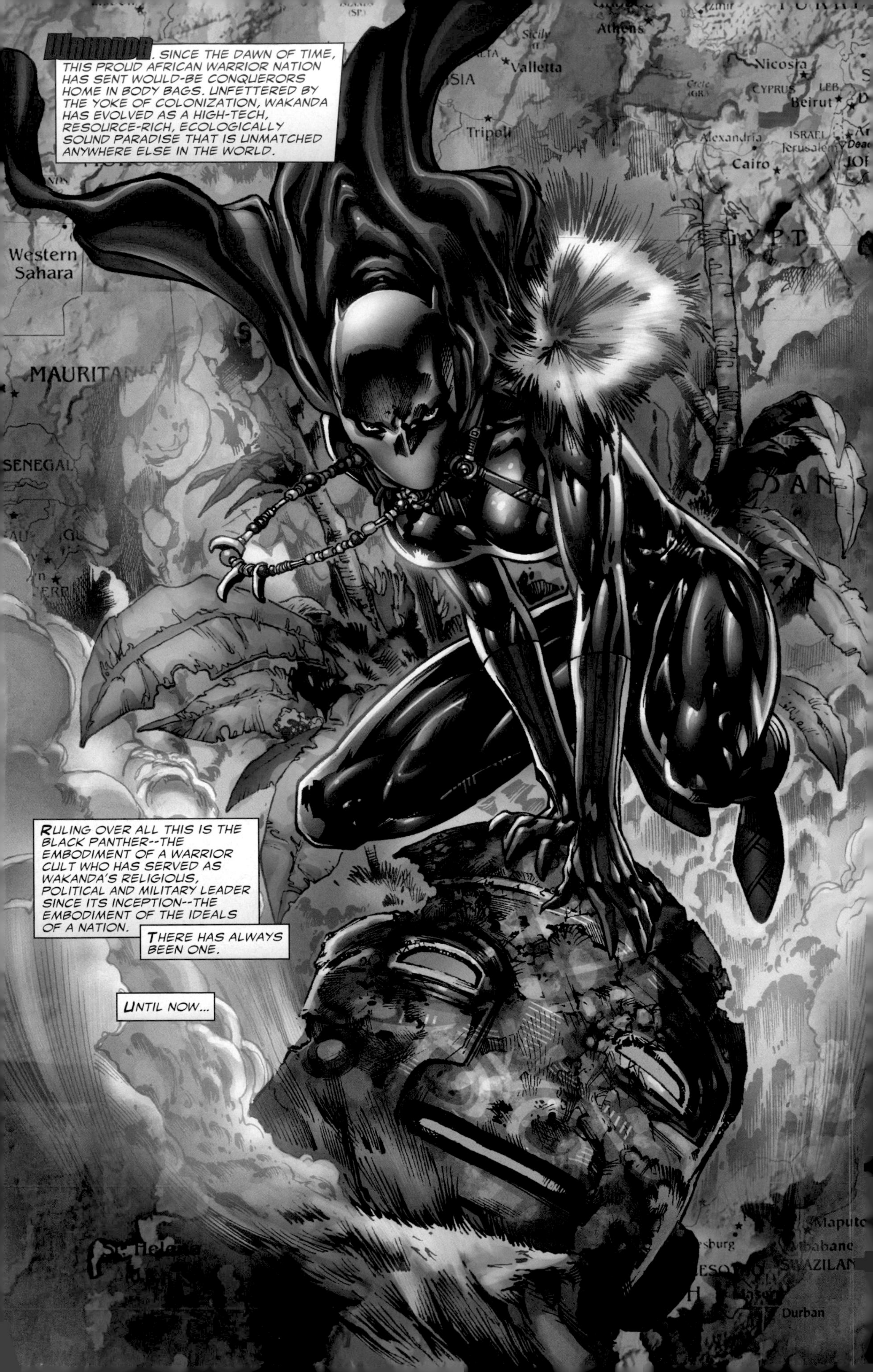
WAKANDA. SINCE THE DAWN OF TIME, THIS PROUD AFRICAN WARRIOR NATION HAS SENT WOULD-BE CONQUERORS HOME IN BODY BAGS. UNFETTERED BY THE YOKE OF COLONIZATION, WAKANDA HAS EVOLVED AS A HIGH-TECH, RESOURCE-RICH, ECOLOGICALLY SOUND PARADISE THAT IS UNMATCHED ANYWHERE ELSE IN THE WORLD.
RULING OVER ALL THIS IS THE BLACK PANTHER--THE EMBODIMENT OF A WARRIOR CULT WHO HAS SERVED AS WAKANDA'S RELIGIOUS, POLITICAL AND MILITARY LEADER SINCE ITS INCEPTION--THE EMBODIMENT OF THE IDEALS OF A NATION.
THERE HAS ALWAYS BEEN ONE.
UNTIL NOW...
Athens
Valletta
Nicosia
CYPRUS
Beirut
Tripoli
Alexandria
ISRAEL
Cairo
Western Sahara
SENEGAL
Maputo
Durban

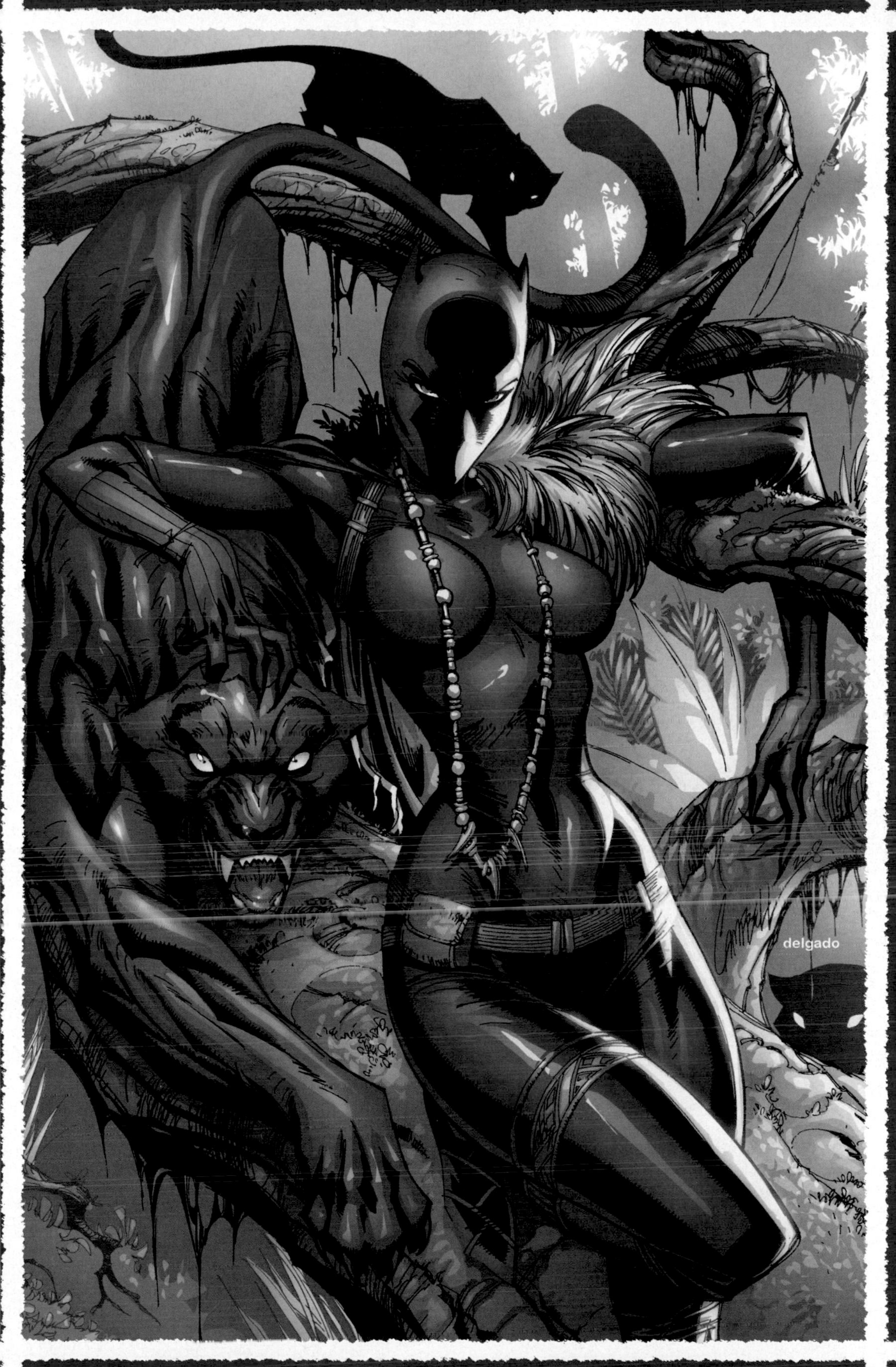
delgado

I

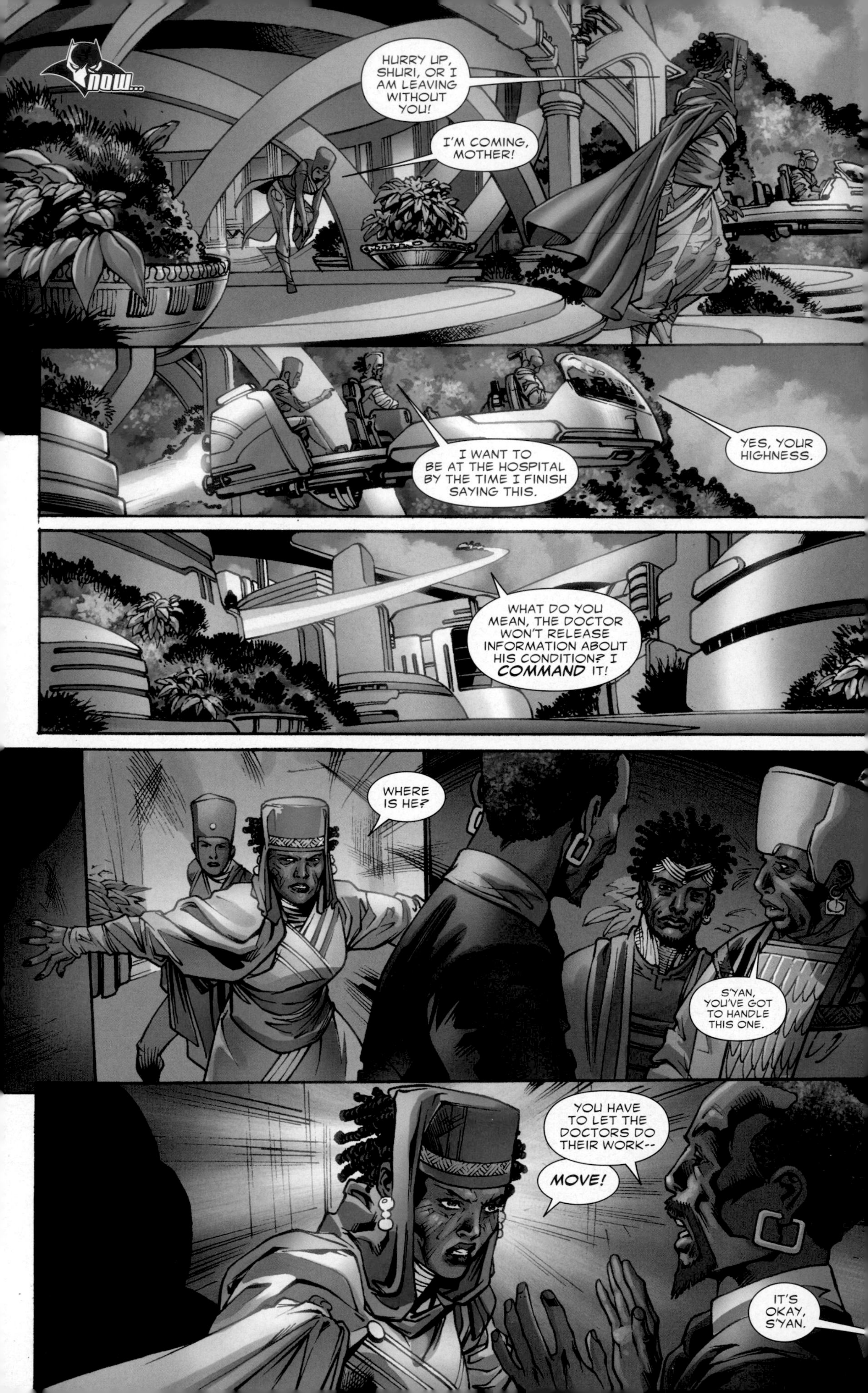
NOW...
HURRY UP, SHURI, OR I AM LEAVING WITHOUT YOU!
I'M COMING, MOTHER!
I WANT TO BE AT THE HOSPITAL BY THE TIME I FINISH SAYING THIS.
YES, YOUR HIGHNESS.
WHAT DO YOU MEAN, THE DOCTOR WON'T RELEASE INFORMATION ABOUT HIS CONDITION? I COMMAND IT!
WHERE IS HE?
S'YAN, YOU'VE GOT TO HANDLE THIS ONE.
YOU HAVE TO LET THE DOCTORS DO THEIR WORK--
MOVE!
IT'S OKAY, S'YAN.

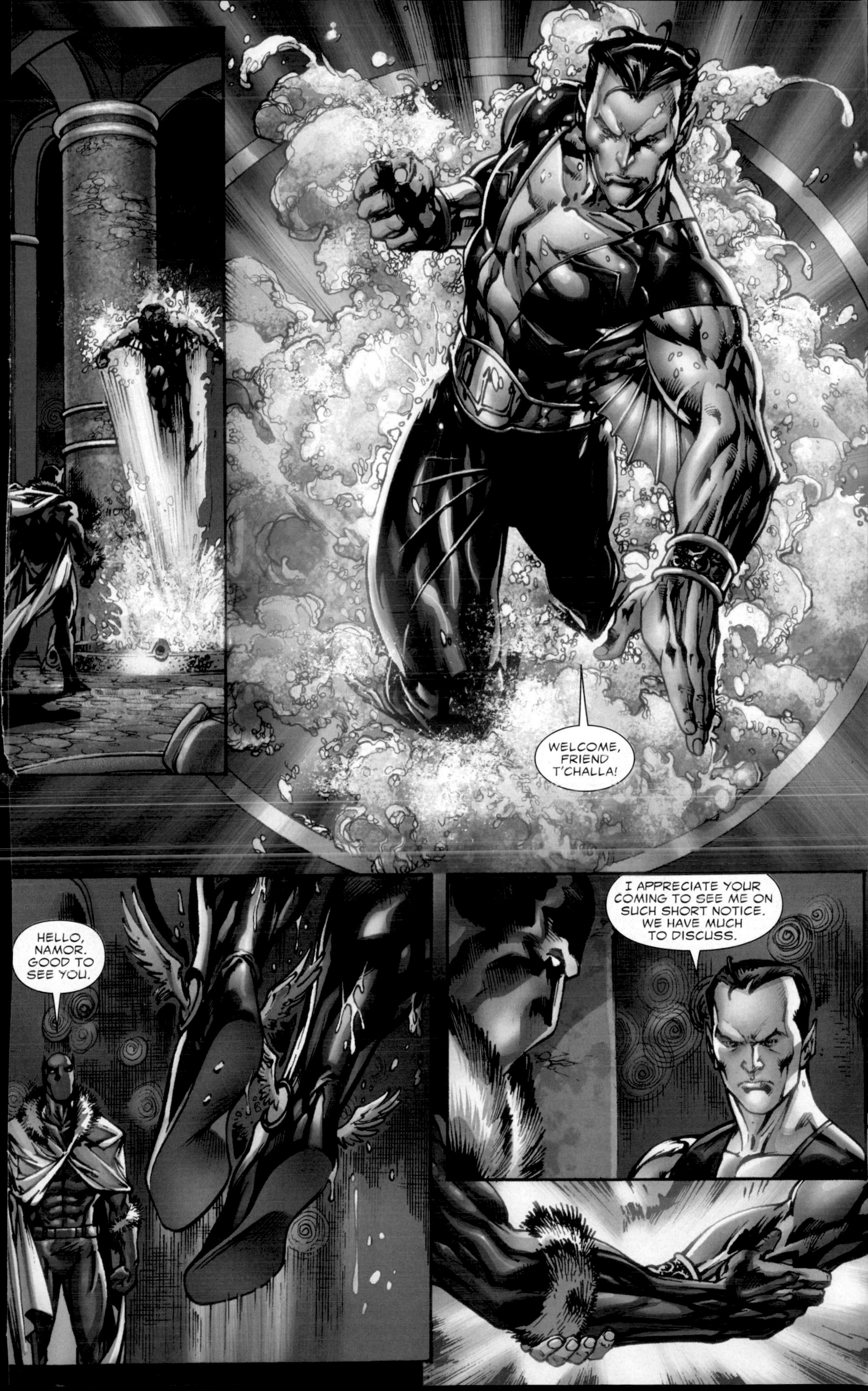
WELCOME, FRIEND T'CHALLA!
HELLO, NAMOR. GOOD TO SEE YOU.
I APPRECIATE YOUR COMING TO SEE ME ON SUCH SHORT NOTICE. WE HAVE MUCH TO DISCUSS.

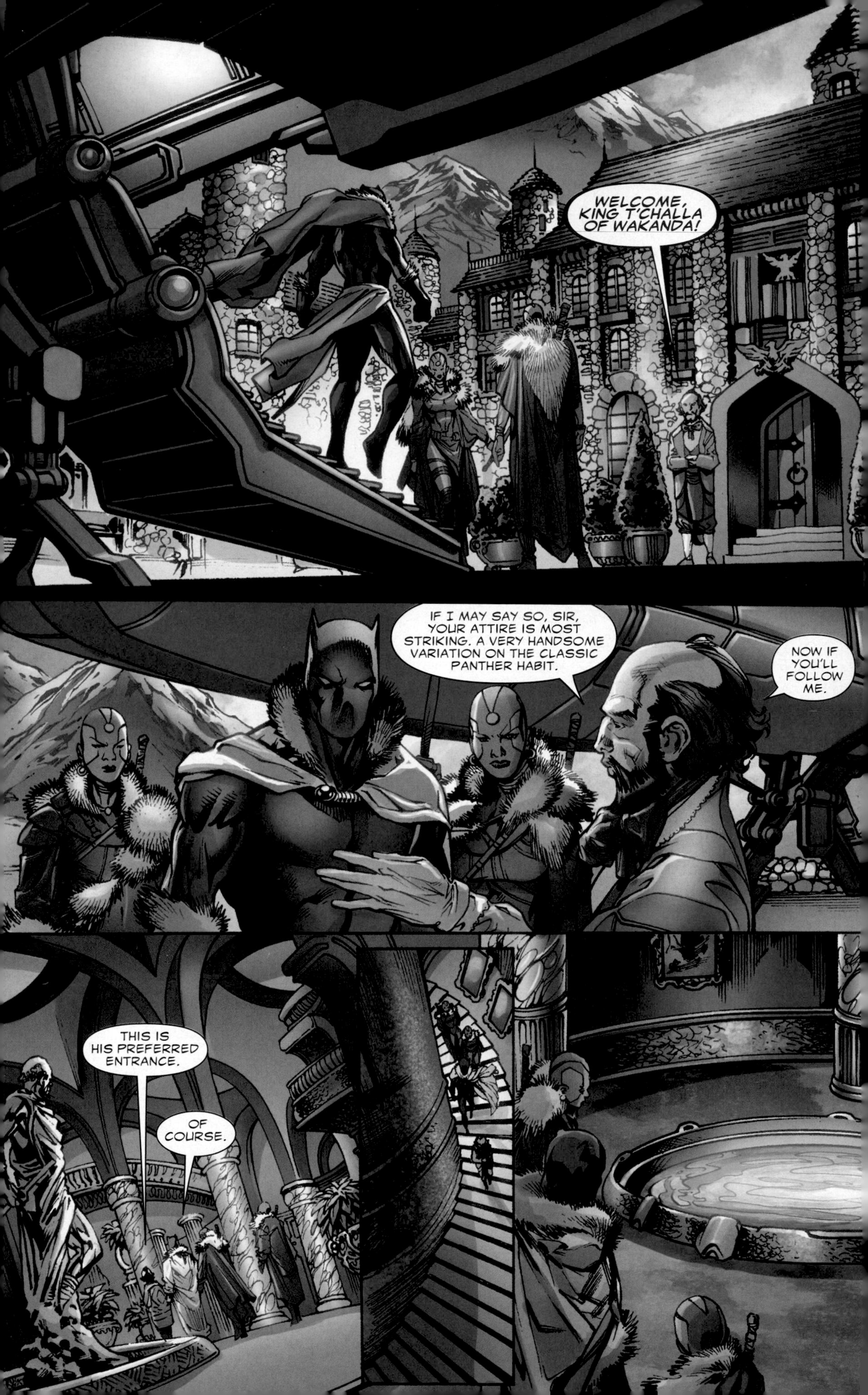
WELCOME, KING T'CHALLA OF WAKANDA!
IF I MAY SAY SO, SIR, YOUR ATTIRE IS MOST STRIKING. A VERY HANDSOME VARIATION ON THE CLASSIC PANTHER HABIT.
NOW IF YOU'LL FOLLOW ME.
THIS IS HIS PREFERRED ENTRANCE.
OF COURSE.

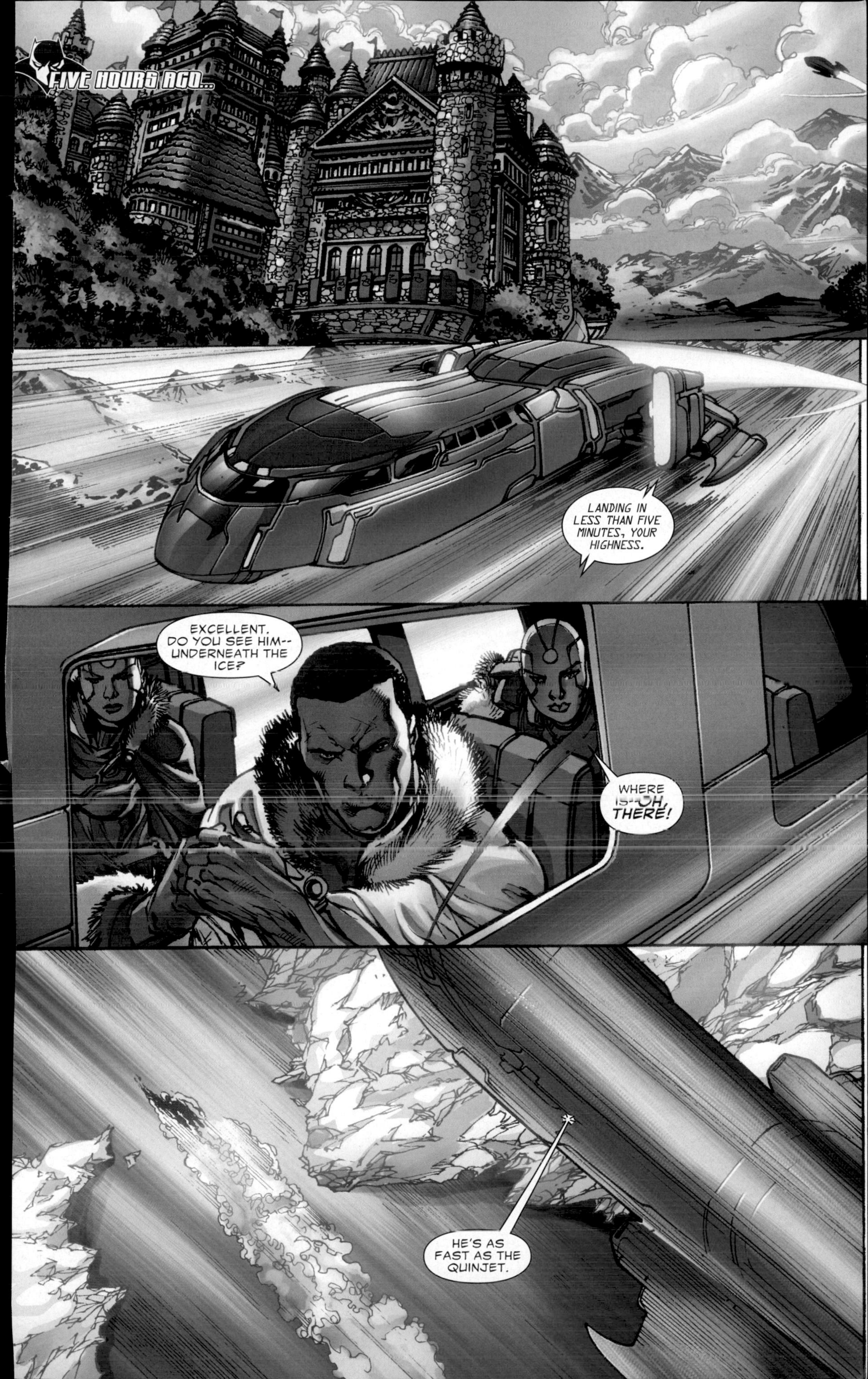
FIVE HOURS AGO...
LANDING IN LESS THAN FIVE MINUTES, YOUR HIGHNESS.
EXCELLENT. DO YOU SEE HIM--UNDERNEATH THE ICE?
WHERE IS--OH, THERE!
HE'S AS FAST AS THE QUINJET.